国家双高“铁道机车专业群”系列　多语种教材
——铁道车辆技术专业

Application and Management of Railway Vehicles
铁道车辆运用与管理
（中英对照版）

主　编　余建勇　许卫红　班希翼
副主编　杨　阳　冯　辉

西南交通大学出版社
·成　都·

图书在版编目（C I P）数据

铁道车辆运用与管理：中英对照版/余建勇，许卫红，班希翼主编. —成都：西南交通大学出版社，2022.10

ISBN 978-7-5643-8940-6

Ⅰ. ①铁… Ⅱ. ①余… ②许… ③班… Ⅲ. ①铁路车辆－汉、英 Ⅳ. ①U27

中国版本图书馆 CIP 数据核字（2022）第 182559 号

Application and Management of Railway Vehicles

铁道车辆运用与管理

（中英对照版）

主 编 余建勇 许卫红 班希翼

责任编辑 张文越
封面设计 何东琳设计工作室

出版发行 西南交通大学出版社
（四川省成都市金牛区二环路北一段 111 号
西南交通大学创新大厦 21 楼）
邮政编码 610031
发行部电话 028-87600564 028-87600533
网址 http://www.xnjdcbs.com
印刷 四川森林印务有限责任公司

成品尺寸 185 mm × 260 mm
印张 13.75
字数 347 千
版次 2022 年 10 月第 1 版
印次 2022 年 10 月第 1 次
定价 48.00 元
书号 ISBN 978-7-5643-8940-6

课件咨询电话：028-81435775

PREFACE

This book is compiled in accordance with the latest version of *Railway Technical Management Regulations*, *Operation and Maintenance Regulations for Railway Passenger Cars*, *Operation and Maintenance Regulations for Railway Freight Cars*, *Rules for Investigation and Handling of Railway Traffic Accidents* and other relevant rules and regulations, and is compiled in accordance with the production organization mode and working content of the railway vehicle operation department.This book draws on the practical experience of experts and practitioners, and introduces the main work in the process of vehicle operation in detail, mainly including vehicle operation management, freight car operation and maintenance, passenger car operation and maintenance, railway production safety, etc. During the compilation process, the editors designed a series of professional skills and language learning tasks based on the application and maintenance of railway vehicles in the framework of task teaching. Using Chinese and English as the teaching media, the editors not only imparted professional knowledge and skills, but also focused on cultivating learners' ability to read English literature on railway vehicles, as well as their English communication ability in the work setting. By reading this book, readers can basically understand the basic situation of railway vehicle operation and maintenance. This book is suitable for the English teaching of vehicle majors in railway vocational colleges, and can also be used as a reference for on-site staff in countries along "The Belt and Road" that adopt Chinese railway standards.

This book is compiled by teachers of Zhengzhou Railway Vocational and Technical College, with Yu Jianyong, Xu Weihong and Ban Xiyi as chief editors, Yang Yang and Feng Hui as deputy chief editors, and Shang Yu as chief reviewer. Among them, Yu Jianyong is responsible for the first and second chapters of the Chinese part, Ban Xiyi is responsible for the third chapter of the Chinese part, Feng Hui is responsible for the fourth chapter of the Chinese part, Xu Weihong is responsible for the first, second and fourth chapters of the English part, and Yang Yang is responsible for the third chapter of the English part.

We would like to express our heartfelt thanks for the support and help from the Locomotive and Vehicle Department of China National Railway Group Co., Ltd., Zhengzhou Bureau Group Corporation of China Railway, and Chengdu Bureau Group Corporation of China Railway and other relevant departments in the process of compiling the textbook.

Due to the limited level of editors, inaccuracies are inevitable, and we hope that readers who use this book could provide any constructive criticism and feedback.

Editor

March 2022

前　言

本书依据最新版《铁路技术管理规程》《铁路货车运用维修规程》《铁路客车运用维修规程》《铁路交通事故调查处理规则》等相关规章规程，按照铁路车辆运用部门生产组织方式及内容，借鉴专家及从业人员的实践经验，对车辆运用过程中的主要工作进行了详细介绍，主要包含车辆运用管理工作、货车运用维修、客车运用维修、铁路生产安全等内容。在编写过程中，编者以任务教学为框架设计了一系列基于铁路车辆运用维修的专业技能学习和语言学习任务，以中英双语为教学媒介，既传授专业知识和技能，又注重培养学习者阅读铁道车辆方面英文文献的能力，以及在工作场景中的英语交流能力。通过阅读本书，读者可基本了解铁道车辆运用维修工作基本情况。本书适合铁道类职业院校车辆专业英语教学使用，也可供采用中国铁路标准的“一带一路”沿线国家的现场工作人员参考。

本书由郑州铁路职业技术学院余建勇、许卫红、班希翼担任主编，杨阳、冯辉担任副主编，由郑州铁路职业技术学院尚宇主审。其中，余建勇负责编写中文部分第一、二篇，班希翼负责编写中文部分第三篇，冯辉负责编写中文部分第四篇，许卫红负责编写英文部分第一、二、四篇，杨阳负责编写英文部分第三篇。

在教材编写的过程中，编者得到了中国国家铁路集团有限公司机辆部，中国铁路郑州局、成都局集团公司等相关部门的支持和帮助，在此表示衷心感谢。

由于编者水平有限，不妥之处在所难免，希望使用本书的各位读者予以批评指正。

编　者

2022 年 3 月

CONTENTS

目　录

Chapter 1

Vehicle Management

As one of China's major infrastructures, railway is the main artery of national economy, as well as the backbone of transportation system. Railway transportation is featured by highly concentrated, closely connected and coordinated working links.

Railway transportation system consists of transport, maintenance, cars, public works, electrical and other departments. In order to ensure its safety, punctuality, convenience and efficiency, railway system must be operated by strictly following the transportation rules and the unified commands of China Railway Co., Ltd. (hereinafter referred to as China Railway Group), so as to transport passengers and goods to their destinations accurately, timely and safely. Railway employees must strictly abide by labor and operating disciplines, strictly implement the rules and regulations, keep in mind their own responsibilities, and ensure safe production with an extremely responsible attitude to the country and the people.

Learning Objectives

(1) Understand the tasks of vehicle operation.

(2) Master the requirements for marshalling and coupling of passenger trains and freight trains.

(3) Master the technical indicators of railway passenger cars and freight cars.

Learning Content

1. Vehicle management and maintenance

Vehicle operation includes management and maintenance. Freight trains are used throughout the country. Except for special cars and exclusive-used cars, we generally implement the responsibility system for maintenance by sections on national railways, rather than the allocation system.

1) Tasks of vehicle operation

The basic task of vehicle operation is to implement regulations and orders during maintenance, abide by operation disciplines, labor disciplines, and operation standardization, and find and deal with the faults of cars in operation to ensure driving safety.

(1) Correctly implement relevant regulations and orders.

(2) Correctly formulate production plans and technical measures, strengthen overall quality management, implement inspection and repair regulations, and improve car repair quality.

(3) On the basis of ensuring the quality of vehicle maintenance, strive to shorten the vehicle maintenance time and accelerate the cyclic utilization of vehicles.

(4) Repair the cars assigned to the depot and the cars within the jurisdiction to prevent accidents and ensure safety.

(5) Do well in labor protection, improve the working conditions of employees, and ensure safe production.

(6) Carry out technical training to improve the professional skills in train braking technology.

(7) Regularly investigate and analyze the technical status of vehicles in use, collect, process, and analyze the faults in operation and maintenance, so as to form a quality information feedback system to put forward suggestions for improvement in vehicle maintenance and operation management.

2) Vehicle maintenance work

Regular maintenance of railway vehicles is implemented, and gradually expanded to state repairs, replacement repairs, and professional centralized repairs of major parts.

(1) Operation and maintenance of railway passenger trains.

Passenger trains are inspected and repaired according to the traveled mileage. The repair for passenger trains with a maximum operating speed of 120 km/h are divided into overhaul, depot repair, and auxiliary repair. The maintenance quality of passenger trains is directly related to the safety of passengers' lives and property. The daily maintenance contents are as follows:

➢ Technical servicing station: comprehensively inspect, test and repair the passenger train entering the passenger train technical servicing station.

➢ Passenger train inspection and service point: carry out the technical inspection and maintenance for departure, arrival and passing-by trains.

➢ Passenger train technician crew: conduct technical inspection, maintenance and management on the passenger train on the way.

(2) Operation and maintenance of railway freight trains.

The repair of railway freight trains can be divided into overhaul, depot repair, and auxiliary repair. The overhaul of freight trains is once every 5-8 years, the depot repair is once every 1-2 years, and the auxiliary repair is once every 6 months. Freight trains have poor operating conditions and are subjected to frequent impacts during disassembly, marshalling, and mechanized loading and unloading operations. Perishable goods cause corrosion to parts. Trains with heavy-loaded goods and heavy haul trains collide during operation, causing great wear and tear, deformation, looseness, corrosion on train components. Therefore, the train must be inspected and repaired in time, which is divided into car detached repair and in-train repair.

a. Car detached repair.

Detach the cars with faults from the train, send them to the special repair line or repairing points. This is known as the car detached repair. Implementation of the car detached repair can make full use of fixed platform and mechanized repair equipment in accordance with technical standards to repair cars, eliminate failures, and to ensure quality. But this will increase the workload of shunting operations and car waiting time. This will effect transport efficiency. Cars with the faults that can be repaired in train must have the car detached repair.

b. In-train repair.

When doing the technical inspection after the arrival of the train, or before the departure of train, the car failures found in the parking line can be repaired in the dwell time, this is said in-train repair. The implementation of in-train repair can quickly eliminate the traffic safety failure, speed up car turnover and improve transport.

2. Operational indicators for vehicles

1) Present freight car

Present freight cars refer to all existing freight cars in the Railway Bureau jurisdiction at 18:00 every day. They can be divided into freight cars in operation and serviceable freight cars, as shown in Figure 1-1 and 1-2.

(1) Freight cars in operation refer to all the empty, loaded cars that are used in the railway transport operations, collectively referred to as the freight cars in operation. It is an important indicator of the transport capacity.

(2) Serviceable freight cars refers to freight cars that do not participate the railway transport operations. They include the non-production freight cars and empty freight cars provided and rented by enterprises.

A certain number of serviceable freight cars is necessary for transport production. But it cannot take up too many cars; otherwise it will affect the utilization rate of freight cars. Thus all the vehicle-related departments should improve car maintenance efficiency, shorten the repair time, and make efforts to reduce the number of maintenance cars, increase the number of freight cars in operation and mine up transport potential.

Figure 1-1 Freight cars in operation

Figure 1-2 Serviceable freight cars

2) Freight car kilometers

A freight car traveling one kilometer is called one car kilometer. Freight cars in operation kilometer is the total distance traveled by freight cars in operation; it is the indicator that reflects the running amount of the freight cars. To a certain extent, it reflects the degree of wear of the wheel sets.

3) Freight car kilometers per car per day

Freight car kilometers per car per day refers to the running mileage of one freight car in a day and night in a certain period of time for a railway bureau or the railway cooperation.

The number of kilometers for freight car per day = kilometer of freight cars in operation / number of freight cars in operation

= average car-kilometers in one complete turnround / car turnround time (km/d)

The freight car kilometers per car per day is the index to reflect the degree of freight car flow. Under the condition of a certain percentage of empty to loaded car kilometers, the greater the flow of freight car, the larger loading amount of freight car will accomplish.

4) Average car-kilometers in one complete turnround and turnround time of freight car

(1) Average car-kilometers in one complete turnround: refers to the average running distance of one complete turnround. It includes all the travelling distance of the freight car in the loaded and empty state. The average car-kilometers in one complete turnround of the freight car is positive to the turnaround time of the freight car. If the other factors remain unchanged, the longer the whole turnaround distance, the longer the turnaround time. Therefore, the average car-kilometers in one complete turnround should be shortened under the premise of ensuring normal work.

(2) Turnaround time of freight car: refers to the average time spent in turnover of freight cars in operation. It reflects the overall efficiency of the entire process of the car turnover, which is often used as a comprehensive indicator of the efficiency of the car operation.

5) Car loading capacity

The car loading capacity is an indicator of the degree of utilization of the car load capacity. It is divided into static load of car and dynamic load of car.

(1) Static load of freight car refers to the average tonnage of goods loaded by each car in the station, railway bureau or the whole railway in a certain period of time. It directly affects the number of loading cars and the number of operating cars required to complete a certain tonnage of goods.

(2) Dynamic load of freight car refers to the tonnage kilometers of goods completed by the whole railway and one Railway Bureau per car kilometer in a certain period of time.

The static load of freight car only reflects in the utilization of the load capacity of the goods under the static conditions of loading or loaded car. The dynamic load of freight car reflects the the average turnover of goods completed by each loaded car kilometer or operational freight car kilometer. It reflects the operational degree of the freight car in the whole process of transporting goods.

6) Present passenger cars

Present passenger cars include serviceable passenger cars and non-serviceable passenger cars, as shown in Figure 1-3 and 1-4.

(1) Serviceable passenger cars: all passenger cars dealing with transporting passengers collectively are referred to as serviceable passenger cars. Such as soft and hard seat cars for passengers, soft and hard sleeper cars, luggage cars and dining cars for passengers.

(2) Non-serviceable passenger cars: all passenger cars that do not handle passenger business and those that are in poor technical condition and cannot be coupled to the train for operation are non-serviceable passenger cars. Such as spare cars, official cars, welfare cars, special purpose cars and various maintenance cars, etc.

Figure 1-3 Serviceable passenger cars

Figure 1-4 Non-serviceable passenger cars

7) Number of passenger cars on hand

Railway passenger cars usually are respectively assigned to each unit, so the number of cars ownership for each unit is relatively stable, namely the number of all passenger cars each unit owns.

Number of passenger cars on hand can also be obtained by the formula:

$$P = (1+\alpha)\sum Lm$$

P—number of allocated passenger cars;

α—non-serviceable passenger cars retention factor, generally take 0.36 (of which spare car of 0.10, volatility of 0.20, maintenance rate of 0.06);

L—passenger train set number;

M—number of car sets.

Purpose of calculation of passenger cars ownership: one is to better grasp the distribution of passenger cars, to complete the railway transport task evenly; the other one is using the amount of car ownership multiplied by the repair cycle coefficient of various repair process, we can calculate the amount of maintenance tasks.

8) Passenger train kilometers and serviceable passenger car kilometers

(1) Passenger train kilometers refers to total kilometers the passenger train sets run attached to each unit of the bureau. The total kilometers of railway corporation passenger train is the sum of the national railway passenger train km. Passenger train kilometers is an important index of assessment and plan for passenger train related expenses.

(2) Serviceable passenger car kilometers refers to the total running kilometers of passenger cars allocated by each depot under the railway administration in each section.

Serviceable passenger car kilometers is an important part of passenger car kilometers and an important index for planning and assessment of passenger car maintenance costs and other technical expenses.

9) Turnround time of passenger train set

Turnround time of passenger train set refers to the total time from the first time when passenger train set is sent from the departure station to the next time when next passenger train set is sent from the departure station in order to operate the passenger train sets in the train diagram.

The turnround time of passenger train set reflects the efficiency of the whole process of the train set turnover, which reflects the efficiency of all departments related to passenger transport. The length of the turnaround time directly affects the number of cars required for trains in operation, thus affecting the number of passenger cars required for the railway. Therefore, this important indicator of car turnover time is used in the planning the number of passenger train sets.

3. Car maintenance index

1) Existing number of maintenance cars

Existing number of maintenance cars is also named as the number of cars in bad condition, or number of cars with defects. It refers to the number of all cars under repair and to be repaired that have been detained within the jurisdiction of the whole railway, a railway bureau, a vehicle repair factory or depot at 18:00 every day. It include subordinate cars (including corporate rental cars) that are detained for repair due to the expiration of regular inspection or temporary repair, the cars detained for repair, and cars to be scrapped and returned for maintenance. It also includes foreign and enterprise-owned cars with temporary failure that have been detained for repair.

Existing number of maintenance cars can be calculated according to the following formula:

Existing number of maintenance cars = number of remaining maintenance cars at the beginning of the day + number of cars detained for repair today – number of cars repaired today

Existing number of maintenancecars cars reflects the state of railway car reflects the status of vehicles of the whole railway or a railway bureau, as well as the progress of vehicle maintenance work of each vehicle maintenance unit, railway bureau or the whole railway. In order to ensure the factory and depot repair plan step by step and rhythmically, the Ministry of Railways stipulates that each Railway Bureau and repair factory has a certain amount of maintenance vehicles. Each depot and factory shall strive to reduce the number of maintenance cars under their jurisdiction and keep them below the specified quantity. Strengthen the planning of detaining cars and reducing the temporary repair of detached cars are one of the main ways to reduce the number of maintenance cars. Improve the efficiency of maintenance, shorten the maintenance time and improve the daily departure rate of maintenance cars are also important measures to reduce the number of maintenance cars.

2) Rate of cars under repair

Rate of cars under repair, also known as car defect rate, is the indicator to reflect the state of the car with relative figures.

Rate of freight cars under repair: it is the ratio of the number of defective freight cars of the whole railway or a railway bureau to the number of dominant freight cars. Freight cars are generally operated in the whole railway without fixed allocation. The freight car maintenance tasks of each bureau are allocated according to their maintenance capacity.

3) Down time for holding cars for repairing

Down time for holding cars for repairing refers to the average total dwell time of a car repaired by the whole railway or a railway bureau, a vehicle repair factory, a depot or other vehicle repair unit within a certain period of time. Day is used to count the voerhaul and depot repair time. Hour is used to count the time of auxiliary repair and temporary repair.

Down time for holding cars for repairing is an important indicator of the progress of the car repair work. Under the premise of ensuring the quality of the car repair, if down time for holding cars for repairing is shorter, it means the higher of the efficiency of car repair; the longer the down time of car maintenance is, the lower of the efficiency of car repair.

To the depot repair, the total down time of car maintenance for each car includes the time of repair track maintenance, waiting time and repair time; For the vehicles handed over to the factory for maintenance, it is often necessary to add the whole time from the place confirmed to be sent to the factory for maintenance to the train until the factory procedures are completed, which can also be called the return time.

4) Responsibility delay

Responsibility delay is an important indicator to evaluate the quality of the inspection work. Inspection personnel should inspect and maintain the cars in the time specified in the train operation diagram, and ensure the car or train running to the next inspection field and the repaired parts will not have failure. Any delay caused by improper work organization affecting the train to leave according to the scheduled time and due to the maintenance of the train is called the train inspection responsibility delay.

5) Responsible accident

The car operation department shall eliminate the railway traffic accidents and ensure the safety of the train operation. The accident caused by the inspection field or depot should be listed as responsible accident in the railway bureau and depot assessment system in accordance with the provisions of the "Rules for Investigation and Handling of Railway Traffic Accidents". For general accidents, passenger cars are counted according to the number of cars per 100 allocated cars assigned to the depot. Freight cars are counted according to the number of pieces per million vehicle kilometers of freight trains in its jurisdiction.

4. Car marshalling

1) Marshalling of cars in freight trains

The marshalling of freight trains shall comply with the following provisions in addition to the marshalling plan and train operation diagram:

(1) Dangerous and flammable freight cars are required to take some isolation measures during transport to avoid accidents.

(2) In the freight train, it is allowed to close the cut-off cock (hereinafter referred to as the car with closed angle cock) for the cars whose braking effect is stopped due to the loaded goods

and the cars whose automatic brake temporarily fails. But the departure trains marshaled at the inspection field should not have cars with closed angle cock that have brake deformation. The number of cars with closed angle cock marshaled into the trains should not exceed 6% of the total number of cars. If exceeding the number, the force of brake shoe should be calculated, and we should fill the brake performance certificate to the locomotive driver.

The car with closed angle cock shall not be coupled within three cars at the rear of the locomotive; no more than two cars shall be coupled in a row; the last car of the train shall not be the car with closed angle cock; the last second and third trains shall not be the cars with closed angle cock continuously.

For cars that are not suitable for continuous coupling in the middle of the train but with good running part, they can be coupled at the rear of the train with the permission of the train dispatcher. If the automatic brake of the vehicle does not work, the vehicle personnel must take safety measures to ensure that they will not be decoupled.

(3) Mechanical refrigerated cars should be coupled in the middle or rear of the freight train.

2) Coupling requirements for passenger trains

Passenger trains should be coupled in accordance with the type, number and the linked location regulated by the provisions of passenger trains coupling table. The last car should have air gauge and emergency brake valve.

(1) The coupled cars should be coupled according the speed mark of the cars.

(2) The provisions of passenger train linked with freight cars.

Express passenger trains are not allowed to couple freight cars. Other passenger trains in principle are also not allowed to couple freight cars. However, in special circumstances (accident relief, rescue), when freight cars must be coupled to the passenger train, it is subject to the approval of the higher authorities, then freight cars can be coupled to the end of the train, but no more than two freight cars. The technical status and maximum operating speed of the coupled freight cars must conform to the speed requirements of the passenger train. In the passenger train, the end door of the passenger car connected with the freight car must be locked.

(3) Cars not allowed to be coupled into the passenger trains.

Cars that exceed the period of regular maintenance (except the passenger trains according to the provisions in the extension range or identified by vehicle department that are sent for plant repair and depot repair).

Cars that carry dangerous, stinking goods.

Passenger trains that do not have the axle alarm car installed.

(4) Requirements for linking the passenger train and traction locomotive.

Cars loaded with passengers should be isolated with the traction locomotive by the car with no passengers. The luggage car, postal car, electric generator car and other non-passenger cars can be coupled next to the locomotive and at the end of the train as an isolated car. If the isolated car has faults and need to be taken off on the way, the train can continue to run without isolated car. In the absence of isolated car, in order to ensure the safety of passengers and the normal operation of traction locomotives, the front door of passenger car connected with the locomotive should be locked.

(5) Provisions for the car with closed angle cock in passenger train.

Passenger trains are not allowed to marshall cars with closed angle cock. In case of temporary failure of automatic brake during operation and can not be repaired within the parking time, it is allowed to close the angle cock of one car, but the last car of the train shall not be the car with closed angle cock.

3) Confirmation of coupler height difference

The height difference of the center horizontal lines of the couplers (simplified as coupler height difference) should be not more than 75 mm. This height difference is measured by the distances the two nearby coupler's center lines to the track surface. According to the operational restrictions, the maximum height between the coupler center lines to the top of the track surface is 890 mm. The minimum for empty freight car is 835 mm and for loaded freight car is 815 mm.

If the height difference of the coupler exceeds the operational restrictions, when the train runs on the track switches or on the soft foundation of the roadbed, the vehicles may vibrate up and down. Especially on the steep slope line, it is prone to happen decoupling and cause the vehicles to be uncoupled. When the coupler height difference is large, the contact surface of the coupler knuckle is also reduced, resulting in excessive bending moment, which is prone to happen coupler knuckle break accident.

Revision exercises

1. What is the car detached repair and in-train repair?

2. What is the danger if the height of two adjacent couplers exceeds the requirements in marshalling passenger trains?

3. What is the function of freight train's operation indicators and maintenance indicators?

Chapter 2

Freight Car Operation and Maintenance

A majority of our national freight cars enjoy a large number of features as follows: no fixed attachments, no fixed overhauling, no fixed usage, nationwide operation, a variety of car types, complex operating conditions, high safety requirements, high train density, disperse operation fields, short technical inspection time limit, various malfunctions and so on. Therefore, freight car operation will certainly stick to the policy of "safety first, prevention based, comprehensive treatment", establish complete freight car operation management systems, practice scientific production and management methods, provide advanced inspection equipment and make strict rules and regulations. The primary tasks of freight car operation and maintenance are listed below:

(1) To complete technical inspection, automatic brake performance test (hereinafter referred to as train brake test), fault disposal and maintenance of freight cars (hereinafter referred to as freight car fault disposal), etc. To take charge of detaining, repairing and returning the overdue cars, cars with poor technical status, railway freight cars with faults along the way and accident vehicles under regular maintenance. The quality of maintenance and operation freight cars shall meet the specified technical standards to ensure the operation safety of operation trains.

(2) To take charge of operation and maintenance management of freight car safety monitoring systems.

(3) To take charge of maintenance of freight cars that need to be detached and repaired temporarily among the freight cars in opeartion, and the regular maintenance of railway freight cars in rauxiliary repair.

(4) To make technical handover inspection and deal with malfunction of car dumpers before dumping and after unloading and freight cars after defrosting in the defrost garages with bulk goods (hereinafter referred to as the defrost garage); to make technical handover inspection and deal with malfunction of freight cars in and out of factories and mines, ports, local railways,

joint-ventured railways, specific railways, enterprise private railways and temporary engineering railways; to manage technical handover of international combined transport freight cars.

(5) To prepare the operation of express freight block trains in round trips and circling operation and fixed marshalling express trains within the jurisdiction of bureaus.

(6) To conduct technical quality analysis, assessment management and technical quality monitor of freight cars, make periodic investigation and analysis of operation car technical states, collect, handle and analyse malfunctions happening in the process of car operation; design, create and inspect freight cars and make quality supervision and feedback of main accessories;put forward improvement suggestions for car structure, design, manufacture, repair and operation management.

(7) To take care for freight cars ((hereinafter referred to as love trains), advertise the Love Trains activities, guide, supervise and check freight cars, stop anyone from damaging them, and claim for compensation of man-made damaged trains and manage them .

(8) To take charge of key products, trains with off-gauge goods, technical operation of mechanically refrigerated cars and train crew related work in accordance with the regulations.

(9) To assist the operation test of new car models, new technology and new accessories in accordance with the regulations.

(10) To participate railway traffic accident investigation and accident rescue, assist to handle and manage traffic accident investigation, and investigate, handle and manage equipment faults.

(11) To finish other related work stated by China Railway.

Unit 1 Freight Car Operation and Maintenance

Learning Objectives

(1) To know production and living facilities on car inspection fields.

(2) To grasp the primary tasks for freight car operation maintenance.

(3) To grasp the different kinds of freight car operation fields.

Learning Content

1. Freight car operation maintenance tasks

(1) To complete technical inspection, automatic brake performance test (hereinafter

referred to as train brake test), fault disposal and maintenance of freight cars (hereinafter referred to as freight car fault disposal) and so on within the regulated train technical operation time (hereinafter referred to as technical inspection time); to take charge of buckle repair and return of due date or expired cars during periodic repair, cars with bad technical conditions or breaking down on the road and accident cars; to make sure that freight cars in operation meet quality technical standards and run safely.

(2) To take charge of operation and overhaul management of freight car safety monitoring systems.

(3) To take charge of maintenance of freight car in need of temporary car-attached repair and make periodic auxiliary repair.

(4) To make technical handover inspection and deal with malfunction of car dumpers before dumping and after unloading and freight cars after defrosting in the defrost garages with bulk goods(hereinafter referred to as the defrost garage); to make technical handover inspection and deal with malfunction of freight cars in and out of factories and mines, ports, local railways, joint-ventured railways, specific railways, enterprise private railways and temporary engineering railways; to manage technical handover of international combined transport freight cars.

(5) To prepare the operation of express freight block trains in round trips and circling operation and fixed marshalling express trains within the jurisdiction of bureaus.

(6) To conduct technical quality analysis, assessment management and technical quality monitor of freight cars, make periodic investigation and analysis of operation car technical states, collect, handle and analyse malfunctions happening in the process of car operation; design, create and inspect freight cars and make quality supervision and feedback of main accessories; put forward improvement suggestions for car structure, design, manufacture, repair and operation management.

(7) To take care for freight cars (hereinafter referred to as love trains), advertise the Love Trains activities, guide, supervise and check freight cars, stop anyone from damaging them, and claim for compensation of man-made damaged trains and manage them.

(8) To take charge of key products, trains with off-gauge goods, technical operation of mechanically refrigerated cars and train crew related work in accordance with the regulations.

(9) To assist the operation test of new car models, new technology and new accessories in accordance with the regulations.

(10) To participate railway traffic accident investigation and accident rescue, assist to handle and manage traffic accident investigation, and investigate, handle and manage equipment faults.

2. Freight train operation fields

Freight train operation fields are composed of train inspection fields, dynamic inspection fields, technical handover fields and preparation fields and so on. They are the front lines for technical inspection and repair and the required parts of transportation service and safe driving. Freight car operation fields' layout, labor organization, work group setting and staffing requirements must meet the need of safe production and transportation.

(1) Train inspection fields are usually set up on marshalling stations, district stations and intermediate station and primarily responsible for freight car technical inspection. Freight car technical operation includes technological processes of received train for break-up, technological processes of outgoing train made-up at station, technological processes of transit train without resorting and technological processes of transit train with partial resorting.

① Technological processes of received train for break-up: to break up all trains arriving at technical stations. Technical operations includes car inspection and maintenance, freight inspection, verification of cars in stock, bill handover and splitting preparation. car inspection operation fields mainly implements technical examination and repair of freight cars.

② Technological processes of outgoing train made-up at station: to mainly conduct technical operation on technical stations or loading stations for marshalling cars. Technical operation includes car inspection and maintenance , freight inspection, verification of cars in stock, car detachment and attachment, bill handover, departure preparation and departure and so on. car inspection operation fields mainly implements technical examination and repair of freight cars.

③ Technological processes of transit train without resorting: only for cars in need of transit operation and then continuing running after arriving technical stations. Technical operation includes car inspection and maintenance, freight inspection, verification of cars in stock, bill handover, departure preparation and departure and so on. Car inspection operation fields mainly implements technical examination and repair of freight cars which are transit trains in a safe distance from inspection fields and cars without inspection fields ahead.

④ Technological processes of transit train with partial resorting: to mainly take charge of cars in need of minor dispatching services such as changing weight or length, detaching or attaching in bunch after arriving technical stations and then continuing running. Technical operation includes car inspection and maintenance (including detaching and attaching cars and train air testing), freight inspection, verification of cars in stock, car detachment and attachment, bill handover, departure preparation and departure and so on. Car inspection operation fields mainly implements technical examination and repair of freight cars which are transit trains in a safe distance from inspection fields and cars without inspection fields ahead.

(2) Dynamic inspection operation fields: to be intensively set or regional intensively set, dynamic inspectors conduct dynamic inspection for splitting cars and non-recompose and

partial- recompose transit freight cars during the operation by Trouble of Moving Freight Car Detection System(TFDS) in accordance with scope of examination and quality standards, and report fault cars to car inspection fields who will check, confirm and handle those problems.

(3) Technical handover operation fields: to be set on enterprise private railways equipped with dumpers and defrosting garages or on factories and mines, ports, local railways, joint-ventured railways, specific railways, enterprise private railways and temporary engineering railways and other stations connected with national railways. Connecting stations which have car inspection operation fields cannot set up technical handover operation fields whose relevant work are transferred to car inspection operation fields. Technical handover operation fields make technical handover inspection and deal with malfunction of freight cars in and out of factories and mines, ports, local railways, joint-ventured railways, specific railways, enterprise private railways and temporary engineering railways and prevent accident and badly damaged freight cars due to derailing by improper loading and unloading and traffic collision from entering national railway in order not to endanger their transportation safety.

(4) Technical handover operation fields on frontier stations: to usually be set up on frontier stations handling international combined transport freight cars. They are primarily responsible for technical handover and fault treatment of Chinese and foreign international combined transport freight cars and ensure their safe operation.

(5) Preparation operation fields: to usually be set up on stations which make periodic and fixed-spot preparation operation for express freight block trains in round trips and circling operation, fixed marshalling express trains within the jurisdiction of bureaus, freight cars entering plateaus and specialized heavy-haul freight cars; conduct technical inspection and repair of the above cars in accordance with scope of examination and quality standards.

3. Train inspection operation fields

(1) Security duty on train inspection operation fields.

Train inspection operation fields ensure that relevant car parts' quality meets the specification after inspecting freights in accordance with scope of examination and quality standards and safely transport to next fields in charge of relevant parts under regular service conditions, and bear corresponding safety and quality responsibility.

The safe distance for pull-up departure car operation should be about 500 km in principle after train inspection operation in accordance with scope of examination and quality standards. According to transportation organization, line conditions, technical states and train inspection operation layout and plateau, heavy-haul and long-routing freight cars should be kept at a safe distance in accordance with the regulations by the Ministry of Railway.

(2) The sorting and setting of train inspection operation fields.

Train inspection operation fields mainly inspect and maintain freights by the ways of manual or manual-machine checking and meet their safe and unblocked transportation. Fields on marshalling stations and relevant stations should be set reasonably according to the quantity of arriving splitting trains (hereinafter referred to as: arriving trains), marshalling departure trains (hereinafter referred to as:departure trains) and transit trains, transportation organizations, locomotive routing, operation conditions and safe distance and so on, which is shown in Figure 2-1.

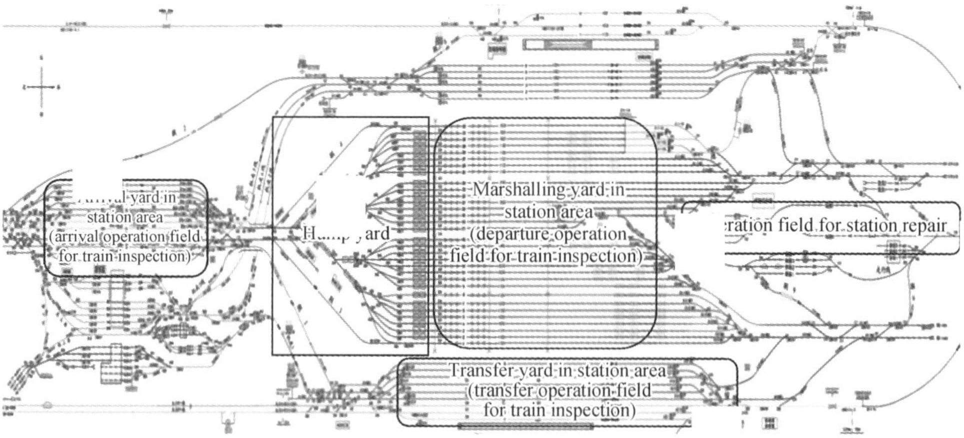

Figure 2-1 Marshalling stations' sketch ma

The grade of car inspection operation fields divides into super class and first class. Super-class car inspection operation fields are set on marshalling stations and district stations marshalling a large number of cars or loading and unloading goods or on district stations and intermediate stations dealing with numerous transit freights during pull-up technical operation.

Train inspection operation fields' names should correspond to their stations, fields, or districts' names in theory. If the districts have several fields, their names are distinguished as up and down, arrival and departure or one and two.

(3) Production and living facilities on train inspection operation fields.

The stations or station area where train inspection operation fields lie have ability to conduct temporary repair. Those who have not the temporary repair ability should set special lines for malfunction freight cars in need of temporary repair;straight line length is no less than 60 m, and equipped relevant facilities and devices and safety protection devices such as electric welding machines and car lifters.

Production and living houses on train inspection operation fields should be set on multiple-use buildings and in theory contains duty room, inspection waiting room, offices, meeting room, shift handover room, material room, multimedia training room, security warning room, computer room, model exhibition room, fault exhibition room and practising bases and other production facilities. Train inspection operation fields also should have charging room, air compressor room, tool room, material and accessory storage and distribution room, outdoor storage sheds for large parts and field-end computer room for controlling brake test devices and so on, as shown in Figure 2-2.

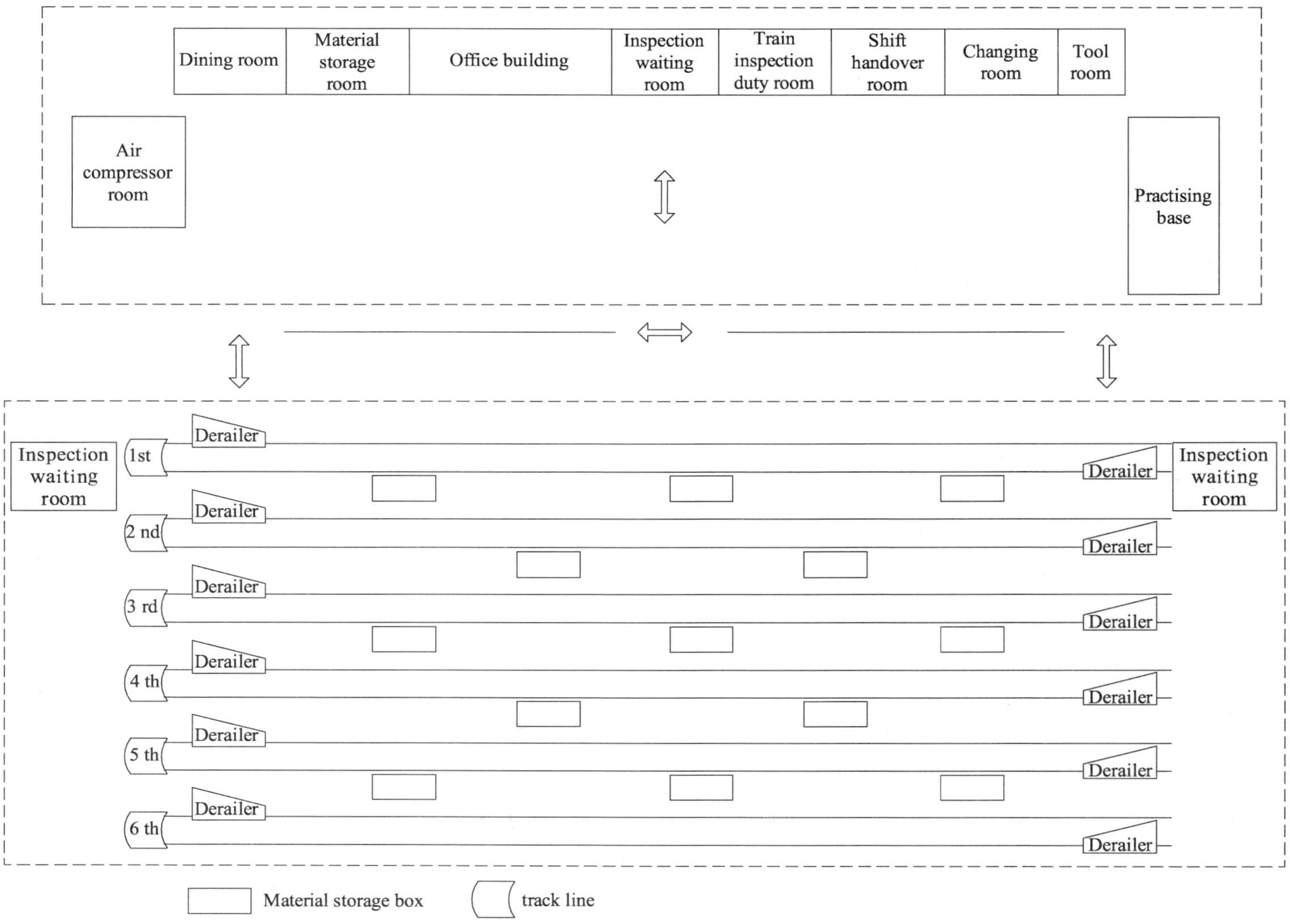

Figure 2-2 Sketch map of car inspection operation layout

Operating lines should build lamp bridges (shown in Figure 2-3) or light houses, of which illumination zones cover all operating area and their illuminance conforms relevant regulations. Lamp bridges or light houses should be at illuminating state when freight inspection is conducted at night or in the dark light.

Figure 2-3　Lamp bridge on car inspection operation fields

Cement prefabricated slabs with 1 m width should be paved between operating lines or outer side of line groups (3 m far from the line center) on the same level with rail bearings and have excellent drainage function. Concrete flat rail bearings should be paved around lines and cinder-prevent walls are set on the outer side of line groups. The fields also have relevant tools, material transport carts, cross-set tool-material distribution and storage boxes and meets requirements for freight fault repair.

(1) Production facilities.

① Freight inspection duty room.

Freight inspection duty room is usually set up on multiple-use buildings or dispatch buildings so as to watch freight arrival and departure; inspection waiting room is set up according to station surrounding or operating lines length or quantity. Freight inspection multiple-use buildings should establish inspection waiting rooms; when a freight inspection multiple-use building is on one end of a field, its inspection waiting room should be on the central part or the other end of the field. If operating lines are above 10, its station or the multiply-use building sets an inspection waiting room on the other side. The inspection waiting room should be equiped with HMIS terminals, printers, straight-through telephones to duty rooms, display terminals of receiving and sending freights and safety information, and seats and so on. Duty rooms and inspection waiting rooms should have clocks and make regular time calibration with stations.

② Operation devices storage room.

Charging room should have deposit counters, tool counters, control panels and charging devices shown as Figure 2-4; tool room has repair tools, devices, accessories and backups, such as work benches, vice benches, grinding machines and bench drilling machines, shown as Figure 2-5.

Figure 2-4 Charging room

Figure 2-5 Tool room

③ Instruction and training aid places.

Model display room should display parts and models of main-type cars and courseware, shown as Figure 2-6; fault exhibition room should put up fault discovery method diagrams and display typical damaged parts, as shown in Figure 2-7.

Figure 2-6 Model display room

Figure 2-7 Fault exhibition rooms

Practising base should meet their area's need and establish different sections for theory training, practice drills, audio-visual education programme, physical parts, damaged parts and so on, shown as Figure 2-8.

Figure 2-8 Practising base

Furthermore, train inspection operation field should have shift handover room, material and accessory storage and distribution room, outdoor storage sheds for large parts, paths connected to outside roads and level crossing railroads on one or two ends of the operating line where road surfaces should harden. If it happens that transport paths cross with main tracks, the fields should build culverts for cars and people. The field should install car approaching speech alarm devices and separation facilities if needing to cross main tracks or near main tracks for inspection operation .

(2) Production facilities.

① Operating lines on car inspection operation fields should install secure derailers with the function of safety protection (shown in Figure 2-9), which have capacity to resist severe weather and thunder. Those derailers' installation sites are decided by the position of annunciators, fouling point indicators, car parking position and car length and so on. The lines also have mobile derailers according to the actual situation (shown in Figure 2-10). Detrailers are used to separate in both ways at the protective section and reliably derail cars intruding into the protective section from either side so as to protect operation personnel.

Figure 2-9 Secure derailer

Figure 2-10 Mobile derailer

② Train inspection operation field should install computer controlling brake test devices which inspect brake performance for car operation in groups and detect and handle their brake problems in time to ensure their safety operation(shown in the Figure 2-11). The quantity and installation of test actuators should be decided by car brake test.

Figure 2-11　Computer controlling brake test devices

Train inspection operation field should install air compressor room which meets maximum air volume of car brake tests and have functions of dedusting, dehumidification and temperature control. Compressed air lines should use corrosion-resistant materials with the pipe diameter of no less than 50 mm, such as stainless steel, take antifreezing measures and be paved under specified trenches or sunken pipes.

③ Train inspection operation field should install car brake test monitor devices and monitor terminals and host computers in the duty rooms.

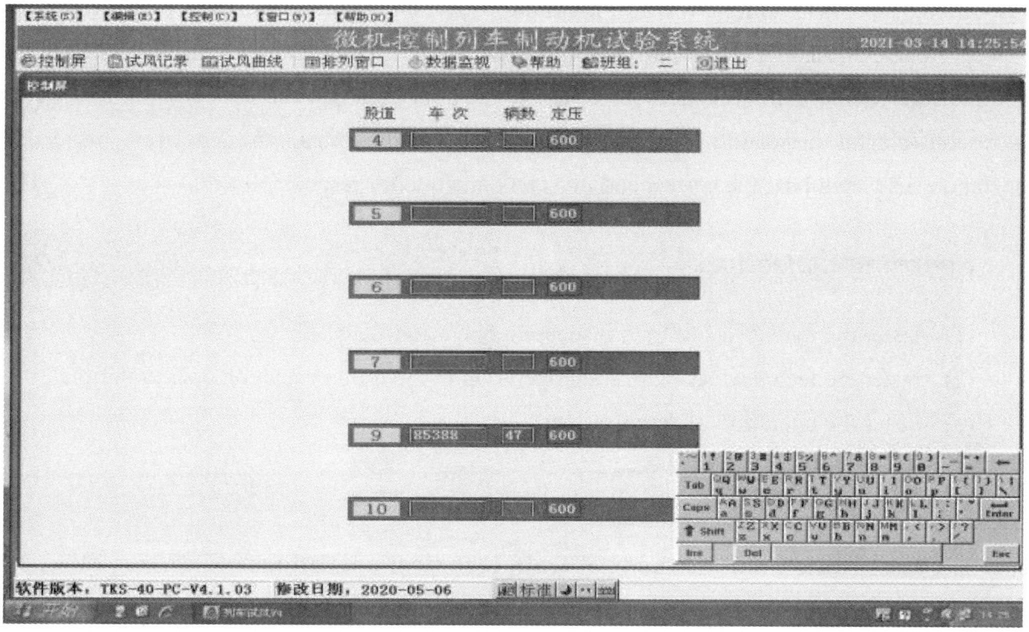

Figure 2-12　Indoor monitor terminal interface

④ Train inspection operation field should install remote supervision terminals of car number automatic identification system, subsystems of Freight Vehicle Management Information System (hereinafter referred to as: HMIS), handheld systems and freight car operation safety monitoring systems and other systems.

⑤ Inspectors on train inspection operation field should have inspecting hammers, inspecting lamps, wireless interphones, handheld sets, fluorescent guide plates, protective red lights or flags, tool straps or waist belts and other tools; the train inspection operation field should possess specialized tools, measuring tools and machines to handle freight breakdown and keep up developing and upgrading new repair methods and tools.

Revision exercises

1. What are sorts of train inspection operation fields?
2. Please make a brief description of freight car operation and maintenance tasks.

Unit 2　Technical Operation for Train Inspection Operation Field

After carrying out technical operations on freight trains in accordance with the prescribed inspection scope and quality standards, the train inspection operation field must ensure that the quality standards of the corresponding parts of the freight trains comply with the regulations, and run safely under normal conditions of use to the next train inspection operation field which is responsible for inspecting the same parts of the freight trains. The first train inspection operation field shall bear the corresponding safety and quality responsibilities.

Learning Objectives

(1) Master the main tasks of train inspection operation field.

(2) Master the technical scope of train operation in the train inspection operation field.

(3) Master the operation of detaining cars.

Learning content

1. Classification and methods of train technical operations

Train technical operations are divided into receiving operations, departure operations, transfer operations, and passing through operations according to the nature of the operations.

There are differences in the operating methods, operating scopes and quality standards adopted.

1) Receiving operation

Receiving operation refers to the operation of the train inspection operation field on the arriving train at the station, which adopts man-machine division of labor inspection or manual inspection. If TFDS is installed on the train route connected to the train inspection operation field, the man-machine division operation mode shall be adopted, and the "Man-machine Division TFDS Dynamic Inspection Scope and Quality Standard" and "Man-machine Division Manual Inspection Scope and Quality Standard of Arrival Train" shall be implemented. If TFDS is not installed on the train route connected to the train inspection operation field or TFDS cannot carry out dynamic inspection normally, manual inspection operation mode shall be adopted, and "Man-machine Division TFDS Dynamic Inspection Scope and Quality Standard" and "Man-machine Division Manual Inspection Scope and Quality Standard of Arrival Train" shall be implemented.

2) Departure operation

Departure operation refers to the operation of the train inspection workplace on the train departing from the station. The train inspection operation adopts the manual inspection mode. Manual inspection shall be implemented for car technical inspection, and the "Inspection Scope and Quality Standard of Departure Train" shall be implemented.

3) Transfer operation

Transfer operation refers to the operation performed on the transfer train. where the train inspection operation field is at the station and at the safety guarantee distance of train inspection operation. The train inspection operation adopts man-machine division inspection or manual inspection. If TFDS is installed on the train route connected to the train inspection operation field, the man-machine division operation mode shall be adopted, and the "Man-machine Division TFDS Dynamic Inspection Scope and Quality Standard" and "Man-machine Division Manual Inspection Scope and Quality Standard of Transfer Train" shall be implemented. If TFDS is not installed on the train route connected to the train inspection operation field or TFDS cannot carry out dynamic inspection normally, manual inspection operation mode shall be adopted, and "Inspection Scope and Quality Standard of Departure Train" shall be implemented. Manual inspection shall be carried out for coupled railway freight trains, and the "Inspection Scope and Quality Standard of Departure Train" shall be implemented.

4) Passing through operation

Passing through operation refers to the operation of freight trains other than the above conditions, using TFDS to carry out dynamic inspection methods, implementing the "TFDS Dynamic Inspection Scope and Quality Standard of Passing through Operation", and handling faults that meet the "TFDS Dynamic Inspection Scope and Quality Standard of Passing through Operation" according to the train stop procedure.

For trains departing from a formation station without train inspection operation field, the train inspection operation shall be carried out on the way through the first train inspection operation field, and the relevant provisions of the transfer operation shall be implemented. For train departing from the formation station without train inspection operation field which belongs to one Railway Bureau Group Company, when the train is not passing through the train inspection operation field of its own Railway Bureau Group Company, the departing Railway Bureau Group Company shall notify the access Railway Bureau Group Company to arrange the first train inspection operation field for train inspection when it passes through, and specify the operation location in relevant documents.

2. Inspection scope of train inspection operation field

According to the actual production requirements, during the technical inspection of railway trains, the vehicles can be divided into the following parts for inspection.

1) Wheel

Vertical wear and inner defect of wheel flange is not out of gauge; tread surface abrasions, stripping, local concave, defect, circumference wear are not out of gauge; flange thickness and rim thickness are not out of gauge, as shown in Figure 2-13.

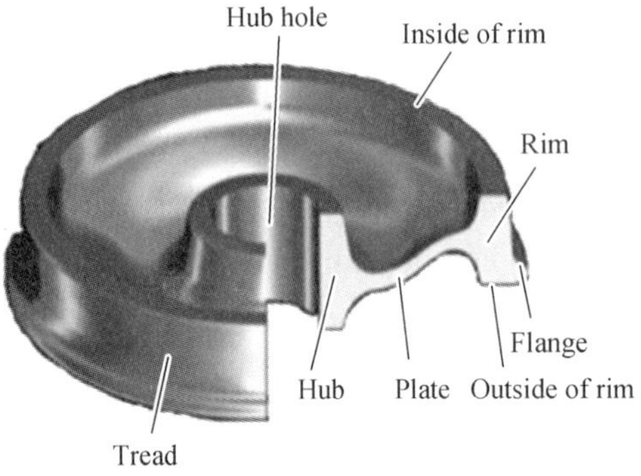

Figure 2-13 Wheel set

2) Axle box and its accessories

Eliminate hot box failure; the rolling bearing has no oil spill, the outer ring, the front cover, the adapter, and the axle box are not cracked, and the shaft end bolts do not fall out; the adapter is not misaligned; as shown in Figure 2-14.

Figure 2-14 Axle box and its accessories

3) Bogie and its accessories

The side frame, bolster and center plate are not cracked; the side frame column wear plate and the main friction plate of the oblique wedge are not damaged, sprang out, or lost; the upper and lower center plate bolts are not broken or lost; the cross rod cover plate and the rod body are not bent, deformed, cracking, the safety chain is not falling off or broke, the support seat is not damaged, the cross rod end bolts is not loosened, the anti-loose pad of clamping washer is not broken off; the axle box and the bolster spring are not broken, sprang out or lost; as shown in Figure 2-15.

Figure 2-15 Bogie and its accessories

4) Coupler

The coupler, knuckle and coupler tail frame are not damaged; the coupler's lifting rod and the seat are complete without damage, and intercoupling difference is not out of gauge; the coupler follower , draft lug, buffer, and coupler pocket are not damaged; yoke support plate, draft flat key and safety hanger bolts and nuts are not lost, and the split pins are not lost; the yoke support plate nuts are not lost, and the bolts and nuts of coupler carrier and coupler pocket stop are not lost; as shown in Figure 2-16.

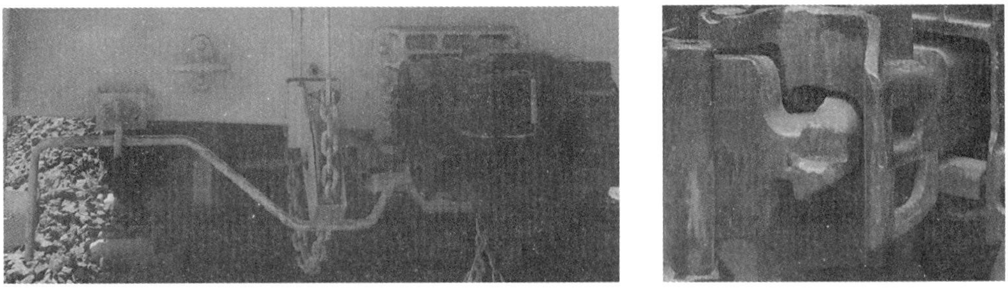

Figure 2-16　Coupler

5) Braking system

The air brake works well:

The brake cylinder and air cylinder have no cracks or fall off , the hanger is not cracked and the fastening bolts are not loose or cracked; the brake valve hanger nut is not loose or missing; there is no leakage of the brake pipe and the connecting pipe, no clips and bolts are lost; no brake hoses are damaged or lost, no brake hose slings are lost; angle cock and cut-out cock are not damaged, and handle is not lost; as shown in Figure 2-17.

Figure 2-17　Braking system

The brake beam frame and strut have no cracks; the brake beam hangers have no cracks, the round pin and cotter pins are not broken or lost; the safety chains of brake beam are not broken or dropped; the brake shoe bolts are not broken or lost, and the brake shoes wear is not out of gauge; none of the tie rods, levers, round pins, and split pins are broken or lost.

6) Hand brake

Hand brake has complete accessories without damage, as shown in Figure 2-18.

Figure 2-18 Hank brake

Figure 2-19 Car body

7) Car body

The inclination or external expansion of the car body is not out of gauge; the automatic identification label of the car number is not invalid or lost; the doors and windows are not damaged or lost; There is no error in door hinge translation, no breakage, and no loss of round pin and cotter pin; the door hinges are not broken, the round pins and cotter pins are not lost; door locking device accessories are complete and in good condition; the rope bolt is not damaged or lost; the pedal shall not be damaged, and the bending shall not exceed the car gauge, as shown in Figure 2-19.

8) Predetermined repairs date

The predetermined repair of empty cars shall not expire.

3. Car detainment for predetermined repairs

1) Detaining car for predetermined repairs

When a freight car's predetermined repair is due or expires during a train inspection outside the scope of the car's distributed jurisdiction of the railway bureau, the station that performs the inspection shall detain the car. Under such circumstances, the train inspector shall insert the prescribed color ticket into the ticket jack mounted on the detained car and informs the on-duty train inspection staff to go through the detaining procedure.

(1) Programmed detainment: According to various overhaul, repair and maintenance, the railway cars shall be detained in light of their models and types in accordance with plans, so as to ensure that all cars of the railway system can be inspected and maintained as scheduled or according to the cars' conditions.

(2) Detainment based on the overhaul period: The center in charge of train inspection and maintenance shall detain and repair the cars within the predetermined repair period according to their markings for repairs and overhauls. Overhauls and depot repairs shall be performed on a monthly basis, and auxiliary repairs and axle inspections shall be performed on a predetermined date. Advanced repairs shall be carried out for the car when its overhaul, depot repair, and auxiliary repair are due at the same time.

(3) Detainment priority: If pursuant to the detainment programs, cars whose repair periods are due or expire or those with different levels of damage cannot be detained at the same time, the expired or more severely damaged shall have the priority of being detained for repairs.

(4) Detainment priority of the empty car: Generally, detainment for the cars whose predetermined repair periods are due shall be carried out first for the empty ones. The loaded cars shall not be detained unless it requires necessary repairs for failures that jeopardize the safety of train operation or it arrives or is about to arrive at the terminus. Otherwise, the loaded car whose predetermined repair periods are due shall be permitted to depart for the next station in charge of inspection and maintenance as long as safe operation of the train is ascertained after careful inspection.

2) Detaining temporary repair cars

In case of car failure found in the train inspection operation field, it shall actively organize maintenance in the train fleet; however, for the major faults that affect the driving safety and cannot be repaired in the train fleet or the faults that exceed the technical inspection time and affect the disassembly operation or on-time departure, the car can be detached for temporary repair.

3) Detaining steps

(1) Master the train detaining plan: the train inspector on duty shall first master the train detaining plan issued by the attendant during the operation time of the shift. Cars should be strictly detained according to the plan (except for temporary repairs).

(2) Check car status: when performing technical inspection on the train, the train inspector shall pay attention to the regular maintenance mark, technical status, and empty and loaded status of the car, so as to determine how to detain the car.

(3) Determine the color ticket for detaining cars: determine the disposal method of cars and select the color ticket according to the car status and detaining plan.

(4) Confirm and fill in the color ticket: in order to prevent human errors, it is necessary to confirm whether the color ticket used is correct, and then fill in it correctly, clearly and neatly according to the regulations.

(5) Insert color ticket and record: insert the color ticket into the color ticket box of the car to indicate the identity of the car in use. Then, record the car type, model, car number, reason for detaining and other information in the Inspector's Work Manual.

(6) Return to the train inspection and service point to complete the formalities: After the operation is completed, the car detention will be reported to the duty attendant immediately and registered. For the insertion of inspection and repair color tickets, such as auxiliary repair, depot repair, overhaul, etc., the duty attendant must fill in "Notification of Car Maintenance".

Revision exercises

1. What are the tasks of the train inspection operation field?
2. What is the train detaining procedure at the train train inspection operation field?

Unit 3 Technical Inspection for Single Car

Technical inspection for sigle car is a basic skill for each railway freight car inspector. In order to ensure the railway traffic safety, each inspector must master the procedures methods, operate orders and operation limit for freight car.

Learning Objectives

(1) Master the operation limit for freight car.

(2) Master the operation methods of technical inspection for single car.

Learning content

1. Work clothes, equipment and tools

Blue and yellow long sleeve blouses with reflective strips, blue pants, yellow work caps with reflective strips, arm badges, safety shoes, split-type raincoats with reflective strips, long boots, 300 × 300 mm monkey wrenches, inspecting hammers, lights,magnet protecting flag, stroboscopic red lights, interphones, portable infrared thermometers, statistical tables on trailer-15A, wheel inspectors, tapelines and recorders and so on, as shown in Figure 2-20.

Figure 2-20 Schematic diagram of staff dress

2. Operation limit for freight car

(1) Car body operation limit for freight car is shown in Table 2-1.

Table 2-1 Car body operation limit for freight car Unit: mm

NO.	Name		Limit	Notes
1	side beam sagging	Empty	≤40	Measure between two bolsters
		Load	≤80	
2	external expansion of pen-top wagon	Empty	≤80	—
		Load	≤150	
3	Car body tilt		≤75	—
4	Damage, corrosion and perforation of end wall, sidewall, floor and door plates and tub plates for empty pen-top wagon		≤50 × 50	—
5	Broken non-metallic plate of box cars and flat casr		≤100 × 100	—

(2) Bogie operation limit for freight car is shown in Table 2-2.

Table 2-2 Bogie operation limit for freight car Unit: mm

<table>
<tr><th>No.</th><th colspan="2">Name</th><th>Limit</th><th>Notes</th></tr>
<tr><td rowspan="2">1</td><td colspan="2">The sum gaps of both side bearings of the same bogie</td><td>2 ~ 20</td><td>Gaps of each side bearing must be above zero, its gap of oversize freight cars with capacity of 280 t and above must be more than 2 mm</td></tr>
<tr><td colspan="2">gaps of double-acting elastic upper and lower side bearings</td><td>0</td><td>—</td></tr>
<tr><td>2</td><td colspan="2">Gaps between upper side bearings and double-acting elastic side bearing roller or nylon support plate</td><td>>0</td><td>—</td></tr>
<tr><td rowspan="2">3</td><td rowspan="2">Vertical distance from each part hung under the rail to rail surface</td><td>inside rails</td><td>≥60</td><td rowspan="2">The each upper part hung under the rail must not be lower than 25 mm</td></tr>
<tr><td>outside rails</td><td>≥80</td></tr>
</table>

(3) Wheel set operation limit table for freight car is shown in Table 2-3.

Table 2-3 Wheel set operation limit table for freight car Unit: mm

<table>
<tr><th>No.</th><th colspan="2">Name</th><th>Limit</th><th>Notes</th></tr>
<tr><td rowspan="2">1</td><td rowspan="2">Thickness of wheel rims</td><td>Spoke plate hole</td><td>≥23</td><td rowspan="2">—</td></tr>
<tr><td>Non-spoke plate hole</td><td>≥24</td></tr>
<tr><td rowspan="2">2</td><td rowspan="2">Thickness of wheel flanges</td><td>Box cars, container flat cars, container-flat cars,transport cars and railway wagon with speeds of 120 km/h</td><td>≥25</td><td>—</td></tr>
<tr><td>Others</td><td>≥23</td><td>Train inspection of thickness of middle wheel flange set in 3-axle and multiaxle bogies could not be included</td></tr>
<tr><td>3</td><td colspan="2">Vertical wear height of wheel Flange(contact position)</td><td>≤15</td><td>—</td></tr>
<tr><td rowspan="2">4</td><td rowspan="2">Inner defect of wheel flange</td><td>Length</td><td>≤30</td><td rowspan="2">—</td></tr>
<tr><td>Width</td><td>≤10</td></tr>
<tr><td>5</td><td colspan="2">Depth of tread circumference wear</td><td>≤8</td><td>—</td></tr>
<tr><td>6</td><td colspan="2">Depth of abrasions and local concave of wheel tread</td><td>≤1</td><td>—</td></tr>
</table>

Continue

No.	Name		Limit	Notes
7	Flaking length on wheel tread	One	≤50	1. Measure it at circumferential direction 2. the measurement rules as follows: ① The width less than 10 mm should be excluded. ② The widest point of the stripped flaking less than 20 mm should be excluded. ③ Its length should be no more than 35 mm if the distance of two flaking outboards is less than 75 mm. The total length of continuous flaking should be no more than 350 mm if its flaking is less than 35 mm at several points. ④ The unshed parts of flaking in the earlier stage should be excluded
		Two（each）	≤40	
8	Tread defect	Length from opposite flange outboard to defected inner edge	≥1508	Measure from the defected inner edge
		Defect length	≤150	Measure it at tread circumferential direction
9	Circumference crack at the edge of wheel spoke plate holes		≤30	—
10	Temperature rise of rolling bearing		≤55 °C	—

(4) Brake operation limit table for freight car is shown in Table 2-4.

Table 2-4 Brake operation limit table for freight car Unit: mm

No.	Name				Limit	Notes	
1	Brake cylinder piston stroke	Single brake shoe installed with the brake-shoe adjuster	356×254 brake cylinder	Empty	115～135	Uninstalled with the brake-shoe adjuster	85～135
				Load	125～160		110～160
			305×254 brake cylinder	Empty	145～165	—	
				Load	145～195	—	
			254×254 brake cylinder	Empty	145～165	—	
				Load	145～195	—	
			203×254 brake cylinder	Empty	115～145	—	
				Load	125～160	—	

Continue

<table>
<tr><th>No.</th><th colspan="4">Name</th><th>Limit</th><th>Notes</th></tr>
<tr><td rowspan="5">1</td><td rowspan="5">Brake cylinder piston stroke</td><td rowspan="3">Compound brake shoes installed with the brake-shoe adjuster</td><td rowspan="2">B_{21}、$B_{22\text{-}1}$-type car</td><td>Empty</td><td>120 ~ 130</td><td>—</td></tr>
<tr><td>Load</td><td>150 ~ 160</td><td>—</td></tr>
<tr><td colspan="2">B_{19}、$B_{22\text{-}2}$、B_{23}-type car</td><td>130 ~ 150</td><td>—</td></tr>
<tr><td rowspan="2">Integrated brake equipment</td><td colspan="2">BAB series</td><td>Travel indicator in the hole of the brake sign</td><td rowspan="2">—</td></tr>
<tr><td colspan="2">DAB series</td><td>Travel indicator in the circle of the travel sign</td></tr>
<tr><td>2</td><td colspan="4">Remaining thickness of high and low friction composition brake shoe</td><td>≥20</td><td rowspan="2">—</td></tr>
<tr><td>3</td><td colspan="4">Remaining thickness of two-axle or three-axle bogie brake shoe in C_{100}-type open top car</td><td>≥25</td></tr>
<tr><td>4</td><td colspan="4">Thickness difference of brake shoe in the same brake beam</td><td>≤20</td><td rowspan="2">Confirm after changing brake shoe</td></tr>
<tr><td>5</td><td colspan="4">Thickness difference of brake shoe in the same brake beam of two-axle or three-axle bogie brake shoe in C_{100}-type open top car</td><td>≤10</td></tr>
</table>

(5) Coupler operation limit table for freight car is shown in Table 2-5.

Table 2-5 Coupler operation limit table for freight car Unit: mm

<table>
<tr><th>No.</th><th>Name</th><th colspan="2">Limit</th><th colspan="2">Notes</th></tr>
<tr><td rowspan="2">1</td><td rowspan="2">Distance between NO. 13 knuckles and guards</td><td colspan="2">Locked position</td><td>≤135</td><td rowspan="2"></td></tr>
<tr><td colspan="2">Full open position</td><td>≤250</td></tr>
<tr><td rowspan="2">2</td><td rowspan="2">Distance between 13A and 13B knuckles and guards</td><td colspan="2">Locked position</td><td>≤132</td><td></td></tr>
<tr><td colspan="2">Full open position</td><td>≤247</td><td></td></tr>
<tr><td rowspan="2">3</td><td rowspan="2">Distance between NO.16 and NO.17 knuckles and guards</td><td colspan="2">Locked position</td><td>≤100</td><td></td></tr>
<tr><td colspan="2">Full open position</td><td>≥219</td><td></td></tr>
<tr><td>4</td><td colspan="3">Slack allowance of coupler release rods</td><td>40 ~ 55</td><td></td></tr>
<tr><td>5</td><td colspan="3">Height difference of connecting couplers</td><td>≤75</td><td></td></tr>
<tr><td rowspan="3">6</td><td rowspan="3">Coupler center height</td><td colspan="2">Maximum</td><td>≤890</td><td rowspan="3"></td></tr>
<tr><td rowspan="2">Minimum</td><td>Empty</td><td>≥835</td></tr>
<tr><td>Loaded</td><td>≥815</td></tr>
</table>

3. Responsibility distinction on train inspection operation

According to technical inspection for arrival, transferring and departure freight cars, train inspection field operation will take freight car's longitudinal central line as the dividing line to carry out faceted checks. In order not to miss inspection of some parts, confused boundaries are divided as follows:

① Couplers' connection state, three states of coupler operation for head and tail car, coupler release rod and chain, anti-skipping pin, sling chain and lower lock pin are all in the charge of the car inspector at the side where the coupler release rod is located; the height of coupler and the height difference between two connecting couplers shall be in the charge of the inspectors on both sides; if the upper part of the coupler and the longitudinal center line of the impact seat are damaged, the vehicle inspector on the side where the coupler release rod is not located shall be responsible for it.

② The bottom surface of the coupler body (lower pin holes), lock legs, coupler carriers, coupler support seats, oil-bearing nylon wear plates, coupler yoke keys, safety hanger bolts and brake hose sling chains are in the charge of cross rail inspectors.

③ Bogie side bears,central plates,swing bolsters, inner bolster spring(not including damper springs),brake beam body and post's clip bolts, cross levers, cross beams, safety chains, unloaded/loaded adjusting valves are in the charge of cross rail inspectors.

④ Inside and outside of bogies are divided at the top point of wheel flanges.

⑤ Brake cylinder connecting pipes' leakage is in the charge of brake inspectors.

⑥ Fixation of the inner and outer bogies and floating levers, upper levers, fixation of lever fulcrums and sockets, fixation of lever chain hoof rings and round pins and cotters (rivet pin sets) are in the charge of inspectors of this side.

4. Manual inspection of a freight car from the division of man and machine operation on the transit trains

Manual inspection of a freight car from the division of man and machine operation on the transit trains takes the faceted inspection method of "cross-bend-lean", among which "cross: cross the rail to check bogie outer end on the same side of brake hoses; bend: bend to check hanging accessories under the central underframes; lean: lean forward to check bogie inner end on the same side of brake hoses and the inner and outer ends of the other bogie. The process is shown as Figure 2-21.

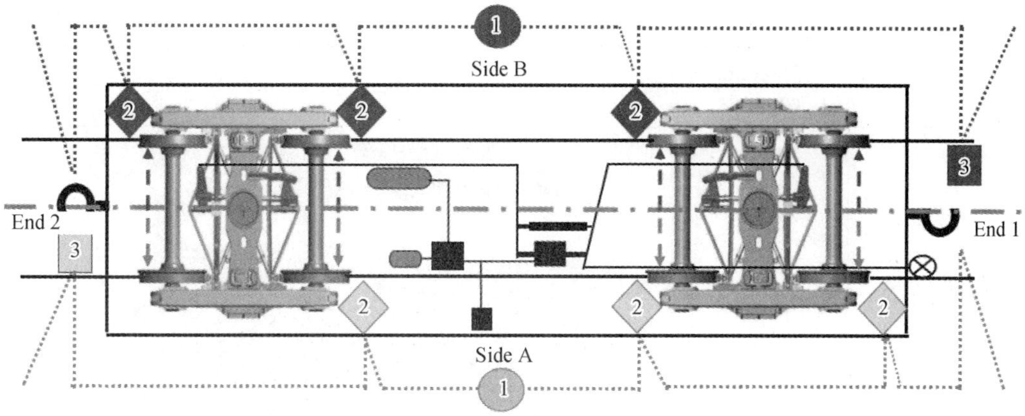

Lnspection method: 1-Bend； 2-Detect； 3-Cross Through

Figure 2-21　Plan sketch of the faceted inspection method of "cross-bend-lean"

The contents and quality standards for manual inspection of a freight car are shown in Table 2-5.

Table 2-5　Manual inspection methods of a freight car

No.	Pace and pose	Inspection contents	Quality standards
1	Step into the rail on left foot and make a visual check	Corner post, end sill on his side, coupler pocket and coupler on his side, flat car end plate (foot plate)hinge and round cotter, air brake equipment and car side fence on the end plate	① Corner posts and end sills are without breaking; the degree of panel's corrosion, perforation and damage should be within limit; external expansion of pen-top wagon should be within limit. ② Couplers have no damage; coupler pockets have no damage, rivets are not missing or broken up. ③ End sills on the open top cars and rope lugs have not been broken. ④ Flat car end plates,foot plate hinges and pockets are not broken, round cotters are not missing and rope lugs have not been broken. ⑤ Tank cars have no leakage,top running boards and guard railings and other parts are not fallen off or stand out. ⑥ Ore cars, tank cars, grain cars, double-deck container flat cars (brake cylinders are installed on the underframe end.) the actual parts are inspected according to underframe brake equipment: auxiliary reservoirs, accelerate relief cylinders, volume reservoirs and step-down reservoirs are not broken, hangers are not broken, nuts are not missing; clips and nuts which fasten the brake piping and connect piping and flange nuts are not missing. Telecentric and combined dust collectors and release valves have no damage, rod hangers of release valves have no damage; cutout cocks are not broken.

No.	Pace and pose	Inspection contents	Quality standards
1	Step into the rail on left foot and make a visual check		
2	Bend and make a visual check	(1) Angle cock,brake hose	Angle cocks,straight end cocks and brake hoses have no damage

		(2) Each beam, rivets from plate holds, brake piping clips and nuts	① Side beams, end beams, sleeper beams, cross beams and draft sills are without cracking; rivets from plate holders are not broken and missing. ② Clips and nuts which fasten the brake piping and connect piping and flange nuts are not missing

Continue

<table>
<tr><th>No.</th><th>Pace and pose</th><th>Inspection contents</th><th>Quality standards</th></tr>
<tr><td rowspan="4">2</td><td rowspan="4">Bend and make a visual check</td><td rowspan="2">(3) Derail automatic brake devices, side bearing, bolster springs</td><td>① Adjustable levers of derail automatic brake devices are not broken, pull rings are not connected to axles, round pins on pull rings are not missing.
② Side bearings are not broken or missing, nylon wear plates of double-acting elastic upper and lower side bearings have no gap, side bearing rollers or side bearing support plates have no touch with upper side bearing wear plates, the gap of side bearing should be within the limit.
③ Bogie bolster springs with spring planks and rivets of top center plates are not broken;nuts and cotter connected auxiliary frames with joint levers are not missing.
④ Bogie inner bolster springs with spring planks and damper springs are not broken, excluded or missing</td></tr>
<tr><td>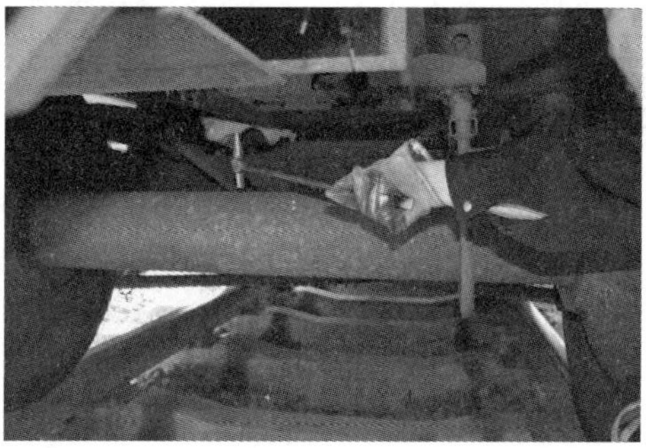</td></tr>
<tr><td rowspan="2">(4) Foundation brake</td><td>① Brake beam cranes are not broken, round pins and cotters are not broken or missing,cotters assembled by K3 bogie brake beam end and brake heads are not broken or missing, brake beams are at their right position.
② Dead lever fulcrum brackets,dead lever fulcrums and dead lever fulcrum chain hoof rings, top rods and cotters on the foundation brakes facing the side are not broken or missing, and pull rivet pin rings are not missing</td></tr>
<tr><td></td></tr>
</table>

Continue

No.	Pace and pose	Inspection contents	Quality standards
2	Bend and make a visual check	(5) Integrated brake equipment	Brake cylinder coupling hoses on the integrated brake equipment are not broken,push rods of brake cylinders and β -type bolts are not missing; brake cylinder piston stroke indicators and signs are not missing

		(6) Wheels	Inner defect of wheel flange is within the limit. Plate hole edges have no crack at radial direction, and the degree of cracks at the circumference direction is within the limit

3	Free step out, face the scheme repair marks and stand,make visual check	Car body, side beam, mark of scheme repair	① Side beams are not broken,top side beams on the open top cars are not broken; side beam sagging, car body tilt and external expansion should be within limit. ② Date of scheme repair on empty cars does not expire (except for return maintenance cars)

Continue

No.	Pace and pose	Inspection contents	Quality standards
4	Free step, bend, make visual check	(1) Wheels, bearing, adapters	① Vertical wear and inner defect of wheel flanges is without overrun, tread surface abrasions, stripping, local concave, defect, circumference wear does not exceed the limit; flange thickness and rim thickness does not exceeded the limit. Plate hole edges have no crack at radial direction, and the degree of cracks at the circumference direction is within the limit, wheel rims are not broken. ② Rolling bearing outer rings and adapters are without cracking, bolts at axle ends do not loosen or fall off, the top surface of K2-type bogie adapters do not grind out metal; side guide frames and accessory guide frames have no touch with rolling bearing at the vertical direction

		(2) Wheels, brake head	① Fold-head bolts and rivets on side frame column wear plate are not broken or missing. ② Vertical wear and inner defect of wheel flange is without overrun, tread surface abrasions, stripping, local concave, defect, circumference wear does not exceed the limit; flange thickness and rim thickness does not exceeded the limit.Plate hole edges have no crack at radial direction, and the degree of cracks at the circumference direction is within the limit, wheel rims are not broken. ③ the top surface of brake shoes are not broken,brake shoe keys are not broken or missing;wear and tear of brake shoes are within limit and they do not grind out metal filings. ④ Rivets on the brake head are not missing; Brake beam cranes are not broken, round pins and cotters are not broken or missing,cotters assembled by K3 bogie brake beam end and brake head are not broken or missing, brake beams are at their right position. ⑤ Rivets on end cross rods do not loosen or fall off

Continue

No.	Pace and pose	Inspection contents	Quality standards
5	Stand, make visual check	Car body	① Side posts are not broken;upper side beams on the open top cars; side beam sagging, car body tilt and external expansion do not exceed the limits. ② Doors, windows of cars are without damage and loss; the degree of panel's corrosion, perforation and damage should be within limit; the accessories of door lock devices are complete and in good condition; folding and sockets of car doors are without break; round pins and split pins are without loss; ③ Belay devices and stake pockets are without missing and cracking; tapered neds and door shields of containers are not broken or missing; tank body and valves have no leakage, tank bands are not broken,tight nuts and jam nuts do not loosen,round pins and split pins are without loss, upper running boards on the tank and guard railings do not fall off 
6	Free step, bend, make visual check	(1) Column wear plate, wedge	① Side frame column wear plates, wedges and main friction plates are not broken,missing or out. ②Swing bolster wedge friction surface and wear plates are not out; folding head and bolts on the swing bolster wedge wear plates 

Continue

<table>
<tr><th>No.</th><th>Pace and pose</th><th>Inspection contents</th><th>Quality standards</th></tr>
<tr><td rowspan="4">6</td><td rowspan="4">Free step, bend, make visual check</td><td rowspan="2">(2) Wheels, brake head</td><td>The same to the sub-term 2st, Term fourth</td></tr>
<tr><td></td></tr>
<tr><td rowspan="2">(3) Wheels, bearing and adapters</td><td>The same to the sub-term 1st, term fourth</td></tr>
<tr><td></td></tr>
<tr><td rowspan="2">7</td><td rowspan="2">Bend forward, make visual check</td><td rowspan="2">(1) Beams and brake, brake piping</td><td>① Central sills, side sills, body bolsters and cross bearers are not broken.
② Clips and nuts which fasten the brake piping and connect piping and flange nuts are not missing</td></tr>
<tr><td></td></tr>
</table>

Continue

No.	Pace and pose	Inspection contents	Quality standards
7	Bend forward, make visual check	(2) Brake beams, empty/load automatic adjuster devices	① Brake beam cranes are not broken, round pins and cotters are not broken or missing, cotters assembled by K3 bogie brake beam end and brake head are not broken or missing, brake beam cranes are at the right position. ② Bogie bolster springs with spring planks and rivets of top center plates are not broken;nuts and cotter connected auxiliary frames with joint lever are not missing. ③ Sensor valves on empty/load automatic adjuster devices are not broken

		(3) Accessories of derail automatic brake devices, foundation brake gear, round pins	① Adjustable levers on derail automatic brake devices are not broken, pull rings have no touch with axles, pull rings and round pins are not missing. ② Dead lever fulcrum brackets, dead lever fulcrums and dead lever fulcrum chain hoof rings, top rods and cotters on the foundation brakes facing the side are not broken or missing, and pull rivet pin rings are not missing

Continue

No.	Pace and pose	Inspection contents	Quality standards
7	Bend forward, make visual check	(4) Heterolateral inner wheel flanges, side bearing, bolster springs	① Side bearings are not broken or missing, nylon wear plates of double-acting elastic upper and lower side bearings have no gap, side bearing rollers or side bearing support plates have no touch with upper side bearing wear plates; the gap of side bearing should be within the limit. ② Bogie inner bolster springs with spring planks and damper springs are not broken, excluded or missing. ③ Inner infect of wheel flanges are within the limit

8	Free step, make visual check	Car body	① Side posts are not broken;upper side beams on the open top cars are not broken; side beam sagging, car body tilt and external expansion do not exceed the limits. ② Sliding tracks of car doors are not broken, car door pullers do not get off the tracks,doors, windows of cars are without damage and loss; the degree of panel’ s corrosion, perforation and damage should be within limit; the accessories of door lock devices are complete and in good condition;folding and sockets of car doors are without break; round pins and split pins are without loss; ③ Belay devices and stake pockets are without missing and cracking; tapered neds and door shields of containers are not broken or missing; tank body and valves have no leakage,manhole covers and safety valves are not missing,lower dump oil discharge pipes, heating pipes and their covers do not fall off, upper running boards on the tank and guard railings do not fall off

No.	Pace and pose	Inspection contents	Quality standards
9	Free step, bend, make visual check	(1) Central beams, side beams and cross beams	Central beams, side beams and cross beams are not broken; cotters on bottom door shafts are not broken or missing

		(2) Foundation brake	Break cylinders rear lever fulcrums, round pins and cotters are not broken or missing; pull rivet pin rings are not missing

		(3) Manual brake	Additional lever holders, round pins and cotters of manual brakes are not missing.

Continue

No.	Pace and pose	Inspection contents	Quality standards
9	Free step, bend, make visual check	(4) Air brake	Auxiliary reservoirs, accelerate relief cylinders, volume reservoirs and step-down reservoirs are not broken, hangers are not broken, nuts are not missing; brake cylinder hangers and nuts are not broken, hanger nuts in middle brake valves are not missing; clips and nuts which fasten the brake piping and connect piping and flange nuts are not missing, relief valves and adjusting valves on empty/load automatic adjuster devices are not broken; telecentric and combined dust collectors and release valves have no damage, rod hangers of release valves and hangers of empty/load car adjusting levers have no damage;manual empty/load carport are at the right position;cutout cocks are not broken 
10	Bend, make visual check	(1) Beams, brake piping clips	The same to sub-term 1st, term seventh 
		(2) Derail automatic brake devices, foundation brakes and round pins	The same to sub-term 3rd, term seventh 

Continue

No.	Pace and pose	Inspection contents	Quality standards
10	Bend, make visual check	(3) Heterolateral inner wheel flanges, side bearings, bolster springs	The same to sub-term 4st, term seventh 
11	Free step, bend forward, make visual check	(1) Wheels, bearing and adapters	The same to sub-term 1st, term fourth 
		(2) Wheels, brake head	The same to sub-term 2st, term fourth 

Continue

<table>
<tr><th>No.</th><th>Pace and pose</th><th>Inspection contents</th><th>Quality standards</th></tr>
<tr><td rowspan="2">12</td><td rowspan="2">Stand,make visual check</td><td rowspan="2">Car body</td><td>The same to term fifth</td></tr>
<tr><td></td></tr>
<tr><td rowspan="4">13</td><td rowspan="4">Free step, bend forward, make visual check</td><td rowspan="2">(1) Column wear plate, wedge</td><td>The same to sub-term 1st, term sixth</td></tr>
<tr><td></td></tr>
<tr><td rowspan="2">(2) Wheels, brake head</td><td>The same to sub-term 2st, term 4th</td></tr>
<tr><td></td></tr>
</table>

Continue

No.	Pace and pose	Inspection contents	Quality standards
13	Free step, bend forward, make visual check	(3) Wheels, bearing and adapters	The same to sub-term 1st, 4th 
14	Bend, make visual check	Each beams, rivets from plate holders	(1) Side beams, end beams, cross beams and draft sills are without cracking. (2) Rivets from plate holders are not broken and missing 
		2. Derail automatic brake devices,foundation brake and round pins	The same to sub-term 3st, term seventh 

Continue

No.	Pace and pose	Inspection contents	Quality standards
15	Stand, make visual check	(1) Foot steps, ladder handholds and car end guard fences	Foot steps, ladder handholds and car end guard fences are without crack or missing, bending degree of foot steps and ladder handhold doesn't exceed the limit

		(2) Car body	Corner posts and end beams are not broken; the degree of wall plate's corrosion, perforation and damage should be within limit; external expansion of pen-top wagons should be within limit; end sills on the open top cars has not been broken. Flat car end plates,foot plate hinges and pockets are not broken, round cotters are not missing and rope lugs have not been broken

		(3) Manual brake	Folders of folding manual brakes are not broken, round pins and cotters are not missing and brackets are not broken

Continue

No.	Pace and pose	Inspection contents	Quality standards
16	Free step, make visual check	(1) Coupler release rod bracket and coupler release rod chain, height difference of couplers	Coupler release rod brackets are without cracking and nuts are not missing; loose length of coupler release rod chains meets requirement; height difference of couplers do not exceed the limit

		(2) Coupler pockets, couplers on this side	The couplers, coupler pockets and their rivets are without crack or missing

		(3) Three states of coupler operation test for head and tail car	Coupler knuckle's S side of head and tail train stock; function of three states of coupler operation is good

17	The same to term 1th to term 16th	The same to term 1th to term 16th	The same to term 1th to term 16th

Revision exercises

1. What is the operation limit for each part of freight cars?
2. Please make a brief description of the content of technical inspection for one car.

Unit 4 Train Brake Overall Test for Departure Train

The train brake test is to adjust the speed of the train and stop at a designated location when the train is running, and to decelerate or stop in time in case of an emergency, to ensure the safe and punctual operation of the train, and to prevent the train from rash advancing, conflict and personal injury accidents. The performance of the car air automatic brake in the train is an important factor related to the safe operation of the train. Therefore, the function of the automatic air brake of the car in the train should be ensured to be good and meet the specified technical standards. Therefore, before the train departs, the air brake function of the car in the train should be tested in accordance with the regulations.

Learning objectives

(1) Master the operation standard of train brake test.

(2) Master the hand signal representation of train brake test.

(3) Master the hand signal transmission method of train brake.

Learning content

1. Key points of operation

In the test of the train brake, the on-site inspector runs on the left side of the running direction of the train, and runs inspection according to the allocated number of cars, and visually confirms the braking and release state of the brake. For cars that affect the on-site inspector's confirmation of brake cylinder status due to their structures, when the whole train is marshalled, the on-site operation fleet can be adjusted to two fleets to conduct brake test on both sides of the train at the same time; cars that are sporadically marshalled into the train must be reported to the foreman (the foreman or a person designated by the foreman will confirm the performance of the brake on the other side of the train). When the brake test is performed on both sides of the train, the work of the inspector on the left in the running direction of the train is the main task, and the inspector on the right side shall only confirm the brake cylinder status and brake performance on this side, and report to the inspector on the left side of the same section after each test item is completed.

1) Leakage test

Close the angle cock at the front of the first car, maintain the pressure of the train pipe system for 1 minute, and the dropped pressure of the train main pipe displayed by the wireless wind pressure monitor shall not be greater than 20 kPa. Open the angle cock after the test.

2) Sensitivity test

Set the car to the service braking position and reduce the pressure by 50 kPa (70 kPa when marshalling more than 60 cars), the whole train must have a braking effect, and no natural release shall occur within 1 min. Then set the running position to relieve the air filling, and the whole train must be relieved within 1 minute.

3) Stabilization pressure test

Set the car to the service braking position and reduce the pressure by 140 kPa (170 kPa when the pressure of train pipe is 600 kPa), no emergency braking shall occur, and confirm that the piston stroke of the brake cylinder must meet the requirements; retain the pressure at the same time, the pressure drop of the train pipe displayed by the wireless wind pressure monitor within 1 minute is not more than 20 kPa.

2. Operating procedures and standards

1) Reach the air testing position

The on-site inspectors arrive at their respective starting positions for the air testing, and carry out the train brake test according to the running diagram of train brake test. See Figure 2-22.

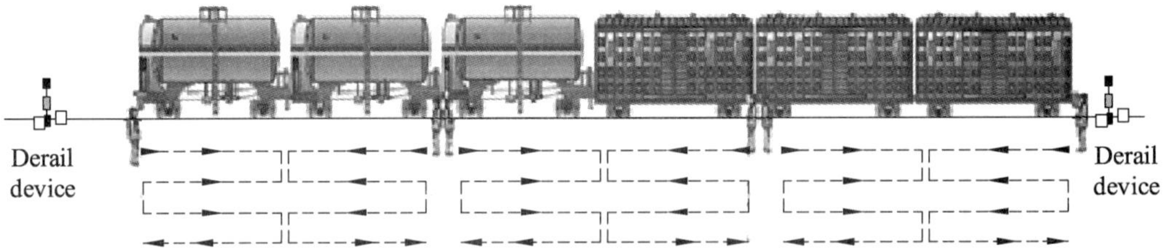

Figure 2-22 the running diagram of train brake test.

Note: As shown in the figure, the left side is the train travel direction. The first inspector is the inspector of the train head, and the last train inspector is the end train inspector. Therefore, from left to right, they are designated as the first inspector, No. 2 train inspector, No. 3 train inspector, No. 4 train inspector, No. 5 train inspector and end train inspector.

2) Leakage test

(1) Confirm train pipe pressure.

Method 1: The positive number inspector of rear car visually confirms that the train pipe pressure displayed by the wireless wind pressure monitor reaches the specified pressure.

Method 2: The positive number inspector of rear car uses the walkie-talkie to contact the on-duty train inspector to confirm that the pressure of the train pipe reaches the specified pressure (standard term: "please confirm × Track × Sub-air pressure"). On the main interface of the system, the on-duty train inspector responds according to the actual value of "pressure" (standard term: " × Track × Sub-air pressure × kPa"); if it reaches the constant pressure of the train pipe, reply " × Track × Sub-air pressure × kPa meet the requirements".

Train pipe pressure: 600 kPa.

(2) Transmit pressure retaining signal.

① Pressure retaining signal: if the daytime visibility can meet the requirements, the inspection hammer shall be used to horizontally extend one arm to the train direction, and if the night or daytime visibility cannot meet the requirements, the inspection lamp with white light shall be used to swing laterally in front of the chest.

Figure 2-23 Hand signal representation mode of retaining pressure

② In case of bad weather and curve lines, walkie talkie can be used to assist in transmitting braking signal at the same time. Standard terms:

Transmitting person: " × Track × Section (or recipient name), pressure retaining";

Recipient: " × × Track × Section (or the name of the sender), received".

③ The pressure retaining signal shall be displayed and transmitted section by section in turn. Over-transmission, missed transmission, wrong transmission, and substitution transmission are not allowed. Speculative judgment is strictly prohibited.

④ It is forbidden to use red flag (red light) to replace inspection hammer (inspection light) to display transmission.

⑤ Pressure retaining signal transmission procedures and standards

a. The positive number inspector of rear car stands at the starting position of air testing, facing the head of the train, and transmits the "pressure retaining signal" to the positive number inspector of middle car and negative number inspector of rear car, and stops displaying after confirming that the other party has received the "pressure retaining signal" not less than 2 times.

b. The negative number inspector of rear car and the positive number inspector of middle car stand in line at the starting position of the air testing, facing the rear of the train. When the positive train inspector of rear car transmits the "pressure retaining signal", the "pressure retaining signal" shall be received at least twice; turned 180°, facing the head of the train, the negative number inspector of rear car and the positive number inspector of middle car transmit the "pressure retaining signal" to the negative number inspector of middle car and the negative number inspector of head car together, and stop the transmission after confirming that the other party has received the "pressure retaining signal" not less than 2 times.

c. The negative number inspector of middle car and the negative number inspector of head car stand in line at the starting position of the air testing, facing the rear of the train. When the positive number inspector of middle car and the negative number inspector of rear car transmits the "pressure retaining signal", the "pressure retaining signal" shall be received at least twice; turned 180°, facing the head of the train, the negative number inspector of middle car and the negative number inspector of head car transmit the "pressure retaining signal" to the positive number inspector of head car, and stop the transmission after confirming that the other party has received the "pressure retaining signal" not less than 2 times.

d. The positive number inspector of head car stands at the starting position of the air testing, facing the rear of the train; when the negative number inspector of middle car and the negative number inspector of head car transmit the "pressure retaining signal" to themselves, they should receive the "pressure retaining signal" not less than 2 times.

(3) Start leakage test.

① The positive number inspector of head car slowly closes the angle cock at the front of the first car, so that the center line of the angle cock handle and the center line of the auxiliary pipe are at an angle of 90° (the opening line of the angle cock and the center line of the auxiliary pipe are 90°), and report to the on-duty train inspector (standard term: " × Track × Times angle cock closed").

Figure 2-24 Close the angle cock

②On the main interface of the system, the on-duty train inspector uses the left mouse button to click the “leakage test start” button once (the “leakage test start” button changes from a convex state to a concave state).

Abnormal situation: The “leakage test start” button cannot be pressed during the rising phase of air pressure. If the “leakage test start” button cannot be pressed down (that is, the button cannot be changed from the convex state to the concave state), check whether the pressure of the train pipe has reached the effective constant pressure range. If the pressure does not reach the specified pressure, use the car radio to notify the positive number inspector of head car, he will open the angle cock at the front of the first car and notify the driver of the leading locomotive to continue charging.

(4) Transmit confirmation signal

① Confirmation signal: the inspection hammer shall be used if the daytime visibility can meet the requirements, and the inspection lamp with white light shall be used if the visibility can not meet the requirements at night or in the daytime, which shall be inclined at 45° toward the train direction.

Figure 2-25 Hand signal representation of confirmation

② In bad weather and curve lines, walkie talkie can be used to assist in transmitting braking signals at the same time. Standard terms:

Transmission confirmation signal: “ × Track × Section (or receiver’s name), the signal is back”.

Receive confirmation signal: “ × Track × Section (or the name of the sender), received”.

③ The confirmation signal shall be displayed and transmitted section by section in turn. Over-transmission, missed transmission, wrong transmission, and substitution transmission are not allowed. Speculative judgment is strictly prohibited.

④ It is forbidden to use red flag (red light) to replace inspection hammer (inspection light) to display transmission.

⑤ Confirmation signal transmission procedures and standards.

a. The positive number inspector of head car stands at the starting position of air testing, facing the rear of the train, and transmits the "confirmation signal" to the negative number inspector of middle car and negative number inspector of head car, and stops displaying after confirming that the other party has received the "confirmation signal" not less than 2 times.

b. The negative number inspector of middle car and the negative number inspector of head car stand in line at the starting position of the air testing, facing the rear of the train. When the positive train inspector of head car transmits the "confirmation signal", the "confirmation signal" shall be received at least twice; turned 180°, facing the head of the train, the negative number inspector of middle car and the positive number inspector of head car transmit the "confirmation signal" to the negative number inspector of rear car and the positive number inspector of middle car together, and stop the transmission after confirming that the other party has received the "confirmation signal" not less than 2 times.

c. The negative number inspector of rear car and the positive number inspector of middle car stand in line at the starting position of the air testing, facing the head of the train. When the negative number inspector of middle car and the negative number inspector of head car transmits the "confirmation signal", the "confirmation signal" shall be received not less than 2 times; turned 180°, facing the rear of the train, the negative number inspector of rear car and the positive number inspector of middle car transmit the "confirmation signal" to the positive number inspector of rear car, and stop the transmission after confirming that the other party has received the "confirmation signal" not less than 2 times.

d. The positive number inspector of rear car stands at the starting position of the air testing, facing the head of the train; when the negative number inspector of rear car and the positive number inspector of middle car transmit the "confirmation signal" to themselves, they should receive the "confirmation signal" not less than 2 times.

(5) Confirm the leakage.

Method 1: The positive number inspector of rear car visually observes the train pipe pressure displayed by the wireless wind pressure, and confirms that the pressure of the train pipe displayed by the wireless wind pressure monitor does not drop more than 20 kPa within 1 minute, and uses the walkie-talkie to notify the operation crew. Standard term: " × Track × Time leakage test is qualified."

Method 2: the on-duty train inspector observes in real time that the "retaining pressure" value displayed in the "leakage test" item at the bottom of the "air testing window" interface reaches 60 seconds, and the “leakage” value is not greater than 20 kPa, and uses the car-mounted radio (or walkie-talkie) to notify the on-site operators (Standard term: “ × Track × Time leaking test is qualified, leakage volume × kPa”).

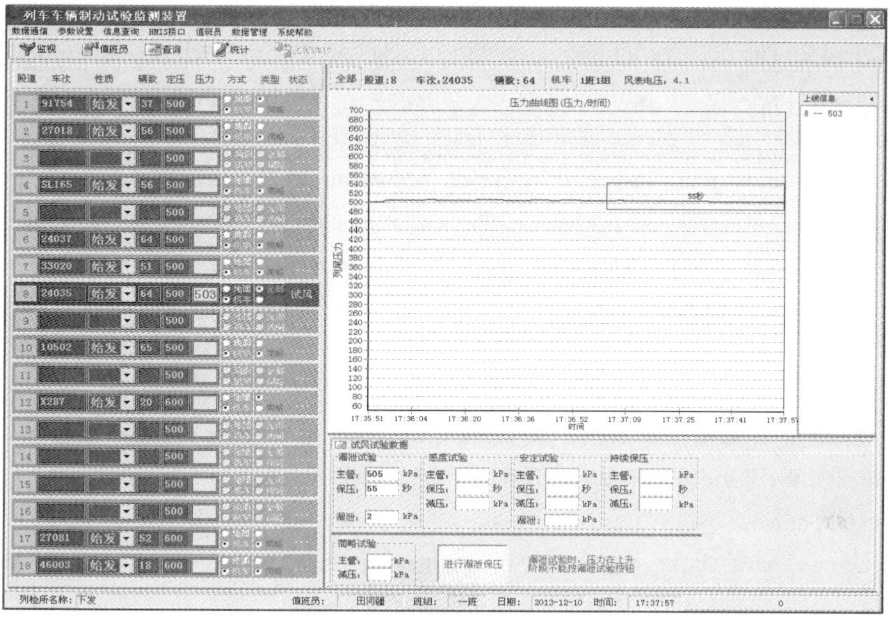

Figure 2-26 Confirmation of leakage

(6) End the leakage test.

After receiving the notification of passing the leakage test by the positive number inspector of rear car or the on-duty train inspector, the positive number inspector of head car shall slowly open the angle cock of the head car to make the center line of the handle of the angle cock consistent with the center line of the auxiliary pipe (the opening line of the angle cock is consistent with the center line of the auxiliary pipe). See Figure 2-27.

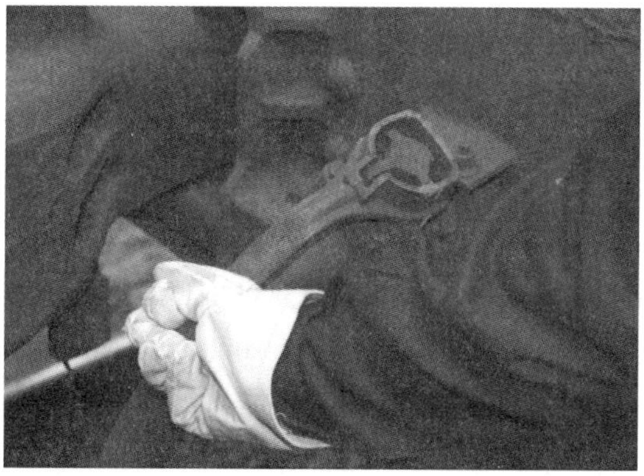

Figure 2-27 Closing the angle cock

3) Sensitivity test

(1) Confirm the train pipe pressure.

Method 1: The positive number inspector of rear car visually confirms that the train pipe pressure displayed by the wireless wind pressure monitor reaches the specified pressure.

Method 2: The positive number inspector of rear car uses the walkie-talkie to contact the on-duty train inspector to confirm that the pressure of the train pipe reaches the specified pressure (standard term: “please confirm × Track × air pressure”). On the main interface of the system, the on-duty train inspector responds according to the actual value of “pressure” (standard term: “ × Track × air pressure × kPa”); if it reaches the constant pressure of the train pipe, reply “ × Track × air pressure × kPa meets the requirements.”

Train pipe pressure: 600 kPa.

(2) Transmit braking signal.

① Braking signal: If the daytime visibility can meet the requirements, the inspection hammer shall be used to raise above the head; if the night or daytime visibility cannot meet the requirements, the inspection lamp with white light shall be used to raise above the head and shake up and down.

Figure 2-28 Hand signal representation of braking

② In case of bad weather and curve lines, walkie talkie can be used to assist in transmitting braking signal at the same time. Standard terms:

Transmitting person: “ × Track × Section (or recipient name), braking”;

Recipient: “ × Track × Section (or the name of the sender), received”.

③ The braking signal shall be displayed and transmitted section by section in turn. Over-transmission, missed transmission, wrong transmission, and substitution transmission are not allowed. Speculative judgment is strictly prohibited.

④ It is forbidden to use red flag (red light) to replace inspection hammer (inspection light) to display transmission.

⑤ Braking signal transmission procedures and standards.

a. The positive number inspector of rear car stands at the starting position of air testing, facing the head of the train, and transmits the "braking signal" to the positive number inspector of middle car and negative number inspector of rear car, and stops displaying after confirming that the other party has received the "braking signal" not less than 2 times.

b. The negative number inspector of rear car and the positive number inspector of middle car stand in line at the starting position of the air testing, facing the rear of the train. When the positive train inspector of rear car transmits the "braking signal", the "braking signal" shall be received not less than 2 times; turned 180°, facing the head of the train, the negative number inspector of rear car and the positive number inspector of middle car transmit the "braking signal" to the negative number inspector of middle car and the negative number inspector of head car together, and stop the transmission after confirming that the other party has received the "braking signal" not less than 2 times.

c. The negative number inspector of middle car and the negative number inspector of head car stand in line at the starting position of the air testing, facing the rear of the train. When the negative number inspector of middle car and the negative number inspector of rear car transmits the "braking signal", the "braking signal" shall be received not less than 2 times; turned 180°, facing the head of the train, the negative number inspector of middle car and the negative number inspector of head car transmit the "braking signal" to the positive number inspector of head car together, and stop the transmission after confirming that the other party has received the "braking signal" not less than 2 times.

d. The positive number inspector of head car stands at the starting position of the air testing, facing the rear of the train; when the negative number inspector of middle car and the negative number inspector of head car transmit the "braking signal" to themselves, they should receive the "braking signal" not less than 2 times. Then they should turn 180° to display "braking signal" to the driver and informed the leading locomotive driver to set the service braking position for sensitivity test and decompression. It is allowed to use walkie talkie to inform the driver of braking. Standard terms: " × Track × Test, please reduce the pressure by 50 (70) kPa."

(3) Confirm the pressure reduction of the sensitivity test.

Method 1: The positive number inspector of rear car observes the train pipe pressure displayed by the wireless wind pressure monitor in real time and confirms that the pressure reduction of the sensitivity test meets the requirements.

Method 2: The positive number inspector of rear car uses the walkie-talkie and the on-duty train inspector to jointly control the pressure reduction of the sensitivity test (standard term: "please confirm × Track × sensitivity test pressure reduction"), after confirming the pressure reduction of the sensitivity test displayed on the system terminal, the on-duty train inspector shall contact the operation field (standard term: " × Track × sensitivity test pressure reduction volume × kPa").

(4) Confirm braking performance.

After the train reaches the specified pressure reduction volume for 1 minute, the on-site inspectors start from the starting position of the air test, and run and check according to the number of cars allocated to the air test meeting position, bend over and lean over one by one to check and confirm the braking effect of cars within the scope of responsibility with the inspection hammer pointing (illuminated by the car inspection lamp at night), and confirm that there is no natural release within 1 minute. See Figure 2-29.

Figure 2-29 Confirmation of brake performance

(5) Monitor air test curve.

The on-duty train inspector shall observe the air pressure curve of the rear car and prompt information displayed on the system terminal in real time, confirm that the sensitivity test result shows "qualified", and then contact the operation field (Standard term: " × Track × sensitivity test is qualified"). See Figure 2-30.

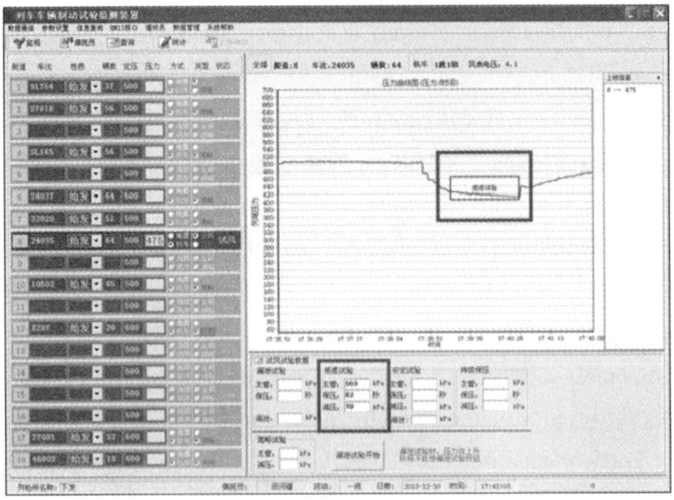

Figure 2-30 Air test curve

Abnormal situation: if the on-duty train inspector finds that the test items are not completed, the test is unqualified, the air test data is interrupted, etc., he shall notify the on-site train inspector to find out the causes and handle them, and then conduct the train braking test again.

(6) Transmit release signal.

① Release signal: the inspection hammer shall be used if the daytime visibility can meet the requirements, and the inspection lamp with white light shall be used if the night or daytime visibility can not meet the requirements, swinging left and right at the lower part of the body. See Figure 2-31.

Figure 2-31 Hand signal representation of release

② In case of bad weather and curve lines, walkie talkie can be used to assist in transmitting braking signal at the same time. Standard terms:

Transmitting person: " × Track × Section (or recipient name), release";

Recipient: " × Track × Section (or the name of the sender), received".

③ The release signal shall be displayed and transmitted section by section in turn. Over-transmission, missed transmission, wrong transmission, and substitution transmission are not allowed. Speculative judgment is strictly prohibited.

④ It is forbidden to use red flag (red light) to replace inspection hammer (inspection light) to display transmission.

⑤ Release signal transmission procedures and standards

a. The positive number inspector of rear car and the negative number inspector of rear car stand at the meeting position of air testing, facing the head of the train, and transmits the "release signal" to the positive number inspector of middle car and negative number inspector of middle car, and stops displaying after confirming that the other party has received the "release signal" not less than 2 times.

b. The positive number inspector of middle car and the negative number inspector of middle car stand in line at the meeting position of the air testing, facing the rear of the train.

When the positive train inspector of rear car and the negative train inspector of rear car transmits the "release signal", the "release signal" shall be received not less than 2 times; turned 180°, facing the head of the train, the positive number inspector of middle car and the negative number inspector of middle car transmit the "release signal" to the positive number inspector of head car and the negative number inspector of head car together, and stop the transmission after confirming that the other party has received the "release signal" not less than 2 times.

c. The positive number inspector of head car and the negative number inspector of head car stand in line at the meeting position of the air testing, facing the rear of the train. When the positive number inspector of middle car and the negative number inspector of middle car transmits the "release signal", the "release signal" shall be received not less than 2 times; turned 180°, the positive number inspector of head car and the negative number inspector of head car transmit the "release signal" to the locomotive driver together, and inform the leading locomotive driver to charge air for release. It is allowed to use walkie talkie to inform the driver of release. Standard term: " × Track × release."

(7) Confirm release performance.

After the train is charged with air, the on-site inspector shall start from the air test meeting position, run and check according to the allocated number of cars, return to the starting position of air test, bend over and lean over one by one to check with the inspection hammer in the daytime (illuminated by the car inspection light at night), confirm that the cars within the scope of responsibility must be relieved within 1 minute, and the pull rod chain of hand brake is in a relaxed state. See Figure 2-32.

Figure 2-32 Release performance confirmation

4) Stabilization pressure test

(1) Confirm the train pipe pressure.

Method 1: The positive number inspector of rear car visually confirms that the train pipe pressure displayed by the wireless wind pressure monitor reaches the specified pressure.

Method 2: The positive number inspector of rear car uses the walkie-talkie to contact the on-duty train inspector to confirm that the pressure of the train pipe reaches the specified pressure (standard term: "please confirm × Track × air pressure"). On the main interface of the system, the on-duty train inspector responds according to the actual value of "pressure" (standard term: " × Track × air pressure × kPa"); if it reaches the constant pressure of the train pipe, reply " × Track × air pressure × kPa meets the requirements."

Train pipe pressure: 600 kPa.

(2) Transmit braking signal.

① Braking signal: If the daytime visibility can meet the requirements, the inspection hammer shall be used to raise above the head; if the night or daytime visibility cannot meet the requirements, the inspection lamp with white light shall be used to raise above the head and shake up and down. See Figure 2-33.

Figure 2-33 Signal representation of brake hand

② In case of bad weather and curve lines, walkie talkie can be used to assist in transmitting braking signal at the same time. Standard terms:

Transmitting person: " × Track × Section (or recipient name), braking";

Recipient: " × Track × Section (or the name of the sender), received."

③ The braking signal shall be displayed and transmitted section by section in turn. Over-transmission, missed transmission, wrong transmission, and substitution transmission are not allowed. Speculative judgment is strictly prohibited.

④ It is forbidden to use red flag (red light) to replace inspection hammer (inspection light) to display transmission.

⑤ Braking signal transmission procedures and standards

a. The positive number inspector of rear car stands at the starting position of air testing, facing the head of the train, and transmits the "braking signal" to the positive number inspector of middle car and negative number inspector of rear car, and stops displaying after confirming that the other party has received the "braking signal" not less than 2 times.

b. The negative number inspector of rear car and the positive number inspector of middle car stand in line at the starting position of the air testing, facing the rear of the train. When the positive train inspector of rear car transmits the "braking signal", the "braking signal" shall be received not less than 2 times; turned 180°, facing the head of the train, the negative number inspector of rear car and the positive number inspector of middle car transmit the "braking signal" to the negative number inspector of middle car and the negative number inspector of head car together, and stop the transmission after confirming that the other party has received the "braking signal" not less than 2 times.

c. The negative number inspector of middle car and the negative number inspector of head car stand in line at the starting position of the air testing, facing the rear of the train. When the positive number inspector of middle car and the negative number inspector of rear car transmits the "braking signal", the "braking signal" shall be received not less than 2 times; turned 180°, facing the head of the train, the negative number inspector of middle car and the negative number inspector of head car transmit the "braking signal" to the positive number inspector of head car together, and stop the transmission after confirming that the other party has received the "braking signal" not less than 2 times.

d. The positive number inspector of head car stands at the starting position of the air testing, facing the rear of the train; when the negative number inspector of middle car and the negative number inspector of head car transmit the "braking signal" to themselves, they should receive the "braking signal" not less than 2 times. Then they should turn 180° to display "braking signal" to the driver and informed the leading locomotive driver to set the service braking position for pressure reduction of stabilization pressure test. It is allowed to use walkie talkie to inform the driver of braking. Standard terms: "× Track × stabilization pressure test, please retain the pressure after decompressing 170kPa."

(3) Confirm the pressure reduction of the stabilization pressure test.

Method 1: The positive number inspector of rear car observes the train pipe pressure displayed by the wireless wind pressure monitor in real time and confirms that the pressure reduction of the stabilization pressure test meets the requirements.

The positive number inspector of rear car uses the walkie-talkie and the on-duty train inspector to jointly control the pressure reduction of the stabilization pressure test (standard term: "please confirm×Track × pressure reduction of the stabilization pressure test"), after confirming the pressure reduction of the stabilization pressure test displayed on the system terminal, the on-duty train inspector shall contact the operation field (standard term: "× Track × stabilization pressure reduction volume × kPa").

(4) Confirm braking performance.

After the train reaches the specified pressure reduction volume, the on-site inspectors start from the starting position of the air test, and run and check according to the number of cars allocated to the air test meeting position, bend over and lean over one by one to check and confirm that the cars within the scope of responsibility shall not have emergency braking effect with the inspection hammer pointing (illuminated by the car inspection lamp at night), and the piston stroke of the brake cylinder shall comply with the provisions in the table below.

Figure 2-34 Confirmation of braking performance

(5) Monitor air test curve.

The on-duty train inspector shall observe in real time that the "pressure retaining" value displayed under the "stabilization pressure" test item on the "air test data" interface of the system reaches 60 seconds, and the "leakage (kPa)" value shall not be greater than 20kPa (the pressure retaining time shall be calculated automatically by the system). After the stabilization pressure test result shows "qualified", he shall contact the operation field (standard term:"× Track × stabilization pressure test is qualified").

Abnormal situation: if the on-duty train inspector finds that the leakage exceeds the standard, the test items are not completed, the test is unqualified, the air test data is interrupted, etc., the test must be repeated.

(6) Transmit release signal.

① Release signal: the inspection hammer shall be used if the daytime visibility can meet the requirements, and the inspection lamp with white light shall be used if the night or daytime visibility can not meet the requirements, swinging left and right at the lower part of the body.

② In case of bad weather and curve lines, walkie talkie can be used to assist in transmitting braking signal at the same time. Standard terms:

Transmitting person: "× Track × Section (or recipient name), release";

Recipient: "× Track × Section (or the name of the sender), received."

③ The release signal shall be displayed and transmitted section by section in turn. Over-transmission, missed transmission, wrong transmission, and substitution transmission are not allowed. Speculative judgment is strictly prohibited.

④ It is forbidden to use red flag (red light) to replace inspection hammer (inspection light) to display transmission.

⑤ Release signal transmission procedures and standards

a. The positive number inspector of rear car and the negative number inspector of rear car stand at the meeting position of air testing, facing the head of the train, and transmits the "release signal" to the positive number inspector of middle car and negative number inspector of middle car, and stops displaying after confirming that the other party has received the "release signal" not less than 2 times.

b. The positive number inspector of middle car and the negative number inspector of middle car stand in line at the meeting position of the air testing, facing the rear of the train. When the positive train inspector of rear car and the negative train inspector of rear car transmits the "release signal", the "release signal" shall be received not less than 2 times; turned 180°, facing the head of the train, the positive number inspector of middle car and the negative number inspector of middle car transmit the "release signal" to the positive number inspector of head car and the negative number inspector of head car together, and stop the transmission after confirming that the other party has received the "release signal" not less than 2 times.

c. The positive number inspector of head car and the negative number inspector of head car stand in line at the meeting position of the air testing, facing the rear of the train. When the positive number inspector of middle car and the negative number inspector of middle car transmits the "release signal", the "release signal" shall be received not less than 2 times; turned 180°, the positive number inspector of head car and the negative number inspector of head car transmit the "release signal" to the locomotive driver together, and inform the leading locomotive driver to charge air for release. It is allowed to use walkie talkie to inform the driver of release. Standard term: " × Track × release."

(7) Confirm release performance.

After the train is charged with air, the on-site inspector shall start from the air test meeting position, run and check according to the allocated number of cars, return to the starting position of air test, bend over and lean over one by one to check with the inspection hammer in the daytime (illuminated by the car inspection light at night), confirm that the cars within the scope of responsibility must be relieved, and the pull rod chain of hand brake is in a relaxed state. See Figare 2-35.

(8) Paint checking mark of brake cylinder piston stroke

The on-site inspector shall confirm that the automatic brake is released and the basic braking device is released (the pull rod chain of the hand brake is in a relaxed state), and paint the "brake cylinder piston stroke inspection mark" as required.

Inspection mark of brake cylinder piston stroke: chalk the connecting line on the front cover and piston cylinder of brake cylinder one by one, with the length of no less than 100 mm; when the brake cylinder is on the other side of the car, after confirming the release, draw a line with chalk on the head of the stay arm opposite to the brake cylinder one by one. See Figure 2-36.

Figure 2-35 Confirmation of release performance

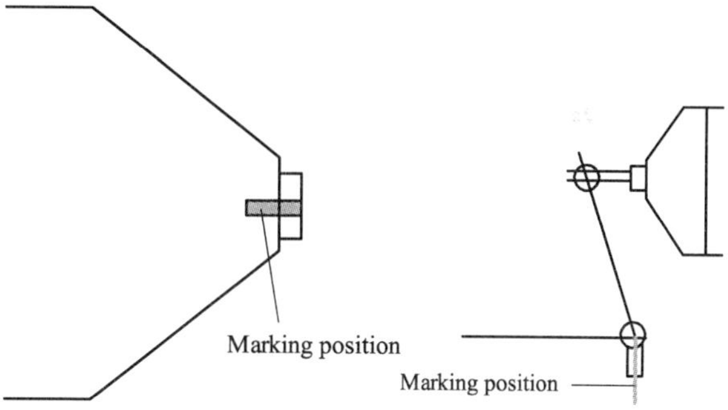

Figure 2-36 Marking position of brake cylinder piston stroke inspection

5) End the stabilization pressure test

(1) Confirm the train pipe pressure.

Method 1: The positive number inspector of rear car visually confirms that the train pipe pressure displayed by the wireless wind pressure monitor reaches the specified pressure.

Method 2: The positive number inspector of rear car uses the walkie-talkie to contact the on-duty train inspector to confirm that the pressure of the train pipe reaches the specified pressure (standard term: "please confirm × Track × air pressure"). On the main interface of the system, the on-duty train inspector responds according to the actual value of "pressure" (standard term: "×Track ×air pressure ×kPa"); if it reaches the constant pressure of the train pipe, reply " × Track × air pressure × kPa meets the requirements."

(2) Save testing results.

After the on-site inspector turns off the wireless wind pressure monitor, the "pressure curve" will be saved automatically.

(3) Check air pressure curve.

The on-duty train inspector shall click the “query” button, click the corresponding train number in the pop-up window to view the air test curve, and when he finds that the system prompts “operated” or blank, the air test items are incomplete, the air test curve is incomplete, the air test curve is not standardized, etc., he shall notify the on-site inspector to find out the cause and re-implement the train brake test after handling. See Figure 2-37.

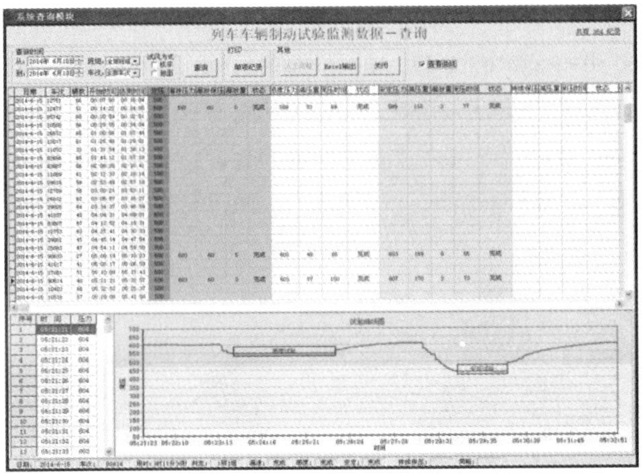

Figure 2-37 Air pressure curve

(4) Paint the test mark of train brake.

When the normal use of the train brake test monitoring device is affected due to power failure or temporary fault, the train brake test is completed. After confirming that the last car is released, clear chalk marks shall be painted on the outside of the front cover of the rear car brake cylinder. See Figure 2-38.

Figure 2-38 Marking test position of train brake

Marking format: abbreviation, month and day of train inspection operation field.

(5) Remove the wireless wind pressure detector.

a. The positive number inspector of rear car presses the "off" key on the control panel of the wireless wind pressure monitor to turn off the power supply. See Figure 2-39.

b. The positive number inspector of rear car shall close the angle cock at the rear of the train so that the center line of the handle of the angle cock is at an included angle of 90° with the center line of the auxiliary pipe (the opening line of the angle cock is at an included angle of 90° with the center line of the auxiliary pipe). See Figure 2-40.

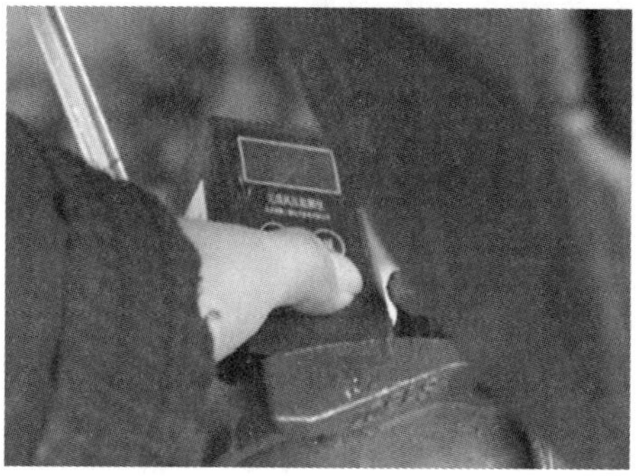

Figure 2-39 Power off the wireless wind presswre cletector

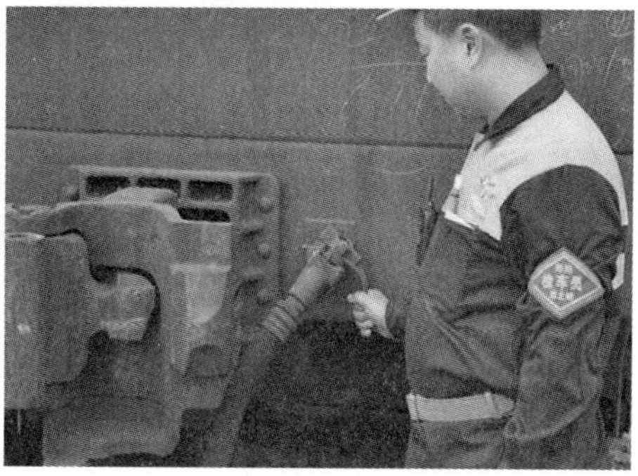

Figure 2-40 Close the angle cock

c. The positive number inspector of rear car slowly moves the handle (transmitting antenna) towards the wind pressure monitor to remove the pressure air from the rear car brake hose. See Figure 2-41.

d. After the hook of the wireless wind pressure monitor leaves the hose connector, remove the wireless wind pressure monitor. See Figure 2-42.

Figure 2-41 Removethe pressure air from the rear brake hose

Figure 2-42 Remove the wirekss wind pressure monitor

(6) Confirm the tail train mark.

When the tail device is used as the tail mark of the train, it is not necessary to lift the brake hose of the rear car. The positive number inspector of the rear car must connect the car brake hose with the tail device hose and open the rear angle cock of the last car. See Figure 2-43.

Figure 2-43 Tail train mark

(7) Transmit test completion signal.

a. Completion signal of air test: if the daytime visibility can meet the requirements, an inspection hammer must be used. If the night or daytime visibility can not meet the requirements, an inspection lamp with white light must be used to rotate in a circular direction from the top to the train set. See Figure 2-44.

b. Confirmation signal: if the visibility in daytime can meet the requirements, the inspection hammer shall be used to incline 45° towards the train direction; if the visibility at night or in daytime cannot meet the requirements, the inspection lamp with white light shall be used to incline 45° towards the train direction. See Figure 2-45.

Figure 2-44 Completion signal of air test

Figure 2-45 Confirmation signal

c. In case of bad weather and curve lines, walkie talkie can be used to assist in transmitting signal at the same time. Standard terms:

Transmitting test completion signal: "× Track × Section (or recipient name), the signal has passed";

Receiving test completion signal: "× Track × Section (or the name of the sender), received".

Transmitting confirmation signal: "× Track × Section (or recipient name), the signal is back";

Receiving confirmation signal: "× Track × Section (or the name of the sender), received".

d. The signal shall be displayed and transmitted section by section in turn. Over-transmission, missed transmission, wrong transmission, and substitution transmission are not allowed. Speculative judgment is strictly prohibited.

e. It is forbidden to use red flag (red light) to replace inspection hammer (inspection light) to display transmission.

f. Test completion signal transmission procedures and standards

- The positive number inspector of rear car stands at the starting position of air testing, facing the head of the train, and transmits the "test completion signal" to the positive number inspector of middle car and negative number inspector of rear car, and stops displaying after confirming that the other party has received the "test completion signal" not less than 2 times.
- The negative number inspector of rear car and the positive number inspector of middle car stand in line at the starting position of the air testing, facing the rear of the train. When the positive train inspector of rear car transmits the "test completion signal", the "test completion signal" shall be received not less than 2 times; turned 180°, facing the head of the train, the negative number inspector of rear car and the positive number inspector of middle car transmit the "test completion signal" to the negative number inspector of middle car and the negative number inspector of head car together, and stop the transmission after confirming that the other party has received the "test completion signal" not less than 2 times.

c. The negative number inspector of middle car and the negative number inspector of head car stand in line at the starting position of the air testing, facing the rear of the train. When the positive number inspector of middle car and the negative number inspector of rear car transmits the "test completion signal", the "test completion signal" shall be received not less than 2 times; turned 180°, facing the head of the train, the negative number inspector of middle car and the negative number inspector of head car transmit the "test completion signal" to the positive number inspector of head car together, and stop the transmission after confirming that the other party has received the "test completion signal" not less than 2 times.

d. The positive number inspector of head car stands at the starting position of the air testing, facing the rear of the train; when the negative number inspector of middle car and the negative number inspector of head car transmit the "test completion signal" to themselves, they should receive the "test completion signal" not less than 2 times. Send "confirmation signal" to the negative number inspector of middle car and the negative number inspector of head car, and stop the display after confirming that the other party has received it for at least 2 times.

- The negative number inspector of middle car and the negative number inspector of head car stand in line at the starting position of the air testing, facing the head of the train. When the positive number inspector of head car transmits the "confirmation signal" to the other party, the "confirmation signal" shall be received not less than 2 times; the negative number inspector of middle car and the negative number inspector of head car turn 180°, facing the head of the train; the negative number inspector of middle car and the negative number inspector of head car transmit the "confirmation signal" to the positive number inspector of middle car and the negative number inspector of rear car together, and stop the transmission after confirming that the other party has received the "confirmation signal" not less than 2 times.
- The positive number inspector of middle car and the negative number inspector of rear car stand in line at the starting position of the air testing, facing the head of the train. After the positive number inspector of head car and the negative number inspector of middle car return to the "confirmation signal", the "confirmation signal" shall be received not less than 2 times; then turn 180°, and face the rear of the train; the positive number inspector of middle car and the negative number inspector of rear car return the "confirmation signal" together, and stop the display after confirming that the other party has received it not less than 2 times.
- The positive number inspector of rear car faces the head of the train, when the positive number inspector of middle car and the negative number inspector of rear car transmits the "confirmation signal" to the positive number inspector of rear car, the "confirmation signal" shall be received not less than 2 times.

(8) Remove protection signal.

a. The positive number inspector of head car removes the stop signal on the left body in train running direction of the head car which is behind the locomotive, reports to the on-duty train inspector, who shall repeat it for confirmation. The protective red flag shall be rolled up after removal, and the protective red light shall be closed after removal, and shall be carried. Standard term:

The positive number inspector of head car: "× Track × end, remove the red flag (red light)."

The on-duty train inspector: "× Track × end, remove the red flag (red light)."

b. The positive number inspector of rear car removes the stop signal on the left body in train running direction of the rear car, reports to the on-duty train inspector, who shall repeat it for confirmation. The protective red flag shall be rolled up after removal, and the protective red light shall be closed after removal, and shall be carried. Standard term:

The positive number inspector of rear car: "× Track × end, remove the red flag (red light) and wind meter."

The on-duty train inspector: "× Track × end, remove the red flag (red light) and wind meter."

6) Operation completed

After the test, the operator returns to the starting position.

Revision exercises

1. What are the hand signal display methods of braking, release, pressure maintaining, confirmation, and air test completion signal during train brake test?

2. What is the operation procedure of sensitivity test ?

3. What is the operation procedure of leakage test ?

4. What is the operation procedure of stabilization pressure test ?

Chapter 3

Operation and Maintenance of Passenger Trains

Railway passenger trains are an essential instrument for railway passenger transportation and the maintenance of passenger trains is an important part of railway transportation. The quality of maintenance work is directly related to the safety of passengers' lives and property. Providing good equipment, ensuring safe driving, and serving passenger transportation are the basic tasks of railway passenger trains operation and maintenance.

Passenger trains are subject to fixed allocation management. Its operation and maintenance work includes passenger trains management, operation maintenance management and operation safety management, etc., mainly conducted by the passenger car technical maintenance station (warehouse inspection), passenger train inspection and repair station and passenger trains crew. The railway bureau and the depot to which the passenger trains belong together constitute the main body responsible for the safety and quality of passenger trains. The operation and maintenance of passenger trains should follow the guidance of equal emphasis on maintenance, condition monitoring and prevention, continue to strengthen the application foundation, and continuously improve the management mechanism to achieve objectives as "normative management, standard operating, professional team, advanced equipment, eligible quality, safety and reliability."

Unit 1 Passenger Train Technical Servicing Point

The passenger train technical servicing point is an important base for passenger trains operation and maintenance. It has the functions of auxiliary repair, warehousing inspection, passenger trains renovation and temporary repair. After maintenance, the passenger train shall meet "Outbound Quality Standard of Operating Passenger Train", and ensure that there is no liability accident within a warehousing maintenance cycle.

Learning Objectives

(1) Understand the responsibilities of the passenger train technical servicing point.

(2) Master the conditions of scrapping passenger cars.

(3) Master the operation procedures of train technical inspection by passenger train technical servicing point.

Learning Content

1. Conditions of scrapping passenger trains

Passenger trains with excessive natural consumption, corrosion or serious accident damage that meet one of the following conditions can be applied for scrapping:

- Exterior walls and roof plates must be completely disassembled, and iron pillars must be replaced by 2/3.
- The middle beam needs to be replaced.
- The vertical bending of the middle and side beams exceeds 200 mm or the lateral bending exceeds 100 mm.
- Two side beams are broken or one side beam and two end beams are broken.
- The underframe of the vehicle is twisted, and its inclination exceeds 70 mm within 1 m of the underframe or over 300 mm for the entire underframe.
- The underframe has a high degree of damage and serious deformation after the fire accident, identified as no repair value.

2. Procedures for the maintenance of the passenger train technical servicing point

The maintenance procedures and contents of passenger train technical servicing point are shown in Figure 3-1.

(1)Technological processes of received train (Crew & Passenger Train Inspection and Service Point)

(2) Into Depot

(3) Train Transferred by Crew (Crew& Technical Maintenance Station of Passenger Trains)

(4) Recompose train

(5) Technical Inspection/ In-train Repair/ AC Inspection& Repair/ Train Detached Repair/ Train Minor Repair

(6) Train Transferred by Crew (Crew& Technical Maintenance Station of Passenger Trains)

(7) Out Depot

(8) Technological processes of outgoing train (Crew & Passenger Train Inspection and Service Point)

Figure 3-1 The maintenance procedures and contents

3. Train technical inspection of the passenger train technical servicing point

1) The division of labor and operation routes of the car set maintenance personnel

The car set inspection is carried out by 4 persons for inspection and 4 persons for repair; 4 persons for inspection are numbered ①~④, two persons for each pair, and the two pairs work from both sides of the car ends to the middle until they meet each other.

The four repairers are numbered ⑤ ~ ⑧, two for each pair, and the two pairs respectively start from the two sides of the car ends and follow the corresponding inspectors to the middle according to the mark, until they meet. No. ① and No. ⑤ are the leaders of the inspection and repair team respectively.

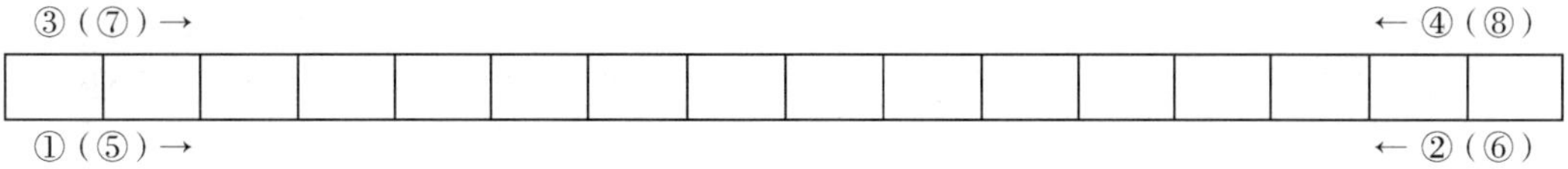

Figure 3-2 Diagram of the division of labor and operation route of the car set maintenance personnel

2) Safety precautions for train technical inspection operations

Safety precautions: ① Before and after the overhaul and maintenance of vehicles on the track, safety protection signals should be set and removed in accordance with regulations. ② Wear work clothes, safety helmets and other protective equipment according to regulations, and slippers, sandals, and high heels are forbidden. ③ As drilling under the vehicle, avoid the head from hitting the accessories. When handling the brake malfunction, close the door and exhaust the air. It is strictly forbidden to put fingers into the round pin hole. ④ The work should be adequate rather than simplified. ⑤ Concentrate on working during operation, strictly implement regulation as "first, stop; second, look around; third, confirm; fourth, pass the crossroad", and pay attention to avoiding the other trains during operation. ⑥ Be careful when going up and down the trench, and jumping is strictly prohibited.

3) Train technical inspection operation procedure

Operation procedure: assign tasks → set protection signals →technical detection → eliminate vehicle malfunctions→ fully test train brakes → acceptance inspection after repair → remove protection signals→ return to the office filling in the ledger.

(1) Assigning tasks.

As vehicle bottom enters the depot, the worker (group) leader handles the handover with the return crew, then back to group calling together the team (group) personnel, including repair personnel, assigning work tasks, conveying the precautions and the parking position of the vehicle bottom, and checking each person's carry-on tools and materials, and then setting off in pairs.

(2) Setting protection signals.

Numbers ① and ⑤ are responsible for inserting protection signals (safety plates, derailment devices), including a derailment device installed on the left side of the rail in the direction of the train, with a protection distance of no less than 20 m, and a protection signal set on the same side of the derailment device (red flags during the day and red lights at night), hanging up small cards indicating the type of work. In addition, connect the air source of the train brake tester to relieve the air filling of the train (check the anti-skid measures under the vehicle). After displaying the signal to ③ and ⑦ that the safety protection has been installed, start the operation.

(3) Inspecting car technical status.

Check from both ends of the car set to the middle, 2 people in 1 pair, 4 people working in parallel, calling for response. If a malfunction is found, it should be written in chalk on the malfunction point or other obvious place (but not on the wagon skin), and record it in "Vehicle Records-15".

(4) Eliminating the malfunctions.

The repair personnel firstly deal with the malfunctions transferred by the return crew in "Passenger trains Technical Status Transfer Book (Vehicle Records-181)", and then follow the inspectors to deal with the malfunctions marked by the inspectors one train after another in accordance with the prescribed quality standards. After treatment, mark "√" at the original mark. For those who need welding, cooperate with the electric welder for welding repair. When it is necessary to uncouple wagons for repair, the foreman shall notify the duty officer after confirmation. When it is necessary to replace the wheel pair, contact the relevant team in time to make preparations for the wheel replacement, and propose a delivery plan to the duty officer.

(5) Rechecking vehicle malfunctions.

After the inspectors complete all the technical inspections for the underside of vehicle, they must go back and recheck the malfunctions handled by the repairers. If qualified, erase the mark; if not, notify the repairer to handle it again.

(6) Testing train brakes.

After the trains are fully repaired, 4 inspectors will conduct the test of the train brakes for a certain period of time in accordance with the specified test requirements. For vehicles that replace the distribution valve (three-way valve), a single-vehicle test should be carried out first, and after confirming that it is in good condition, the test of the train brakes for a certain period of time should be carried out. The repaired vehicles should meet the quality standards for passenger trains out of the depot.

(7) Removing the safety protection signals.

After the work is completed, check the signs and display the completion signals one by one from the rear to the front. The check hammer is used during the day and the white light is used at night to swing with the train body at an angle of 45. After receiving all the completion signals, personnel No. ①, ⑤ remove the safety protection signals and the type of work cards.

(8) Returning to the office and filling in the ledger.

Line up to return the station and notify the duty room that the work is completed.

The worker (group) leader summarizes the overhaul situation, filling in "Car Records-181", and reports and submits "Car Records-181" to the duty officer. In addition, the leader should fill in other ledgers (such as maintenance records Car Records-81).

(9) Completion.

Collect waste materials, accessories, etc., sort and maintain tools, and the worker leader calls a completion conference.

4. Quality standards for passenger trains delivery

Through the implementation of daily maintenance and special maintenance, the passenger train technical servicing point must ensure that the passenger trains into service meet the "Outbound Quality Standard of Operating Passenger Train", as shown in Table 3-1.

Table 3-1 Use of quality standards for passenger car delivery

Parts	Quality Standards
Wheel Set	1. There should be no cracks on the axle, no looseness of the hub; the size of each part meets the specified limits. 2. There are no cracks in the brake disc hub, disc seat, and half disc joints, no through cracks in the heat dissipation ribs (sheets), no obvious partial wear on the friction surface of the brake disc, and the brake disc wear and thermal cracks on the friction surface do not exceed the limit. The plate, bolt and pin sleeve are tight; the bolt cotter is not damaged or lost
Bogie	3. The frame, bolster, spring plank carrier and all installation seats (including the installation seats connected to the bogie accessories on the vehicle body) have no cracks and deformation, bolster hanger and bolster hanger shafts, lateral lever, side-tumble-proof twist pole, traction bars (Horizontal bars), traction pin, upper and lower center plate, axle box guide column, locating swing arm and clamping band, all safety hangers have no cracks, and the bolster spring and axle box spring are not damaged. 4. The elastic positioning bushing of the guide post does not fall off or swell; the rubber parts, such as, the axle box positioning node, the traction bar rubber node, and the lateral stop are not damaged or degummed; the rubber stack locator is stacked with no cracks, and the notch direction meets the requirements; anti-roll and torsion rod joint bearings and rubber protective sleeves are not protruded or cracked.

Continue

Parts	Quality Standards
Bogie	5. The gaps of the bolster stop, side bearing, and lateral stop should not exceed the limit; the mounting bolts of each part of the bogie are not loose, and the anti-loose iron wires are well -bound; the center plate pad is not damaged and the lateral stop wear plate does not fall off. 6.The height measuring block of pneumatic suspension should not be missing, the bonding surface of the rubber bag and the metal plate is not separated, the surface cracks of the rubber bag and the rubber stack are not exceeded, and the capsule cord is not exposed. 7.The height adjusting valve and the height valve adjusting rod are installed firmly without cracks or deformation, and the adjusting rod sleeve is intact; the pressure differentiating valve should be installed firmly without cracks; the safety wire rope, round pin, and split pin should not be broken; the air spring exhaust device of AM96 bogie exhausts the air well, and the steel cables, operating levers, springs, split pins, etc. are not damaged. 8.There are no missing parts of the hydraulic damper; the installation of accessories is firm; also, there is no oil leakage or breakage
Basic Braking Device	9. The lever and suspension device of the disc brake unit have no cracks, and the levers can rotate flexibly; the round pins and split pins are not lost, broken or worn to the limit, the matching gap between the round pins and the sleeve is not exceed the limit, and the pin sleeve does not move out. The thickness of the brake pads does not exceed the limit, and there is no pressure on the brake pads or the brake pads leave the brake disc when relieved. 10.The brake brackets, hangers, rods and levers of tread brakes (including tread cleaners) are free of cracks; the rods and supports are not resistant, and the brackets are installed firmly without cracks; the relief springs are installed firmly with no cracks; the wear of brake hanger does not exceed limit; each round pin and split pin are not lost or broken, the matching gap between each round pin and the sleeve is not exceed limit, and the pin sleeve does not move out or crack; the brake head anti-turning device and the brake hanger pin is well-equipped with anti-off stop. 11.The stroke of the brake cylinder piston complies with the regulations. The automatic gap adjuster and the ST1-600 brake adjuster work well. The brake shoe does not contact the wheel and also does not wear off when it is relieved; the distance from all hangings to the rail surface meets the regulations. 12.The hand brake works well and the chain is in a loose state; the wear plates of all wearing parts (including bogies, hooks, etc.) are complete and well lubricated.

Continue

Parts	Quality Standards
Air-Brake Device Device and Main Air Device	13.The train brake test meets the requirements. The braking and mitigation effect is good, the leakage of the braking pipeline system does not exceed the limit, and the unit brake cylinder, brake mitigation display and anti-skid exhaust valve have no leakage; the main air pipeline system is well connected, and the leakage does not exceed the limit. 14.All pipe clamps of the pipe system shall be free from looseness and loss; All valves, cocks and air cylinder accessories shall be free of missing, firmly installed, correctly positioned and in good condition; the hose shall be free of bubbles, loose installation, and in good connection; the dust plug shall be hung firmly, and the dust plug chain shall not be too close to the rail surface after it is hung; the handle cotter pin of angle cock shall be free from damage and loss; the brake release indicator is clean and the display is correct with no crack; the wind meter is not expired ; the lead seal of emergency brake valve is intact. 15.The cylinder and seat of unit brake are not cracked, the positioning pin is well positioned, the dust cover is not damaged, and the metal hose has no looseness, wear, or damage. 16.The integrated electric pneumatic braking chassis, the gas circuit control box body and the mounting seat are not damaged or loose, and the box door is closed well. 17.The routine inspection test of the passenger trains tail are good, the main engine is installed firmly, the pipeline is free of leakage, the rubber hose is free of cracking or aging, and the dedicated DC48V power socket is not loose or damaged, and works normally
Coupler and Draft Gear	18.No cracks on the coupler, coupler yoke, coupler support plate, centering block and hanger, coupler pocket, draft lug of the No. 15 coupler and draft gear, and the draft gear is not cracked; the support plate bolts and the cross bolts of the tail pin are not loose, and the anti-loose iron wire is installed well; the knuckle pivot pin is not broken, the nut is installed well, and the split pin is not broken; the buffer is not upturned, the coupler release rod falls in groove, and does not impact the bottom lock lifter connector; the bottom lock lifter and coupler release rod shall be bound as required ; the three-state function of the front and rear couplers of the train is in good condition, and the couplers height meets the requirements; the difference of the connected couplers does not exceed the limit. 19.There are no cracks and permanent deformations on the mounting seat, buffer shell, and coupler body of the tight-lock coupler and draft gear; all bolts are not loose or missing; the connecting gap between the two couplers and the extension of the inner half cylinder of the buffer relative to the rear end surface of the shell does not exceed the limit ; the uncoupling handle is well positioned without deformation

Continue

Parts	Quality Standards
Car Body and Roof Equipment	20.The regular inspection of the vehicle does not expire; the escalator and anti-climbing box at the end of the vehicle are installed firmly, and the box door is locked well; the vehicle body is not inclined beyond the limit; the beams of the vehicle under-frame are not cracked, and the walls and roof are not damaged. 21.The windshield spring and damping device are installed firmly without breakage; the folding windshield tie rods are composed of moderately tight and firmly connected, the tarp is not cracked, the folding shed lanyards (spring) in the vehicle are complete, and the cross plate is not upturned; the iron windshield folding shed shall be free of bending, cracking and open welding; the crack of the rubber windshield capsule does not exceed 100 mm. 22. The foot step are installed firmly without corrosion and damage; the handlebars are not damaged, lost or loose; each skirt is locked and fastened. 23.The accessories of each hanging device (including the hangings of electrical equipment box) of the under-frame are complete, firmly installed, free of cracks, and the lock nuts are not loose; the appearance of each box (including electrical equipment box) under the vehicle is not damaged, and the door lock of the box is in good condition; there is no leakage from the fuel tank, water tank, and dirt tank. 24. The water injection pipes, drain pipes, ducts, and toilet buckets are installed firmly without any defects; the drain pipes are oriented correctly, avoiding axle boxes, trolleys, wheel sets and basic brake devices; the holes between various drainage pipes, brake pipes, release valve pull rods and the vehicle body shall be blocked reliably, and the cold proof materials shall not be exposed. 25. The roof does not leak rain; the roof equipment is firmly installed, the roof antenna, roof flap, ventilator, waste exhaust hood, muffler cap, etc. Shall be free from loss, and the fixing bolts are not falling off or loose
Inner Equipment of the car	26. Equipped with fire extinguishers and fire hammers in accordance with regulations; fire extinguishers shall not be overhauled, the pressure shall comply with the regulations, and the lead seal shall be intact. Wall panels, floors, and roof panels are intact with no holes, and all bedding strips through counters, toilets, washrooms, small corridor floors and wall panels are complete, and gaps and holes are well sealed. 27. All hinged doors, sliding doors, flaps, springs, locks, door stops, and bumpers are complete and function well; sliding plug doors work well, each lock switch is normal, and the flip pedals are installed firmly and work normally; automatic inner door manual and the electric control position conversion function is good, the function is flexible, and the anti-extrusion works well. 28. The movable window accessories are complete, and the lifting and locking functions are good; the door and window glass is installed firmly without damage; the window frame of the externally embedded riveting structure is not damaged or loose.

Continue

Parts	Quality Standards
Inner Equipment of the car	29. Seats, sleeping berths and slings, handrails, escalators, tea tables, luggage racks, and coat hooks shall be installed without looseness; seat and sleeping berths are not damaged; height signs, seat numbers, shop numbers, and special seat signs for the disabled are complete and clear, also, the position meets the requirements; the floor and floor cloth in the vehicle have no collapse or bubbling that affects walking. 30. The water supply piping system and valve do not leak and works well; the face-wash basin, hand-wash basin, and toilet are installed firmly, and the cracks do not affect the use; the water level meter (liquid level meter) displays accurately, and the maintenance does not expire. 31.The heating device has complete accessories and works well. The temperature gauge and water level gauge indicate accurately; the valves, plugs, couplings, and elbows of the piping system have no water leakage or freezing. Coal-fired warm water boilers, tea stoves and dining car stoves work well, and the chimneys and fire and heat insulation devices are complete. 32.The stool collection device works well, and the toilet flushes evenly without spraying outside
The Electrical Device Under the Car	33. The test of the main line insulation of the train meets the requirements; the appearance of the plugs and sockets of the electrical connectors at the end of the vehicle is not deformed or damaged, and the markings are clear and correct; the sheath of the connecting line is not damaged, and the sealing gasket is not damaged; the connectors are firmly connected; the tail marker lights are installed at the front and rear of the DC48V side light socket of the vehicle has good conduction. 34. The junction boxes, wiring ducts, and wiring pipes are firmly installed; various sensors (including brake air supply system pressure sensors, vehicle body and bogie acceleration sensors, anti-skid speed sensors, axle temperature sensors, and battery temperature detection sensors), The exhaust valve is installed firmly, the wiring is not damaged, the lead sleeves are well connected, and there is no anti-wear; the shaft end grounding device and the car body grounding wire are installed firmly, and the bolts are not loose or missing. 35. All parts of the shaft end generator are complete and work well; no loosening or cracking of the large and small pulleys; the bolts shall be free of damage; the accessories of the suspension device shall be complete without cracks; the clearance between the suspension device and the pin hole shall meet the regulations, and the lubrication shall be in good condition; the belt installation is moderately tight; the bottom groove is not ground; there is no burn mark on the surface of the rectifying element, and the wire has no desoldering.

Continue

Parts	Quality Standards
The Electrical Device Under the Car	36. The battery has no looseness or leakage, and the electrolyte level meets the requirements; the connection line is firm and non-sulfurized with good conductivity; the electrolyte specific gravity and voltage meet the requirements, the fuse capacity meets the requirements, and the regular inspection marks are clear; drainage and exhaust are unobstructed; single block and the battery voltage meets the regulations, and the discharge voltage of the DC 110 V battery pack is not lower than that of the 92 V.
The Electrical Devices in the Vehicle	37.The door locks of electrical integrated control cabinets, power cabinets, air-conditioning control cabinets, lighting distribution cabinets (panels), kitchen electrical control cabinets, etc. are in good condition and closed tightly; the touch screen and indicator lights are normal, and the switches and buttons are operated flexibly and contacted well; the settings of the sensors, thermal relays, PLCs, touch screens, and on-line insulation detection devices are reliable and meet the requirements; electrical components such as electrical switches, contactors, and relays are installed firmly and work well; the wiring terminal shall be free of looseness, desoldering and burning, and the temperature measurement adhesive shall be complete without discoloration; All wiring shall be free of exposure and well insulated; the capacity of each fuse shall meet the requirements. 38.The output voltage and frequency of the charger and inverter are normal; the communication among the charger, the inverter and the electrical integrated control cabinet is normal, and the normal information code is displayed on the touch screen; the indicator light of the under-vehicle power box of the electrical integrated control cabinet is displayed in green. 39.After power on, the control cabinet power conversion and air-conditioning control electrical actions and instructions are normal, and various functions meet the requirements; the working current of each functional unit is normal; the leakage current of DC 600 V bicycle does not exceed 100 mA, and the leakage current of AC 380 V bicycle does not exceed 150 mA; the front and the rear DC 600 V trunk lines are online; the CF card of the insulation monitoring device is intact, the touch screen has no fault or error display, and the voltage of any main line to ground shall not be lower than that of the 130 V. 40.All parts of the air-conditioning device are complete, function well and installed firmly; the evaporator network and the return air network are clean; the air preheater of the unit is installed firmly without burning; check the corresponding functions according to the external temperature power-on test; the system function must be good, and all motors operate normally without abnormal sound. 41.The electric heater is installed firmly and works well. There is no foreign matter between the protective cover and the wall panel, and the heating plate (pipe) is not closely attached; the warm water tank and the heating device works normally; the electric water boiler outlet valve is not loose, leaking, heating and protecting works normally.

Continue

Parts	Quality Standards
The Electrical Devices in the Vehicle	42. The lighting fittings are complete; the type is uniform and the lighting is normal. The passenger information of the display system displays correctly on the carriage; the 48 V emergency power supply rectification, charging, and emergency output functions are normal. The sequence number adjuster works well. The toilet display switch accessories are complete, the installation is firm, and the function is good. Devices such as isolation transformers, electric bells, exhaust fans, electric water pumps, sockets, and public systems such as broadcasting calls are works well. 43. The drain valve and exhaust valve of the electric rice steaming box in the electric kitchen open and close normally (the opening pressure of the automatic exhaust valve is not more than 0.05 MPa); there is no leakage at the pipe fittings; the equipment works normally after being energized. After the electric fryer and range hood are energized, the buttons on the control panel work well and the equipment works normally. The control knob of the induction cooker is flexible and works normally. The air inlet and outlet are unobstructed; the ventilation duct is clean; the air passes through the cooling plate without obstruction; the fan and cooling plate are installed firmly. The door switch of the fresh-keeping heating cabinet is flexible and works normally when it is energized. The refrigerator has complete accessories, no leakage, no damage to the cabinet and door, good sealing, clean heat exchanger and filter; the power output of the matching inverter device is reliable, and the refrigerator works normally after power on. 44. The television picture of the film and television system is clear, the channel is normal and the installation is reliable; the video controller functions normally and the surface is clean. The power switch of the broadcasting system is in the working position, and the volume switch works normally. 45. The communication between the host of the electronic anti-skid device and the PLC of the electrical integrated control cabinet and the carriage level host of the driving safety monitoring device is correct and reliable; The information display of anti-skid device on the touch screen of electrical integrated control cabinet shall be normal information code; The interlocking signal with the door (< 5 km / h) works well. 46. The axle temperature alarm and recorder display accurately, the axle temperature and external temperature display function is normal, and the sound and light alarm is reliable; the static axle temperature difference on the same side <5 °C; the sequence number of alarm car, recorder clock and recording time interval are set correctly; the communication function of the recorder is normal; the communication between the alarm and the PLC in the electrical integrated control cabinet is normal, and there is no "fault" information displayed on the touch screen of the electrical integrated control cabinet. 47. The sound and light alarm function of the pyrotechnic alarm host is good, the power switch is in the working position, and the communication with the PLC in the electrical integrated control cabinet is normal, and there is no "fault" information displayed on the electrical integrated control cabinet's touch screen.

Continue

Parts	Quality Standards
The Electrical Devices in the Vehicle	48. Train safety monitoring device: the vehicle-level electrical equipment monitoring network gateway and the indicator lights of the agent node are displayed normally; the electrical integrated control cabinet touch screen shows that the electrical equipment information of the vehicle is normal, and the vehicle sequence number is consistent with the actual marshalling; the touch screen of the main control station of the train level electrical equipment monitoring network displays normally, without offline vehicle and fault information. The train marshalling number and vehicle sequence number displayed by the train-level host computer should be consistent with the actual information. The content of the "alarm/fault" report of the anti-skid device, brake, and bogie shall not have yellow signs

Revision exercises

1. What are the conditions for scrapping trains?

2. What are the main responsibilities of the passenger train technical servicing point?

3. How to set protection signals when conducting train technical inspection operations in the passenger train technical servicing point?

Unit 2 Technical Inspection of Single Passenger Car

Learning Objectives

(1) Master the operation method of single car technical inspection;

(2) Master the application limit of railway passenger cars.

Learning Content

Single car technical inspection for passenger train is the basic skill that car inspectors must have. The car inspectors must be proficient in the steps, methods and operating sequence of the technical inspection of single passenger cars and related operation limits to ensure the safety of railway transportation.

1. Operation modes

According to the site conditions, single car technical inspection operation is divided into two modes: operation with trench and without trench. The schematic diagrams of the operation routes are shown in Figure 3-3 and Figure 3-4. Generally speaking, the operation procedures are: inserting the red flag → carrying out technical inspection of the passenger car according to the operation process→dictating the fault found → removing the red flag after the operation is completed.

1) Operation without trench

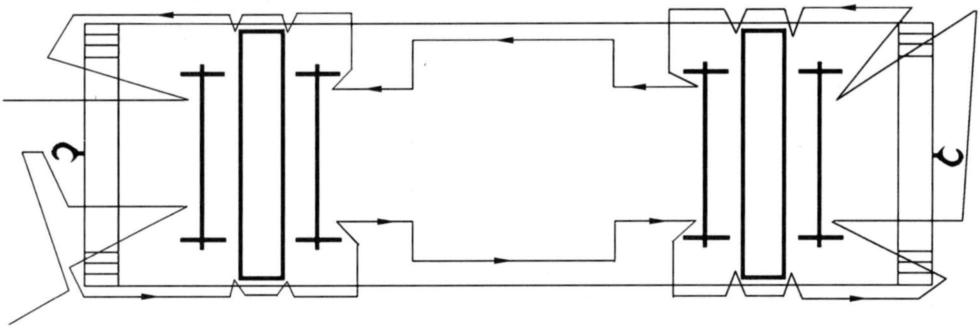

Figure 3-3 Schematic diagram of technical inspection operation route for single cars without trench

2) Operation with trench

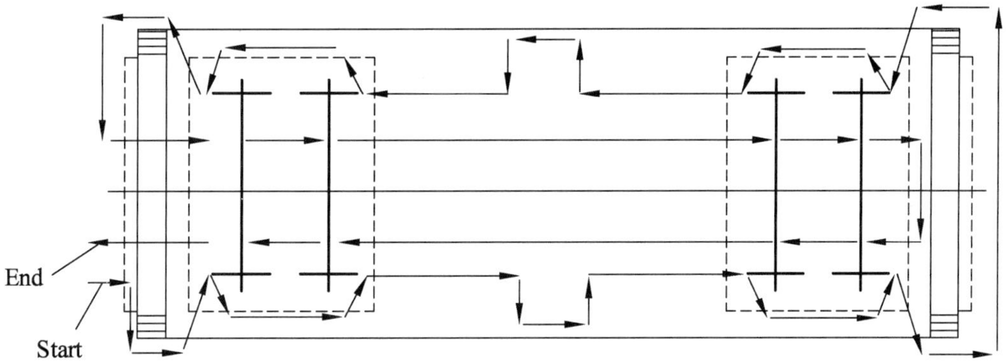

Figure 3-4 Schematic diagram of technical inspection operation route for single cars with trench

2. Operation Steps and Quality Standards

During the operation, the red flag must be inserted firmly and unfolded, the clothes and hats as well as the gloves shall be neatly worn during the operation. The inspector' s body should not slip or fall during the operation, and no part of the body shall be scratched or bleeding. The quality standards and steps of the operation are shown in Table 3-2.

Table 3-2　Technical inspection details and quality standards of ordinary passenger cars

No.	Inspection Sequence	Quality Standard
1	windshield	The windshield and spring are not broken. The nut, round pin and split pin are not lost

2	Turning head during regular inspection and check the inclination	Overhaul and depot inspection are not overdue. The inclination of the car body is no more than 50 mm

3	Testing three states with coupler release rod	The coupler release rod bracket is not loose when the coupler release rod is shaken without touching the lower connecting rod. The clearance between the coupler release rod and the bracket groove is no more than 3 mm. The clearance between the knuckle pin and the knuckle pin hole is no more than 7 mm

Continue

No.	Inspection Sequence	Quality Standard
4	Angle cock, brake hose, coupler carrier bolt and nut, bolt and supporting seat	The brake hose does not deteriorate or blister. The hydraulic testing is not overdue. The accessories have no cracks. There is no leak for the connection part. There is loose allowance for clip bolts. The angle cock can work flexibly and is right in its position and not loose. 
5	Coupler neck, swing block, windshield rod spring	The bolts are not loose. The wear plate is not broken or lost. The windshield rod is not bent. The spring is not broken. The swing block, hanger and coupler neck are not cracked. The clip is not loose 
6	Incoming main pipes and beams	There is no leakage in the piping system. There is no missing or looseness of the pipe clamps. The windshield rod, bolt, split pin are not broken or lost. The coupler carrier is not loose or cracked. The beams are not cracked, and the floor is not corroded 

Continue

No.	Inspection Sequence	Quality Standard
7	Coupler body, coupler follower plate and coupler yoke	There are no cracks in the coupler body, buffer, coupler follower plate or bracket. The wear of the lower part of the coupler body and coupler yoke are no more than 6 mm. The supporting plate is not loose or cracked

8	Center plate,bolster and brake beams	The center plate pin is not lost. The bolt is not loose. The center plate, bolster, bolster spring carrier, frame and brake beam are not cracked. The brake beam is not bent

9	Lever, pull rod and split pin	The wear of each round pin is no more than 3 mm. The distance between each vertical device and the rail surface is no less than 50 mm. Each lever and pull rod shall not compete, or wear the axle body and hub
10	Axle body, wheel back, release spring	The axle is free of cracks. The wear depth of the axle body is no greater than 1 mm. For the defect on the inner side of the rim, the length is no more than 30 mm and width is not more than 10 mm. The inner distance of wheel set is (1353 ± 3) mm, and the error between three places is no more than 3 mm. The release spring is not cracked or loose

Continue

No.	Inspection Sequence	Quality Standard
11	Cross the rail and squad to check brake parts	The wear of the straight part of the brake head hanger and each part of the brake head is no greater than 4 mm. The wear of the end shaft of the brake beam is no greater than 3 mm. The assembly clearance is no greater than 4 mm. The residual wear thickness of each flat split pin is no less than 1.5 mm. The distance between the brake head and the rail surface is no less than 25 mm. The thickness of the brake shoe is no less than 10 mm. the thickness difference of the brake shoe of the same brake beam is no greater than 20 mm. The brake shoe is not close to the wheel
12	Tread, rim and axle box spring	The vertical wear height of the rim is no greater than 15 mm. The thickness of the rim is no less than 23 mm. The circumferential wear depth of the tread is no greater than 8 mm. There is no grinding pile at the top of the rim. The local concave depth of tread scratch is no greater than 1.5 mm. Tread stripping length: no more than 30 mm if there is one stripping, no more than 20 mm if there are two, and no more than 350 mm for continuous stripping. Tread defect: the distance from the outer side of the relative rim to the defect is no less than 1508 mm. The length is no more than 150 mm. The rim thickness is no less than 25 mm. The rear part of the axle box is free of oil rejection. The bolts are not loose, the round springs are not folded or cracked. The positioning sleeve, support ring and buffer are not strung, lost or broken. The pillar bolt split pin is not lost
13	Inspect the pedals from the car end	The pedals are not corroded or deformed. The door armrests are not loose. The accessories of the defecation tube function well 

Continue

No.	Inspection Sequence	Quality Standard
14	Step down, squad to inspect rim	The axle box is free of cracks. The bolts are free of looseness. The rim is free of cracks 
15	Stand up to inspect axle box and wheel tread	The round spring and positioning sleeve are in good condition. The rim, tread and wheel flange are in good condition 
16	Round spring, wheel tread and brake parts	The same as No. 12 and No. 13
17	Turn to inspect bolster guide, bolster hanger and safety bracket	The bolts are not loose. The safety bracket, bolster hanger and hanger seat are free of cracks. The bolster spring and bolster guide are in good condition and without cracks 

Continue

No.	Inspection Sequence	Quality Standard
18	Hanging shaft, supporting board and swing spring	The hanger shaft is free of cracks. The hanger shaft bolts are free of looseness. The bolster springs are free of cracks and breaks. The assembly bolts are in good condition. The bolster spring is right in the groove. The supporting board is in good condition and free of cracks 
19	From damper to bolster guide	Damper accessories are complete without oil leakage and looseness. Traction rod nuts are not loose. And iron stops and rubber pads are in good condition 
20	Inspect frame and axle	The frame is free of cracks.
21	Inspect both sides of side bearing and center plate	The center plate and side bearing bolts are not loose. The center plate is free of cracks 

Continue

No.	Inspection Sequence	Quality Standard
22	Squad to check bolster guide at the other side	The same as No. 19, No. 18 and No. 17
23	Same inspection sequence with the left side to the wheel tread	The same as No. 12, No. 13, No. 14 and No. 15
24	Lean over to inspect the main pipe and beams	The main pipe is free of corrosion and leakage. The pipe clamps are not missing. Each beam and floor is free of crack and corrosion 
25	Inspect another bogie in and out	The same as No. 8, No. 9 and No. 10
26	Inspect pull rod and bracket carefully	The bracket is free of cracks. The bolts are not loose. The lever does not compete 
27	Look forward, inspect the pipes and beams	The same as No. 24

Continue

No.	Inspection Sequence	Quality Standard
28	Branch pipes, cocks and dirt collector	The pipe system is free of leakage. The bolts are free of looseness. The cock and dirt collector are in position. The handle is not broken or lost 
29	Regulator valve and air cylinder	The regulator is not stuck. The mounting bolts are not loose. The valve bolts are not loose. The valve does not leak. The dust-proof rubber pad of the emergency valve is not lost. The pressure reservoir has no leakage. The sling is not loose. The exhaust cock is in good condition 
30	Mark of auxiliary repair and brake cylinder	There is no leakage of the brake cylinder. The bolts are not loose. 

Continue

No.	Inspection Sequence	Quality Standard
31	Brackets and pins	The handbrake, pull rod and bracket are free of cracks. The split pins are in good condition
32	Pull rod, and then forward for floor beam	The middle pull rod and hand brake pull rod accessories are complete. The turnbuckle is not loose. The floor beam is in good condition 
33	Same inspection operation for other bogies	The same as No. 8, No. 9, No 10 and No. 12~25
34	Don' t forget the hand brake accessories	The bolts are not loose. The round split pins are in good condition. The brake chain is in a loose state 
35	Inspect half of the coupler and draft gear and buffer	The same as No. 7 and No. 6
36	Crawl out from the car end to inspect the vestibule diaphragm rod spring	The same as No. 5
37	Coupler head, knuckle pin, sling chain and plug	The knuckle pin and split pin are complete. The hose chain and plug are complete and without cracks
38	Inspect markings and vestibule diaphragm carefully	The same as No. 1. Mark clearly
39	Inspection for one half of the car body is completed after the handrail and pedal inspection	The same as No. 11

Revision exercises

Combined with actual situation, simulate the technical inspection for the lower part of the singe passenger car.

Unit 3 Passenger Train Inspection and Service Point

Passenger train inspection and service point is an important department to ensure the safe operation of passenger trains. It is responsible for the technical operations of departing, passing, and arriving trains, as well as conducting key technical inspections for turnaround and passing passenger trains, so as to eliminate faults that endangering traffic safety.

Learning Objectives

(1) Master the responsibilities of passenger train inspection and service point;

(2) Master the inspection scope of the passenger train inspection and service point;

(3) Master the technical inspection procedures of passenger trains.

Learning Content

1. Responsibilities of passenger train inspection and service point

The main responsibilities of passenger train inspection and service point are:

(1) Passenger train inspection and service point is an important department to ensure the safe operation of passenger trains. It undertakes the key technical inspection for the final arrival, departure and running gear of passing passenger trains, and timely eliminates the faults endangering train safety.

(2) The passenger train inspection and service point must actively repair or properly handle the car faults found or predicted to ensure running safety. Whether the faulty car should be detached shall be confirmed and handled by the passenger train inspection and service point.

(3) Passenger train inspectors must wear armbands during working.

(4) For the departure passenger train, the inspection and service point should be responsible for the connection of the hose that is between the locomotive and the first passenger car behind the locomotive and the electrical connecting line which is at the end of the train, and conduct a brief brake test.

(5) For the final arriving passenger train, the inspection and service point is responsible for uncoupling the coupler between the locomotive and the first passenger car after it, as well as

uncoupling the hose and electrical connecting line at the car end. Turnaround trains that does not enter the depot for maintenance shall be inspected according to the technical inspection operation scope of technical servicing station, and all brake tests shall be conducted.

2. Operation Scope of Passenger Train inspection and service point

1) Operation scope of technical inspection for passing passenger train

(1) Handover of technical status of passenger cars.

(2) Axle temperature: Detach the car if the axle temperature reaches 90 °C or exceeds the external temperature for 60 °C. Notify the crew for key monitoring and informing next inspection and service point beforehand for key inspection if the axle temperature exceeds the external temperature for 45 °C. The cover of the turnaround train must be opened for inspection. If it is found that the bearing parts are damaged, the oil is deteriorated or mixed with sand, water, metal powder and other abnormalities that endanger the running safety, the car should be detached for repair.

(3) Wheel defect, tread peeling and scratch.

(4) Bolster suspension device, foundation brake gear.

(5) Axle box spring, bolster spring and air spring.

(6) Missing, falling off or damage of accessories.

(7) Connection status of coupler, brake hose and main air duct.

(8) Carry out train brake test as required.

2) Non detached inspection scope of passing passenger trains

(1) When the axle box spring of passenger car that is marked speed of 120 km / h and below and equipped with 209 HS bogie is damaged, it shall be replaced. When the broken support ring is confirmed to have no other related faults, it can be replaced at the terminal station right after that running operation. Other damaged axle box springs of passenger cars can also be replaced at the terminal station after running operation.

(2) Deal with foundation brake failure.

(3) Deal with air brake failure.

(4) Replace the couple knuckle and adjust the coupler difference.

(5) Replace traction rod and deal with its faults (except for 25 T passenger trains).

(6) Deal with missing, falling off or damaged parts.

The passenger train inspection and service point must actively repair or properly handle car faults found or predicted to ensure running safety. It should confirm and be responsible for whether the faulty car should be detached. And the crew should obey the decision of the passenger train inspection and service point.

3) Division of Responsibilities of Passenger Train Inspection and Service Point

(1) The passenger train inspection and service point should be blamed if the fault that is within the scope of non-detached inspection is not handled or undertaken detached inspection.

(2) Safe operation to the terminal station should be guaranteed after the fault that is within the scope of non-detached inspection is handled by the passenger train inspection and service point.

(3) Safe operation to the next inspection and service point should be guaranteed after the fault that is within the inspection scope is handled.

4) Operation procedures for technical inspection of passenger trains

Safety precautions for technical inspection of passenger trains:

① Operators should concentrate when they queue out of the waiting-for-inspection room. It is prohibited to crawl under the car body. Implement the regulation of "standing, looking around, confirming and passing" to pass lines. Pass the level crossing quickly after it is confirmed safe. It is prohibited to rush over the track or pass through ahead of the departing train. Stand outside the safety white line when the train arrives.

② Arrive at the receiving point 5 min in advance after receiving the train forecast.

③ Before operation, operators shall insert protective signals: red flags for the day and red lights for the night. Protective signals should be in good condition and in bright color.

④ When working at the other side of the platform, pay attention to passing trains on the adjacent line. If there is a train or a single locomotive passing on the adjacent line of the operated train, stay at a safe place and do not cross the line. The attendant and operators at two ends of the train shall use interphone to timely inform the on-site operators to keep safe, call for a response to remind each other. When an express train or EMU passes through, stop the operation on the adjacent line 10 min in advance, stay at a safe place and proceed to work only after the train passes through.

⑤ It is prohibited to jump up and down the high platform to avoid slipping and falling injury.

1) Operation procedures of technical inspection for passing passenger trains.

Operation procedures: preparation → train receiving → technical inspection work → train braking system performance test → train delivering → returning back to the station.

(1) Preparation.

Passenger train inspectors should wear the required armbands when working on duty. After receiving the operation order from the attendant, they should check the assigned number of trains being inspected, the specified working position and time. Arrive at the post before the train enters the station, stand at a safe place on both sides of the train arrival line, and wait for the train to enter the station. Roll call and task assignment ahead of duty is shown as in Figure

3-5. Set off in queue is shown as in Figure 3-6.

Figure 3-5 Roll call and task assignment ahead of duty

Figure 3-6 Set off in queue

(2) Train Receiving .

When the train arrives at the station, inspectors stand upright to receive the train at the working point facing the train entering direction. When the locomotive passes the train receiving point, the inspector should face the train at an angle of 45°, and conduct "three senses" inspection (visual inspection for parts falling off; auditory inspection for abnormal sound or abnormal jumping sound of the rolling stocks; olfactory inspection for peculiar smell). If problems are found, the location must be accurately recorded. After the train stops steadily, arrive at the faulty location in time for confirmation and deal with it actively and properly.

Receive the train, Insert protection signal are shown as in Figure 3-7 and 3-8.

Figure 3-7 Receive the train

Figure 3-8

(3) Inserting protection signal.

After the passenger train arrives and stops, the train inspector at the front end of the train displays the start signal of the technical inspection to the inspector at the rear end of the train (the middle inspector is responsible for signal transmission), and the inspector at the rear end receives the signal and places the protection signal.

(4) Train technical inspection.

Make full use of the technical inspection time to conduct technical inspection for the train, and repair and deal with the faults found in a timely manner. It is necessary to carefully confirm and decisively decide whether to detach the faulty car that cannot be repaired in the fleet. Car technical inspection is shown as in Figue 3-9.

Figure 3-9　Car technical inspection

(5) Train braking system performance test.

For the departure train and the couple-changed train after the leading locomotive, the inspector at the rear end of the train should install the proofreading wind meter, open the angle cock of the car at the rear of the train, and start the performance test. When the wind meter at the locomotive and rear end are expressed at a constant pressure (the error with wind meter of the rear car does not exceed the specified value), the train inspector at the rear of the train will show the train brake signal to the inspector at the head. Then the inspector should show the train relief signal after the car at the rear of the train has a good release effect and the wind pressure of the main train reaches a constant pressure, close the angle cock, remove the proofreading wind meter, install the dust plug of the air duct and hang the air duct. Then send the signal to the head car inspector that the performance test is completed, remove the protection signal, and take your place to prepare for delivering the train.

(6) Removing protection signal.

After the operation, check the signal and confirm that no operation is being taken under the train, and the train inspector at the head and tail of the train shall remove the safety protection signal.

(7) Train delivering and returning back to the station.

When the departure bell rings, stand at the safe places on both sides of the train. When the train starts, squat to deliver the train at an angle of 45° to the train. After the train passes the operators' position, the operator stands up and continues to watch the train facing the train direction. After the tail of the train passes the fouling post (or departure signal), check the signal from front end to rear end and return back to the station. Deliver the train is shown as in Figure 3-10.

Figure 3-10 Deliver the train

2) Operation procedure of technical inspection for departure trains.

Operation procedure: preparation → coupling locomotive → train braking system performance test → end of inspection.

(1) Preparation.

After receiving the work order, the inspector should immediately check the number of allocated trains being inspected and the determined operation point and enter the post 20 minutes in advance.

(2) Coupling and inspection.

The front car inspector should inspect the coupler's three operation states of the car just behind the locomotive, and check if the connection of the air duct is in good condition. After the locomotive is coupled, confirm the connection status, connect the brake hose and electrical control wiring, open the angle cock to charge air to the train. Inspectors should recheck that there is no leakage for the pipelines of the cars.

(3) Train braking system performance test.

When the main brake pipe of train reaches the constant pressure, the train braking system performance brief test should be carried out as specified. After it is done, the dust plug of the air duct should be installed and the air duct should be hung.

(4) End of inspection.

After all tasks are completed, the inspectors at the head and tail of the train will be notified to remove the protection signal. The inspector working at the head of the train shall stand at a safe place of the connection of the locomotive and rolling stock on the non-platform side, the inspectors working at a place at the tail or middle of the train respectively to deliver the train as specified.

3) Procedures of technical inspection for passenger trains terminal (back to depot)

Operation procedure: preparation → train receiving → locomotive uncoupling → end of inspection

(1) Preparation.

The car inspector shall prepare as required, arrive at the train receiving point 5 min in advance and wait for the receiving.

(2) Train receiving.

After entering the post, turn on the walkie-talkie to monitor the arrival of the train, and receive the train as specified when the train arrives. If problems are found, record them accurately, and confirm and deal with it again after the train has stopped.

(3) Locomotive uncoupling.

Operators set up safety protection signal at the side of the front end of the train. Open the "three bindings" at the front end of the car behind the locomotive. Close the angle cock of the car first, then close the angle cock of the locomotive. Uncouple the brake hose, coupler and electrical control wiring after exhaust the air in hoses of the locomotive and the car.

(4) End of inspection.

After the work is completed, the inspector should report to the attendant after the locomotive leaves. Return to the waiting-for-inspection room, and accept next task.

Revision exercises

1. What is the duty of the passenger train inspection and service point?

2. Which parts of the passing passenger train must be inspected for the passenger train inspection and service point?

Unit 4 Passenger Train Crew

The car crew is the last line of defense to ensure the safety of passenger train operation and the window to display the image of the rolling stock department. It is responsible for the dynamic monitoring of train operation status, emergency handling of equipment failure and technical operation within its scope of responsibility. All units shall, in accordance with the principle of strengthening duty, actively promote the separation of depot and passenger, and gradually abolish the scope of repairs for car crews.

In principle, the work of car crew of passenger train shall implement designated crew system. The car designated crew group is composed of chief steward, crew members, and generator car crew members, collectively referred to as car crew, and the allocation standard shall be implemented in accordance with relevant regulations.

Car crew should wear uniform and keep clean during work, and be polite and courteous. The crew members on duty should wear armbands on the upper left arm (the style is shown in the figure), and consciously abide by labor disciplines, work disciplines and road style regulations. Inter-bureau passenger train should accept the leadership of the local railway bureau, obey the order and command.

Figure 3-11 The style of crew member

Learning Objectives

(1) Get to know the main responsibilities of rolling stock crew.

(2) Master the operation requirements of rolling stock designated crew.

(3) Learn to deal with sudden failures during passenger train operation..

Learning Content

1. Working Requirements for car Designated Crew

1) Before Departure

car designated crew should report to the duty room before departure, undergo an alcohol test, and listen for orders and instructions. Before the train leaves the depot, follow the technical operation procedures to inspect the insulation of the train trunk line, the voltage of the DC110V bus, the lock status of the doors under the car, and the oil volume of the generator car, water level, engine oil level and the operation status of the diesel generator set. Confirm the status of each valve of the oil tank pipe system under the car. Test the alarm function of the fire alarm. Check and sign the fault handling of ct-181 record.

2) On duty

Before the train departs, conduct operation in accordance with the relevant provisions of "car detaching and coupling". Take responsibility for the setting of marker lamp at car rear end and establish the rear end connection of the passenger train. Participate in the train braking system performance test as required.

During operation, the crew member shall inspect the whole train every 3 hours or so, focusing on the train operation status, the working status of the electrical system and "two boilers and one stove", the first inspection after the departure of the air-conditioned train, the first inspection after taking over the shift and the last inspection before the train arrives at the terminus. The car crew shall open the control cabinet and inspect the main wiring row of the power cabinet, the temperature rise status at the inlet and outlet wiring of the main air switch, etc.

During the inspection interval, the car crew shall take their duty at a fixed point, where, in principle, is the crew room at the front and rear cars (which shall not be occupied for a long time). Crew must take their duty in the engineer room if the train is coupled with engineering car.

At the station where there is no passenger train maintenance, the car crew must get off the train to observe whether the car is smoking, tilting or having other abnormal conditions, and confirm and deal with the key faults found during patrol inspection on the way. If there is passenger train inspection at the station, the crew should also hand over car technical status with the passenger train maintenance station.

For locomotive coupling and train reversing, operate in accordance with the relevant provisions of "car detaching and coupling" in this specification, and remove and establish the connection of tails of passenger trains. Be responsible for taking off and hanging the marker lamp at the tail of the train when the train is reversing.

After the train is stopped by emergency braking, the car crew must contact the locomotive crew (running master) to find the reason for stopping. Get off the train if necessary to check the technical status of the wheel treads, coupler connection, etc. Notify the locomotive crew (running master) to start the train, and then strengthen the monitoring of the operation status.

When the device at the rear end of the passenger train fails, if it is confirmed that the LBJ of the locomotive is faulty, the locomotive should be replaced nearby, and if it is confirmed that the main engine of the KLW is faulty and needs to be replaced, the operation should be carried out when the train is stopped at station. During the operation with KLW failure, the crew should inspect the wind pressure in accordance with relevant regulations as notified by the locomotive crew.

The crew of the generator car should be on duty in the monitoring room. When leaving the monitoring room for non-patrolling purposes, it shall not exceed 10 minutes. Every 30 to 60 minutes, enter the generator room and cooling room for a patrol inspection, and fill in the "Generation Car Operation Record" every 1 hour.

In principle, the crew of the generator car should conduct the handover when the station is stopped if he needs to change shifts on the way. The succession crew is responsible for the key inspection for connection status and temperature rise of the power connector of the generator car on the platform side, and the abnormalities in the diesel engine exhaust. And it is also necessary to confirm the remaining fuel in the lower fuel tank at non-high platform stations.

When an emergency needs to be reported during duty, the car chief crew shall send a railway telegram to those with armbands. Without the permission of the competent department, no one shall replace or suspend the work of car crew.

3) After arriving at the terminal

After the train arrives at the terminal, the car crew shall detach the tails of the passenger cars. Operate in accordance with the relevant provisions of "car detaching and coupling" to remove the marker lamp at tail of the train. The passenger train powered by generator cars must be unloaded, powered off and shut down 10 minutes after it reach to the terminal.

For turnaround trains without passenger train maintenance operation, the car designated crew group should make use of the leading locomotives to conduct performance tests of all the train brake systems. At the same time, according to the principle that the parts that may cause faults due to train traction, overload, foreign object strike, etc. must be inspected emphatically, the operation shall be carried out according to the scope of technical inspection of the passing train. Cars with abnormalities on the way shall be inspected emphatically, and the faults predicted by TVDS and THDS (including hot axle faults) shall be handled.

The car designated crew group, who are on the turnaround trains to the depot, should enter the depot with the train to sign in at the inspection duty room, undergo the alcohol test, and carry out the handover of the train system-181 fault. Before the car stock is out of the depot, the designated crew group should report to the duty room, undergo the alcohol test, and listen for related materials conveyed. They should also carry out technical inspection of the train according to the scope of leaving depot operation, check the fault handling of train system 181, and leave the depot with the train.

After the train arrives at the terminal, the car crew shall enter the depot with the train, then report the train operation status to the attendant, accept the alcohol test, hand over the handover Passenger Train Technical Status Handover Book (ct-181), and hand over the discovery and handling of key faults to the train inspection foreman in person.

2. Emergency handling of car Failures During Passenger Train Operation

1) Measures taken in case of fire during operation

(1) Take immediate measures to pull down the emergency brake valve to stop the train and call the local fire alarm.

(2) Assist the train master to evacuate passengers from the fired car in an organized manner.

(3) Take effective measures quickly, cut off the power supply, use fire extinguishers and

other fire-fighting tools to put out the fire in time.

(4) Detach the train as required. First separate the fired car from the rear car, and then from the front car. Do not leave the fired car near bridges, tunnels and major buildings during detachment.

(5) Report to the superior department in time, report the fire, the preliminary causes and the measures taken.

2) Measures taken for axle temperature rise during operation

(1) Causes of axle temperature rise.

Bearing parts damage, poor assembly, lubrication failure, and external faults such as wheel tread faults can all cause the axle temperature rise.

(2) Inspection, judgment and treatments

① When it is found that the temperature of certain axle position increases, the car crew must get off the car in time for verification, and carry out "touch, look and compare" on the axle box. Touch the top of the axle box with hand to compare the its temperature with other axle boxes. If necessary, measure the temperature at the top of the axle box with a point thermometer to confirm whether the temperature of the axle box exceeds the external temperature for 40 °C.

② Cover opening inspection and treatments

For cover opening inspection:

- tighten the clamp bolts at axle head in time if they are found loose;
- add bearing grease in time if there is a lack of grease;
- check the bearing grease with hand if it is found deteriorated. If the grease is mixed with metal powder, it means that the bearing parts have been severely worn, which needs special attention for follow-up inspection;
- check whether the sealing ring of the front cover is invalid if it is found that the axle box is mixed with sand or water. Replace the sealing ring in time when there are spare parts, and add appropriate amount of new grease before closing the cover.
- For cover opening inspection on the way, if it is found that the rolling bearing parts are damaged or stuck, which directly affects running safety, take decisive measures and contact the local section, branch or railway bureau for car detachment, and operate in accordance with the dispatch order of the local bureau and rolling stock depot.

Bearing faults and corresponding treatment must be recorded in detail according to regulations and submitted to train maintenance station or train servicing station after the train arrives at the terminal.

3) Measures taken for stopping due to uncoupling of locomotive and car during

operation

(1) The car crew shall carefully confirm the uncoupling between the locomotive and the car together with the locomotive crew and the operation conductor; Check if there is situation like the locomotive end coupler is in the fully open position or the car end coupler is in the fully open position, and check the mutual coupler difference when both couplers are in the locked position. If the coupler at the locomotive end is in the fully open position, or the height of the locomotive coupler does not meet the requirements after measurement, or the locomotive coupler is faulty, the locomotive crew shall deal with it, obtain proofs, and record the train number, time, place, locomotive model and number, and the names of the driver and the running conductor.

(2) In case of car end, the crew shall carefully inspect: the technical status of the coupler; whether the distance between the coupler knuckle and the inner side of the coupler wrist is greater than 135 mm when the coupler is in locked position; whether the bound second anti-creep device fails; whether the bottom lock pin anti-creep device is good; whether the knuckle lock and thrower are worn; whether the coupler release rod jumps out of the slot; and whether the clearance between the coupler release rod bracket and coupler release rod exceeds the limit; whether the distance between the coupler release rod and the connecting rod of the bottom lock pin is insufficient (no more than 15 mm as specified), etc. Pay special attention to whether the accessories and surrounding devices and components that are easy to cause unlocking have been hit by external force and artificially damaged or lost.

(3) If the coupler knuckle of the car is broken, the steward shall check whether there are old marks on the coupler knuckle section, and the percentage of new and old marks. At the same time, attention shall be paid to the relevant conditions before and after breaking, especially to distinguish whether it is breaking in case of overload after emergency stop or stop after breaking during operation, and make analysis and judgment according to the situation. The car crew should also conduct corresponding inspection and treatment, carefully record the situation and data in detail, draw sketches, and properly keep the damaged products.

4) Measures taken when the air gauge pressure of the whole passenger train fails to meet the requirements

(1) If the air gauge pressure of the whole train is about 500 kPa and does not rise, it is generally because the pressure is not adjusted when the freight locomotive is coupled with the passenger car. The driver is required to adjust the air pressure and then observe the air gauge pressure.

(2) If the locomotive has been charged with air at the release position and the air gauge pressure still fails to meet the requirements, check whether the main and branch pipe systems of

the car have leakage, whether the brake hose connection part and the exhaust cock of reservoir are exhausting a large amount of air, and deal with the leakage in time.

(3) Replace the distribution valve if it has abnormal exhaust.

5) Measures taken when emergency braking occurs during train operation

(1) The car crew should discover the causes of emergency braking and get off the train in time to conduct detailed technical inspection of the car. The key points are: couplers, buffers, traction parts, wheelsets and bogie accessories. Check whether the wheel set is scratched, or the accessories are cracked or fallen off, etc. If there is a defective part or damage of the car, repair it in time or make temporary treatment.

(2) After confirming that the car accessories are not damaged, if the parking time is more than 20 minutes, a brief brake test shall be carried out together with the driver and the running conductor.

(3) If the emergency brake valve is used to stop the train, in addition to the necessary inspections and related records of the car, this should also be recorded and reported to the passenger train inspection station to seal it up.

(4) After departure, the car crew shall strengthen the upper patrol to know the running state of the car.

6) Measure taken for passenger trains with a maximum running speed of more than 120 km/h when the train pipe is damaged and cannot be repaired in case of double pipe air supply

(1) When the train pipe is damaged due to unexpected obstacles and cannot be repaired on the way, the connecting hose of the main pipe of the damaged car shall be connected to the train pipe of the adjacent car, and the car shall act as a bridge.

(2) In this case, the damaged car and cars behind must be changed to single-pipe air supply. However, cocks and handles must be tied up to prevent foreign objects from hitting and causing accidents.

7) What is the position of each cock when the air supply of double pipe needs to be changed to single pipe for air supply due to failure

(1) Close the cock on the pipeline from the main pipe to the air spring (main reservoir).

(2) Open the cock on the pipeline from the auxiliary reservoir to the air spring (main reservoir) to ensure the air supply for the air spring.

(3) When it is necessary to close the cut-out cock to stop action of the air brake due to the failure of the distribution valve:

① Close the cock on the pipeline from the auxiliary reservoir to the air spring (main reservoir).

② Open the cock on the pipeline from the train pipe to the air spring (main reservoir) to ensure the normal air use of the air spring.

8) Measures taken when the air spring leaks during operation

(1) First, confirm whether it is capsule leakage or pipeline leakage. If it is capsule leakage, the only thing can do is to close the small cock in front of the height adjustment valve and stop the air supply of the air spring.

(2) When stopping the air supply of the damaged air spring, the air supply of the air spring of the whole car must be stopped. This is because if only the damaged air spring is closed and other air springs are still supplying air, the car body inclination and coupler height difference will be caused. Therefore, the air spring of the whole car should be closed.

(3) Notify the driver and the operation conductor in accordance with regulations that the train needs to run at a speed limit of 120 km/h.

(4) In case of pipeline leakage, fasten the leakage on the pipeline immediately.

Revision exercises

1. Briefly describe the main responsibilities of the car designated crew group.
2. What are the measures taken in case of emergency braking during train operation.

Chapter 4

Production Safety of the Rolling Stock Department

Railway transportation safety is the comprehensive performance of the normal operation order of the transportation and production system, the safety of passengers' lives and property, and the good condition of goods and transportation equipment. It is also the result of the coordinated operation of all production activities to achieve the above purposes in the whole process of transportation and production. The fundamental task of railway transportation is to safely deliver passengers and goods to their destinations in time. The role, nature and characteristics of railway transportation determine that production safety is the first priority of all the works.

The rolling stock department should abide by the relevant laws and regulations to ensure the safety of railway transportation, car equipment and labour, etc. It should also adhere to the policy of "safety first, prevention priority, management comprehensive" to implement safety risk management thoroughly so as to improve the production safety management.

Learning Objectives

(1) Master the production safety requirements of the rolling stock department.

(2) Master the "Ten Don'ts" of on-site operation.

Learning Content

1. General operation safety

(1) Don't drink before work. Have a good rest to ensure being energetic and focused at work. Protective articles must be worn as required before work. Don't wear slippers, sandals or high heels. Before leaving, switch off the air, gas, water and electricity. Tidy up the tools and materials, and clean the surroundings.

(2) When two or more persons are engaged in the same operation, designate a particular

one to command emplyees to act in a unified manner, cooperate with each other and call for response.

(3) Don't walk through the track center or sleepers while walking along the lines. As is shown in Figure 4-1. When crossing lines and level crossings, abide by the passing rules of "standing, looking around, confirming and passing" strictly in sequence, and pay attention to the locomotives and cars at the same time. It is strictly prohibited to rush with, climb over, jump off or crawl under the cars. As is shown in Figure 4-2.

Figure 4-1　Don't walk through the track center

Figure 4-2　Don't crawl under the car

(4) When crossing the line of the parked car, first confirm that there is no shunting operation and no car likely to move, and then pass over the coupler, grasping firmly and stepping on steadily. Don't step on the coupler lock, coupler neck or the angle cock handle. When crossing the line from the end of the parked car, keep a safe distance: no less than 3 meters when passing barehanded; no less than 5 meters when carrying materials or tools. Pass the track quickly and don't stop.

(5) Walk between two lines and keep away from lines when carrying materials and accessories.

(6) When working and walking on the station yard, pay attention to the locomotives and cars from adjacent lines at any time. Don't sit, stand, chat, rest, take shelter from the rain or enjoy the cool on the sleepers, at the track center, under the car body, at the end of the car or beside the platform.

(7) Don't connect the power cord privately. When the electrical part of the mechanical equipment fails, turn off the power switch immediately and notify the electrician for repair. non electricians are prohibited from repairing the electrical appliances.

(8) The distance between the oxygen cylinder and the acetylene generator should be more than 5 m. The oxygen cylinder and the acetylene generator should be more than 10 m away from the open flame. The oxygen cylinder cannot be contaminated with grease, exposed to the sun, or collided.

(9) In addition to strictly observing the rules of safety in utilizing electric energy, all employees must have the knowledge of first aid for electric shock:

① Quickly disconnect the person who gets an electric shock from the power supply. The discoverer shall quickly cut off the nearby power switch or cut off the power cord with insulated pliers or a wooden handle axe, or separated the person who gets an electric shock from the charged object with an insulator.

② When cutting off the power supply, it is necessary to consider measures to prevent falling injuries after the shocked person is separated from the power supply at the same time.

③ After the person who gets an electric shock is disconnected from the power supply, artificial respiration should be performed immediately on the spot. Send him to the hospital for rescue if needed, and the artificial respiration cannot be stopped on the way to the hospital until he is resurrected or handed over to the doctor for rescue.

2. Operation Safety at the Train Inspection Site

(1) Train inspectors should be familiar with the lines, equipment, buildings and shunting operation in the station. They should also strictly follow the specified route while walking in and out of the operation site.

(2) Have a good rest before going to work (especially for night shift) to ensure being energetic and focused at work. Don't drink before or during work.

(3) Wear uniforms and armbands during train inspection operation. In case of rain or snow, keep good vision and hearing, and watch out for anti-skid.

(4) The operation of picking-up and dispatching trains shall strictly implement the system of setting off in line and also returning back to the station in line after the operation.

(5) The train inspection site should be equipped with protective signals with derailers according to the number of tracks to be repaired, which should be kept in good condition. Designate a particular person to be in charge of its maintenance and storage.

(6) When inspecting, repairing and servicing cars on lines in the station, there must be a particular personnel to insert derailers and protective signals as required. Don't carry out car inspection without protective signals. The joint control safety system shall be strictly implemented in bad weather such as wind, snow, rain and fog.

(7) When the train inspection is completed, check the signals at both ends of the train. When it is confirmed that there is no person under the train, the appointed person shall remove the derailers and protective signals.

(8) When walking in the station, walk between two lines for it is safe. Don't walk on the track center or sleepers, and watch out for cars coming and leaving. Don' t play or walk side by side with more than two people. Don't take the shunting locomotives or cars in the station, let

alone climb up and down.

(9) When crossing lines, abide by the passing rules of “standing, looking around, confirming and passing” strictly in sequence. Pass quickly and safely when it is confirmed that there are no cars from the right, left or adjacent lines. Don’t rush with running locomotives, cars or trains. Don’t pass under trains without protective signal.

(10) When crossing the train, first confirm that there is no shunting operation and no car likely to move, then pass over the coupler, and don’t crawl under the car body. Don’t step on the coupler lock, coupler neck or the angle cock handle.

(11) When crossing lines from the end of the parked car, keep a safe distance: no less than 3 meters when passing barehanded; no less than 5 meters when carrying materials or tools.

(12) When carrying bulky tools or materials in the station, or transferring tools or accessories under the car, call for answers, keep pace with each other, and pay attention to the train dynamics.

(13) When picking up and dispatching trains, stand at a safe place between two lines and watch the train coming and leaving. Pay attention to the conditions of acid and alkali tanker operation, cargo loading, caravan ropes, etc. to prevent accidental injuries.

(14) When inspecting the upper part of the car, confirm the state of the loaded cargo and the closed state of the door to ensure safety before working.

(15) To deal with all brake failures (replace valves, brake shoes or brake beams, wash brake cylinders, etc.), the cut-out cock must be closed first, and the remaining air must be drained off from the auxiliary reservoir. Reset them after the work is over. When adjusting the piston stroke of the brake cylinder, don’t touch the hole when installing pins. Put on safety sleeve and insert safety pin before cleaning the brake cylinder and unloading the bolt of the cylinder head. When unloading the cylinder head nut, the operator’s head should be out of the way. In addition, when repairing large parts, follow the corresponding safety operating procedures.

(16) When resting in the station yard or waiting for inspection, don’t sit on the rail or the edge of the platform, and don’t rest, take shelter from the rain or enjoy the cool under the car.

(17) When passenger trains pass, don’t carry out inspection work on the trains on the adjacent lines.

(18) During the inspection for trackside facilities of train inspection equipment, specific personnel must be assigned for protection, and single person operation is not allowed.

3. Safety of Inspection Work

(1) When inspecting, repairing, and servicing cars on the line in the station, a fixed or mobile signal with a derailer should be installed on the left rail in the train coming direction at

both ends of the train for protection, and the protection distance for both the front and rear ends should be no less than 20 meters. When passenger trains are undergoing technical inspections on arrival and departure lines, they shall be protected by stop signals, and derailers are not required. The train inspection operation line should be level, and no concave cement sleepers or large stone slags shall be laid.

(2) The train inspection station shall prepare adequate protective devices (red flags, red lights, derailers) according to the maximum amount of work, which should be kept and taken over by specific person, and always be in good condition.

(3) Train inspectors should be familiar with the lines, equipment, buildings, train operation, shunting operations, and car pick-up and dispatch in the station. The overhaul of arriving and departing trains shall be carried out in accordance with the operation process. Strictly implement the system of setting off in line and returning back to the station in line after the operation, and it is strictly forbidden to work alone.

(4) Before the train inspection operation starts and ends, it is necessary to strictly implement the interlock transmission method of inserting and removing the protection signal. It is forbidden to carry out the inspection work without the protection signal, or deal with the fault when the train is in operation.

(5) When picking up the car, arrive at the pick-up place in advance and squat at a safe place between two lines. For narrow lines, when trains arrive and depart at the same time on both adjacent lines, picking up and dispatching trains on the outside of the two lines.

(6) When picking up and dispatching trains, watch the train coming and leaving. Pay attention to the conditions of the train operation, cargo loading, caravan ropes, etc. to prevent accidental injuries.

(7) When working on the line, don't wear color glasses or hats that obstruct vision or hearing. You can tie grass ropes or grass on your feet when it is frozen to prevent slipping and falling.

(8) When replacing large accessories, the team leader shall personally organize, command and be responsible for safety work.

(9) In the event of brake failure, first close the the cut-out cock and drain off the residual air from the auxiliary reservoir before proceeding. Reset them after the work is over. When adjusting the piston stroke of the brake cylinder, don't touch the hole when installing pins. Put on safety sleeve and insert safety pin before cleaning the brake cylinder. When unloading the cylinder head nut, the operator's head should be out of the way. When replacing the angle cock, close the angle cock of the car, the other end and that of the neighboring car. When replacing the brake shoe, don't put your hand between the brake shoe and the wheel tread.

(10) When non-inspectors perform axle inspection, detention or other inspection operations in the train fleet, they should contact relevant personnel in advance and take effective safety protection measures before work.

(11) When inspecting, repairing and cleaning the infrared detection device and the fixed derailment device on the trackside, specific personnel must be appointed to protect the passing trains. When a train passes, the operation must be stopped.

Revision exercises

Illustrate the Ten Don'ts of on-site operation.

第一篇　车辆运用管理工作

铁路是国家的重要基础设施之一，是国民经济的大动脉，是交通运输体系的骨干。铁路具有高度集中，各个工作环节紧密联系和协同动作的特点。

铁路运输系统由运输、机务、车辆、工务、电务等业务部门组成，为确保铁路安全正点、方便快捷、高速高效，铁路运输系统必须严格遵守运输纪律，服从运输指挥，在中国国家铁路集团有限公司（以下简称国铁集团）的统一指挥下联合行动，准确、及时、安全地把旅客、货物运输到达目的地。铁路职工必须严格遵守劳动纪律和作业纪律，严格执行各项规章制度，牢记自身职责，以对国家和人民极端负责的态度，保证安全生产。

【学习目标】

（1）了解车辆运用工作的任务。

（2）掌握铁路客、货物列车编挂要求。

（3）掌握铁路客车、货车车辆运用技术指标。

【学习内容】

1. 车辆管理与检修

车辆运用工作包括管理和检修两方面的内容。货车通行全国，除特种车辆和专用车列外，一般不实行配属制，而是实行在全国铁路上按区段维修负责制。

1）车辆运用工作任务

车辆运用工作的基本任务是在检修中执行规章命令；遵守作业纪律、劳动纪律，作业标准化；发现和处理车辆在运用中发生的故障，保证行车安全。

（1）正确执行有关规章命令。

（2）正确编制生产计划及技术措施，加强全面质量管理，落实检修规定，提高修车质量。

（3）在保证车辆检修质量的基础上，努力缩短车辆修车时间，加速车辆周转。

（4）维修好本段配属车辆和管辖范围内的运用车辆，防止事故，保证安全。

（5）做好劳动保护工作，改善职工劳动条件，保证安全生产。

（6）开展技术培训，提高制动技术业务素质。

（7）定期调查分析运用车辆技术状态，对运用维修中的故障进行信息收集、处理、分析，形成质量信息反馈系统，对车辆维修和运用管理提出改进意见。

2）车辆检修工作

铁路车辆实行定期检修，并逐步扩大实施状态修、换件修和主要零部件的专业化集中修。

（1）铁路客车运用维修。

客车按走行公里进行检修，最高运行速度不超过 120 km/h 的客车分为厂修、段修、辅修。客车的维修质量直接关系到旅客生命财产的安全，其日常维修内容为：

➢ 库列检：对于进入客车技术整备所的旅客列车进行全面检查、试验和修理。

➢ 客列检：对始发、到达及通过的旅客列车进行技术检查和维修。

➢ 客车乘务：车辆包乘组对值乘的旅客列车进行途中技术检查、维修和管理工作。

（2）铁路货车运用维修。

铁路货车通常分为厂修、段修、辅修。货车厂修 5 ~ 8 年一次，段修 1 ~ 2 年一次，辅修为 6 个月一次。货车运用条件较差，在解体、编组及机械化装卸作业中承受频繁冲击，易腐货物对配件造成腐蚀，重载货物、长大列车在运行途中冲撞等，使货车零部件产生较大的磨耗、变形、松动、腐蚀等故障。因此必须对货车进行及时的检查维修，分为摘车修和不摘车修。

a. 摘车修：

把有故障的车辆从列车中摘下，送到专用修车线或站修作业场内维修，称为摘车修。实施摘车修可充分利用固定台位和机械化修车设备，按照技术标准修复车辆，消除故障，保证质量。但会增加调车作业的工作量和车辆停留时间，对运输效率有所影响。在列车内无法修复的故障必须施行摘车修。

b. 不摘车修：

在列车到达后、始发前进行技术检查时，对发现的车辆故障，能在停车线上利用站停时间修复的，称不摘车修。实行不摘车修，能较快地消除危及行车安全的故障，加速车辆周转，提高运输效率。

2. 车辆运营指标

1）现在货车

现在货车，是指每日 18:00 现有的全部货车，可分为运用货车和非运用货车。

（1）运用货车：指参加铁路营业运输生产的一切空、重货车，统称运用货车，如图 1-1 所示。它是表明运输生产能力的一项重要指标。

（2）非运用货车：不参加铁路营业运输的非生产性的货车和企业自备、租用的空货车，如图 1-2 所示。

一定数量的非运用货车是运输生产必须的。但不能占用过多，否则会影响货车利用率。为此，车辆相关部门要提高修车效率，缩短停修时间，努力压缩检修车数，增加运用货车数，挖掘运输潜力。

图 1-1　运用货车

图 1-2　非运用货车

2）货车车辆公里

一辆货车走行一公里叫一车辆公里。运用货车车辆公里是运用货车总走行的公里，它是反映货车走行工作量的数量指标，在一定程度上反映了轮对的磨耗程度。

3）货车日车公里

货车日车公里，指在一定时期内铁路局或全路平均每一运用货车在一昼夜内的走行里数。

货车日车公里数=运用货车车辆公里/运用货车数（km/d）

=货车全周转距离/货车周转时间（km/d）

货车日车公里是反映货车流动程度的指标。货车流动程度越大，在空车走行率一定条件下，货车所完成的货运量越大。

4）货车全周转距离及周转时间

（1）货车全周转距离（简称全周距）：货车每周转一次的平均运行距离。它包括货车在重车状态下和空车状态下的全部行程。货车全周转距离与货车周转时间成正比。若其他因素不变，全周距越长，货车周转时间越长。因此，全周距应保证正常工作的前提下力求缩短。

（2）货车周转时间：运用货车在一次周转中平均花费的时间。它反映着整个货车周转过程的总效率，通常把它作为货车运用效率的综合性指标。

5）货车载重量

货车载重量是反映货车载重能力利用程度的指标。分货车静载重和货车动载重两种。

（1）货车静载重：在一定时期内，车站、路局或全路平均每装车一辆所装载的货物吨数。它直接影响到装车数，影响到为完成一定货物发送吨数所需的运用车数。

（2）货物动载重：指在一定时期内，全路、一个路局平均每一货车公里所完成的货物吨公里数。

货车静载重仅反映在装车时或重车状态的静止条件下货车载重能力的利用程度。货车动载重反映的是平均每一重车公里或运用货车公里所完成的货物周转量，表现出货车在运送货物全过程中的利用程度。

6）现在客车

现在客车包括运用客车和非运用客车两种。

（1）运用客车：凡是办理旅客营业的客车统称为运用客车。如供旅客乘坐的软、硬座车，软、硬卧车及为旅客服务的行李车、餐车等，如图 1-3 所示。

（2）非运用客车：凡不办理旅客营业的客车以及技术状态不良，不能编挂于列车中运行的客车，均为非运用客车。如备用车、公务车、福利车、特种用途客车及各种检修客车等，如图 1-4 所示。

图 1-3　运用客车

图 1-4　非运用客车

7）客车保有量

铁路客车一般会分别配属给各单位，所以各单位的客车保有量是相对稳定的数值，即全部配属的客车辆数。

客车保有量也可由下式求得：

$$P=(1+\alpha)\sum Lm$$

式中　P——客车配属辆数；

α——非运用车保有系数，一般取 0.36(其中备用车 0.10，波动率 0.20，检修率 0.06)；

L——旅客列车车底列数；

m——车底组成辆数。

计算客车保有量的目的：一方面是为了更好地掌握车辆的分布情况，以均衡地完成铁路运输任务；另一方面，用保有量乘以各种修程的修理循环系数，可以计算出检修任务量。

8）旅客列车公里及运用客车车辆公里

（1）旅客列车公里：是指由铁路局所属各段配属车底开行的旅客列车公里总数，是计划和考核与旅客列车有关支出的一项重要指标。全路旅客列车公里是全国各铁路局旅客列车公里的总和。

（2）运用客车车辆公里：是指由铁路局所属各段配属客车在各区段走行公里的总和。旅客列车公里，是客车车辆公里的重要组成部分，是计划和考核客车检修费用等有关客运支出的一项重要指标。

9）旅客列车车底周转时间

旅客列车车底周转时间，是指为了开行运行图中某一对旅客列车的车底，从第一次由车底始发站发出之时起，至下一次再由该始发站发出时止，所经过的全部时间。

车底周转时间反映着车底周转全过程的效率，反映着所有与客运有关各部门的工作效率。车底周转时间的长短，直接影响到为开行某对列车所需要的车底数，从而也就影响到铁路所需要的运用客车数。因此，在计划旅客列车车底需要数时，都要使用车底周转时间这一重要指标。

3. 车辆检修指标

1）检修车辆现有数

检修车辆现有数，也叫不良车数、残车数或检修车数，是指每日 18:00 全路、一个铁路局、一个车辆修理工厂或车辆段的管辖范围内所具有的全部已扣修的在修和待修的车辆数。其中包括部属车辆(包括企业租用车)中因定检到期或临修而扣修的车辆；因事故破损和待报废及回送中的检修车辆；也包括在铁路营业线运用中，因临时发生故障而摘车临修的外国车及企业自备车。

检修车辆现有数可按下列公式计算：

检修车辆现有数=日初残存检修车数+本日扣修车数 – 本日修竣车数（辆）

检修车辆现有数可以反映全路或一个铁路局车辆的状况，也可以反映各个车辆检修单位、路局或全路修车工作的进展。为了保证工厂和车辆段修车计划有步骤、有节奏地均衡完成，国铁集团规定了各铁路局和修理工厂有一定的检修车定量。各段、厂要努力减少管内的检修车数，使之经常保持在规定量以下。加强扣车的计划性和减少摘车临修，是减少检修车数的一个主要途径，而提高修车效率、缩短检修时间及提高修车的当日出车率，也是减少检修车辆的重要措施。

2）车辆检修率

车辆检修率，又称车辆不良率，是以相对数字反映车辆状态的指标。

货车检修率：是全路或一个铁路局不良货车数与支配货车数之比。货车通常是全路通用，不固定配属，各局货车检修任务根据各自检修能力分配。

3）车辆检修停留时间

车辆检修停留时间是指在一定时期内，全路或一个铁路局、一个车辆修理工厂、一个车辆段或其他修车单位，平均检修一辆车的全部停留时间。厂、段修的休车时间以天为单位，辅修、临修以小时为单位。

休车时间是表示修车工作进度的重要指标。在保证修车质量的前提下，休车时间 fha 短，则表明修车效率越高；休车时间越长，则表示修车效率越低。

每一检修车辆的全部休车时间，对于交由车辆段修理的车辆来说，大致包括站休时间、待修时间和修理时间；对于交由工厂检修的车辆来说，往往还要加上由确认需要送交工厂检修的地点编入列车，直至送到工厂所在地办理完成入厂手续为止的全部时间，也可称之为回送时间。

4）责任晚点

责任晚点是考核列检工作质量的重要指标。检车人员应在列车运行图规定的时间内检修好车，并确保运行到下一个列检所而该所检修范围的部位不发生故障。凡由于工作组织不当影响列车按图定时间开出的和由于检修列车造成的晚点叫列检责任晚点。

5）责任事故

车辆运用部门应消灭行车事故，确保列车运行安全。由于本列检作业场或段责任造成事故的应按“铁路交通事故调查处理规则”规定，列入责任事故，铁路局、车辆段按件数考核。对一般事故，客车按每百辆配属车发生件数统计；货车按管内货物列车运行量每百万辆公里发生的件数统计。

4. 车辆编组

1）货物列车中车辆的编挂

货物列车编组，除应按照编组计划和列车运行图规定编组外，还应符合下列规定：

（1）装载危险及易燃货物车辆在运输途中须采取隔离措施，以免发生意外。

（2）货物列车中因装载的货物规定停止制动作用的车辆，自动制动机临时发生故障的车辆，准许关闭截断塞门（简称关门车），但列检场所在站编组始发的列车中，不得有制动故障关门车。编入列车的关门车数量不得超过现车总辆数的 6%，超过时，须计算闸瓦压力，并填发制动效能证明书交予司机。

关门车不得挂于机车后部三辆之内；在列车中连续连挂关门车不得超过两辆；列车最后一辆不得为关门车；列车最后第二、三辆不得连续关门。

对于不适于连续连挂在列车中部但走行部良好的车辆，经列车调度员准许，可挂于列车尾部，以一辆为限，如该车辆的自动制动机不起作用，须由车辆人员采取安全措施，保证不致脱钩。

（3）机械冷藏车组应尽量挂于货物列车中部或后部。

2）旅客列车编挂要求

旅客列车应按客车编组表规定的车种、辆数、编挂位置编组，列车最后一辆车后端应有风表、紧急制动阀。

（1）编入的客车应按其标记速度编挂列。

（2）旅客列车加挂货车的规定。

特快旅客列车不准编挂货车，其他旅客列车原则上不准编挂货车。但在特殊情况下（事故救援、抢险），必须由旅客列车挂运时，需经上级主管部门批准，方可在列车后部加挂，但不得超过 2 辆。加挂货车的技术状态和最高运行速度，须符合该列车规定速度要求。旅客列车中乘坐旅客的车辆，与货车相连接的客车端门须加锁。

（3）禁止编入旅客列车的车辆：

a. 超过定期检修期限的车辆(按规定在延期范围内和经车辆部门鉴定送厂、段施修的客车除外)。

b. 装载危险、恶臭货物的车辆。

c. 未安装客车轴温报警装置的客车。

（4）乘坐旅客车辆与牵引机车连挂要求。

旅客列车中乘坐旅客的车辆，应以未搭乘旅客的车辆与机车隔离，可采用行李车、邮政车、发电车等非乘坐旅客的车辆分别挂于机车后第一位和列车尾部作为隔离车，如隔离车在途中发生故障摘下时，可无隔离车继续运行。无隔离车时，为保证乘客安全及牵引机车的正常工作，与机车相连接的客车，前部端门要加锁。

（5）旅客列车中关门车的规定。

旅客列车不准编挂制动关门车。在运行途中如遇自动制动机临时故障，在停车时间内不能修复时，准许关闭一辆，但列车最后一辆不得为关门车。

3）车钩高度差确认

列车中相互连挂的车钩中心水平线的高度差（简称车钩高度差）不超过 75 mm。这个高度差是由相邻两车的车钩中心线分别至轨面的高度差而来。运用限度规定车钩中心线距轨面最高 890 mm；最低限度：空货车 835 mm、重货车 815 mm。

若车钩高度差超过规定，当列车运行至道岔或路基松软地段时，车辆上下振动，尤其在陡坡线路上，容易发生脱钩而造成列车分离。车钩高度差较大时，还使车钩钩舌牵引接触面减少，产生过大的弯矩，容易发生断钩事故。

【复习题】

1. 什么是摘车修和不摘车修？
2. 货物列车编组时对相邻两车钩高有何要求？若超过限度有何危害？
3. 货车车辆运营指标和检修指标的作用有哪些？

第二篇　货车运用维修

由于我国大多数的铁路货车具有无固定配属、无固定检修、无固定使用、全国运行、车型多样，运用工况复杂，又具有安全要求高、列车密度大、作业场地散、技检时间紧、故障形式多等特点和要求。因此，货车运用工作必须坚持“安全第一、预防为主、综合治理”的方针，建立完善的货车运用管理体系，实行科学的生产管理办法，配备先进的检修设备，制定严格的规章制度。货车运用维修的主要任务为以下内容。

（1）在规定的列车技术作业时间（以下简称“技检时间”）内完成货物列车的技术检查、自动制动机性能试验（以下简称“列车制动机试验”）、铁路货车故障处置和修理（以下简称“铁路货车故障处理”）等；负责定期检修的到（过）期车、技术状态不良车、沿途发生故障的铁路货车及事故车的扣修和回送工作；维护运用货车的质量符合规定的技术标准，保证作业列车的运行安全。

（2）负责铁路货车运行安全监控系统的运用和检修管理。

（3）负责对运用货车中需摘车临修的铁路货车进行检修，对需辅修的铁路货车进行定期检修。

（4）负责翻车机翻前卸后、散装货物解冻库（以下简称“解冻库”）解冻后的铁路货车的技术交接检查和故障处理；负责进出厂矿、港口、地方铁路、合资铁路、专用铁路、企业专用线和工程临管线等单位铁路货车的技术交接检查和故障处理。负责国际联运货物列车的技术交接。

（5）负责往返循环开行的快速货物班列、局管内固定编组开行的货物快运列车等整备作业。

（6）对铁路货车运用技术质量的分析、评价和管理，组织开展货物列车技术质量监控，定期调查分析运用车辆技术状态，对铁路货车运用中发现的故障进行信息收集、处理、分析；负责铁路货车设计、新造、检修和主要配件的质量监督与反馈，对车辆结构、设计、制造、修理和运用管理提出改进意见。

（7）负责爱护铁路货车（以下简称“爱车”）工作，组织爱车宣传并指导、监督和检查铁路货车的使用，制止损坏铁路货车的行为，负责损坏铁路货车的索赔和管理。

（8）按规定负责重点物资及超限货物列车和机械冷藏车的技术作业及车辆乘务等工作。

（9）按规定协助进行铁路货车新车型、新技术、新型配件运用考验的相关工作。

（10）参加相关铁路交通事故的调查和事故救援，协助铁路货车交通事故的处理和管理，负责铁路货车行车设备故障的调查、处理和管理。

（11）国铁集团规定的其他有关工作。

单元一　货车运用维修工作

【学习目标】

（1）了解列检作业场的生产生活设施。

（2）掌握货车运用维修主要工作任务。

（3）掌握货车运用作业场的分类。

【学习内容】

1. 货车运用维修工作任务

（1）在规定的列车技术作业时间（以下简称“技检时间”）内完成货物列车的技术检查、自动制动机性能试验（以下简称“列车制动机试验”）、铁路货车故障处置和修理（以下简称“铁路货车故障处理”）等；负责定期检修的到（过）期车、技术状态不良车、沿途发生故障的铁路货车及事故车的扣修和回送工作；维护运用货车的质量符合规定的技术标准，保证作业列车的运行安全。

（2）负责铁路货车运行安全监控系统的运用和检修管理。

（3）负责对运用货车中需摘车临修的铁路货车进行检修，对需辅修的铁路货车进行定期检修。

（4）负责翻车机翻前卸后、散装货物解冻库（以下简称解冻库）解冻后的铁路货车的技术交接检查和故障处理；负责进出厂矿、港口、地方铁路、合资铁路、专用铁路、企业专用线和工程临管线等单位铁路货车的技术交接检查和故障处理。负责国际联运货物列车的技术交接。

（5）负责往返循环开行的快速货物班列、局管内固定编组开行的货物快运列车等整备作业。

（6）对铁路货车运用技术质量的分析、评价和管理，组织开展货物列车技术质量监控，定期调查分析运用车辆技术状态，对铁路货车运用中发现的故障进行信息收集、处理、分析；负责铁路货车设计、新造、检修和主要配件的质量监督与反馈，对车辆结构、设计、制造、修理和运用管理提出改进意见。

（7）负责爱护铁路货车（以下简称爱车）工作，组织爱车宣传并指导、监督和检查铁路货车的使用，制止损坏铁路货车的行为，负责损坏铁路货车的索赔和管理。

（8）按规定负责重点物资及超限货物列车和机械冷藏车的技术作业及车辆乘务等工作。

（9）按规定协助进行铁路货车新车型、新技术、新型配件运用考验的相关工作。

（10）参加相关铁路交通事故的调查和事故救援，协助铁路货车交通事故的处理和管理，负责铁路货车行车设备故障的调查、处理和管理。

2. 货车运用作业场

货车运用作业场主要由列检作业场、动态检查作业场、技术交接作业场、整备作业场等组成，是对列车、车辆进行技术检查、修理的第一线，是服务运输、保证行车安全畅通的必要组成部分。货车运用作业场的布局、劳动组织、作业班组设置和人员配备要求，必须满足运输安全生产的需要。

（1）列检作业场一般设置在编组站、区段站和中间站的车场，主要负责货物列车中铁路货车的技术检修作业。货物列车技术作业分为解体列车到达技术作业、始发列车出发技术作业、无改编（无调）中转列车技术作业、部分改编中转列车技术作业。

① 解体列车到达技术作业：列车到达技术站后全部车列需要进行解体的列车作业，技术作业内容包括：车辆检修技术作业、货运检查、核对现车、票据交接、准备解体。列检作业场主要负责对车列中的铁路货车进行技术检修。

② 始发列车出发技术作业：主要在技术站或装车站进行，对编组出发的列车技术作业，技术作业内容包括：车辆检修技术作业、货运检查、核对现车、摘挂车辆、票据交接、准备发车及发车等。列检作业场主要负责对车列中的铁路货车进行技术检修。

③ 无改编（无调）中转列车技术作业：列车到达技术站后，只办理必要的中转作业后继续运行的列车作业。技术作业内容包括：车辆技术检修作业、货运检查、核对现车、票据交接、准备发车及发车等。列检作业场主要负责对运行达到列检安全保证距离的中转列车和前方无列检作业场车站发出的列车中的铁路货车进行技术检修。

④ 部分改编（有调）中转列车技术作业：列车到达技术站后，变更重量、长度，进行成组甩挂等少量调车作业后继续运行的货物列车作业，技术作业主要包括：车辆技术检修作业（包括摘、挂机车和试风）、货运检查、核对现车、摘挂车辆、票据交接、准备发车及发车等。列检作业场主要负责对运行达到列检安全保证距离中转列车和前方无列检作业场车站发出的列车中的铁路货车进行技术检修。

（2）动态检查作业场：按照集中或区域集中设置，由动态检车员在货物列车运行工况下，利用铁路货车运行安全监控系统（TFDS），按照规定的检查范围和质量标准，对解体列车、无改编中转列车、部分改编中转列车中的铁路货车进行动态检查，对发现的铁路货车故障向列检作业场预报，由列检作业场组织进行检查、确认和处理。

（3）技术交接作业场：设置在有翻车机、解冻库的企业专用线，或实际装卸车数量每昼夜平均 300 辆及以上的厂矿、港口、地方铁路、合资铁路、专用铁路、企业专用线、工程临管线等与国铁接轨的车站。接轨站设有列检作业场的可不设置技术交接作业场，由列检作业场承担技术交接作业场的有关工作。其主要负责对进出厂矿、港口、地方铁路、合资铁路、专用铁路、企业专用线、工程临管线的铁路货车进行技术交接检查和故障处理，防止由于企业装卸作业造成脱轨、撞车等事故和严重损坏的铁路货车进入国铁线运行，危及铁路运输安全。

（4）国境站技术交接作业场：一般设置在办理铁路货车国际联运的国境站。其主要负责国际联运列车的中方、外方铁路货车进行技术交接检查和故障处理，确保参加国际联运的铁路货车运行安全。

（5）整备作业场：一般设置在对往返循环开行的快速货物班列、局管内固定编组开行的货物快运列车、进入高原运行的货物列车中的铁路货车，以及重载货物列车中的专用铁路货车进行定期、定点整备作业的车站，按照规定的检查范围和质量标准，对上述货物列车的铁路货车进行技术检修。

3. 列检作业场

1）列检作业场安全职责

货车运用作业场按规定的检查范围和质量标准，对货物列车或铁路货车进行技术作业后，须保证铁路货车相应部位的质量标准符合规定，并在正常使用条件下安全运行到下一个负责检查该部位的货车运用作业场，承担相应的安全与质量责任。

列检作业场按规定的检查范围和质量标准技术作业后发出的列车，停车技术作业的安全保证距离原则上应为 500 km 左右。高原、重载及长交路等对运输有特殊要求的货物列车，根据运输组织、线路情况、铁路货车技术状态及列检作业布局，按国铁集团的规定确定相应的安全保证距离。

2）列检作业场分类及设置

列检作业场主要负责货物列车的日常检查和维修，以人工检查或人机分工检查方式为主，列检作业场的布局须满足铁路运输安全和畅通的需要，在编组站的车场及相应的车站，根据列车运行图中编制的到达解体列车（以下简称到达列车）、编组始发列车（以下简称始发列车）、中转列车的数量，同时按照运输组织、机车交路、运行工况、列检作业安全保证距离等合理设置。如图 2-1 所示。

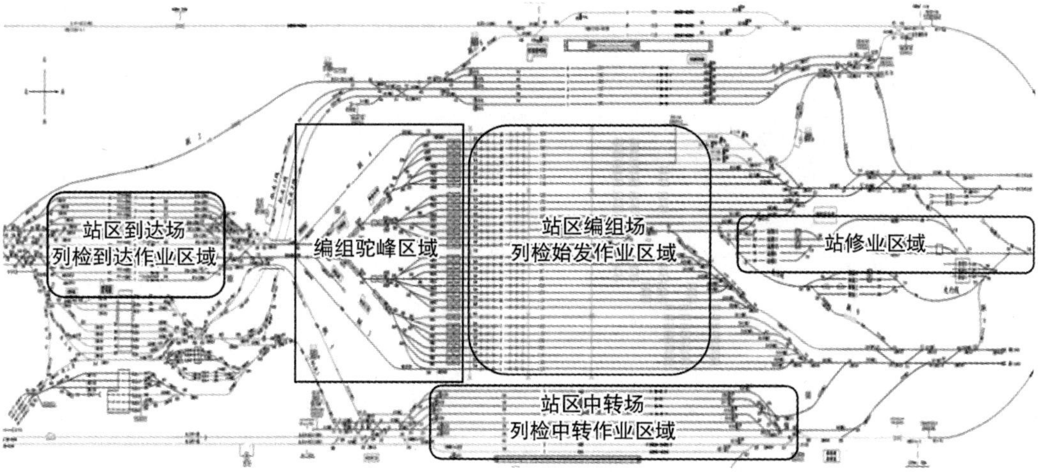

图 2-1　编组站示意图

列检作业场等级分为特级、一级：特级列检作业场设置在日均解体作业 3000 辆以上的编组站的车场；一级列检作业场设置在列车编组作业量较大或大量装卸货物的其他编组站、区段站的车场，以及停车技术作业中转列车较多的区段站、中间站。

列检作业场的名称命名原则上须与所在车站或车场、站区的名称相对应，站区内设多个车场时，原则上采用上行或下行、到达或始发、一或二等方式进行命名。

3）列检作业场生产生活设施

列检作业场所在车站或站区均应有临修能力。暂无临修能力的，应设故障铁路货车临时整修的专用线路，其直线段有效长度不小于 60 m，具备重车架车条件，并配置电焊机、架车机具等临时整修铁路货车故障的设施设备及安全防护设施。

列检作业场的生产生活房屋应相对集中设置在列检综合楼内。原则上应设值班室、待检室、办公室、会议室、交接班室、资料室、多媒体学习培训室、安全警示室、计算机设备机房、模具展示室、故障展览室、练功基地等生产设施。列检作业场还应设充电室、空气压缩机室、工具室、材料配件分存室、室外大型配件存放棚、微机控制列车制动机试验装置的车场端部机房等设施设备。其布局如图 2-2 所示。

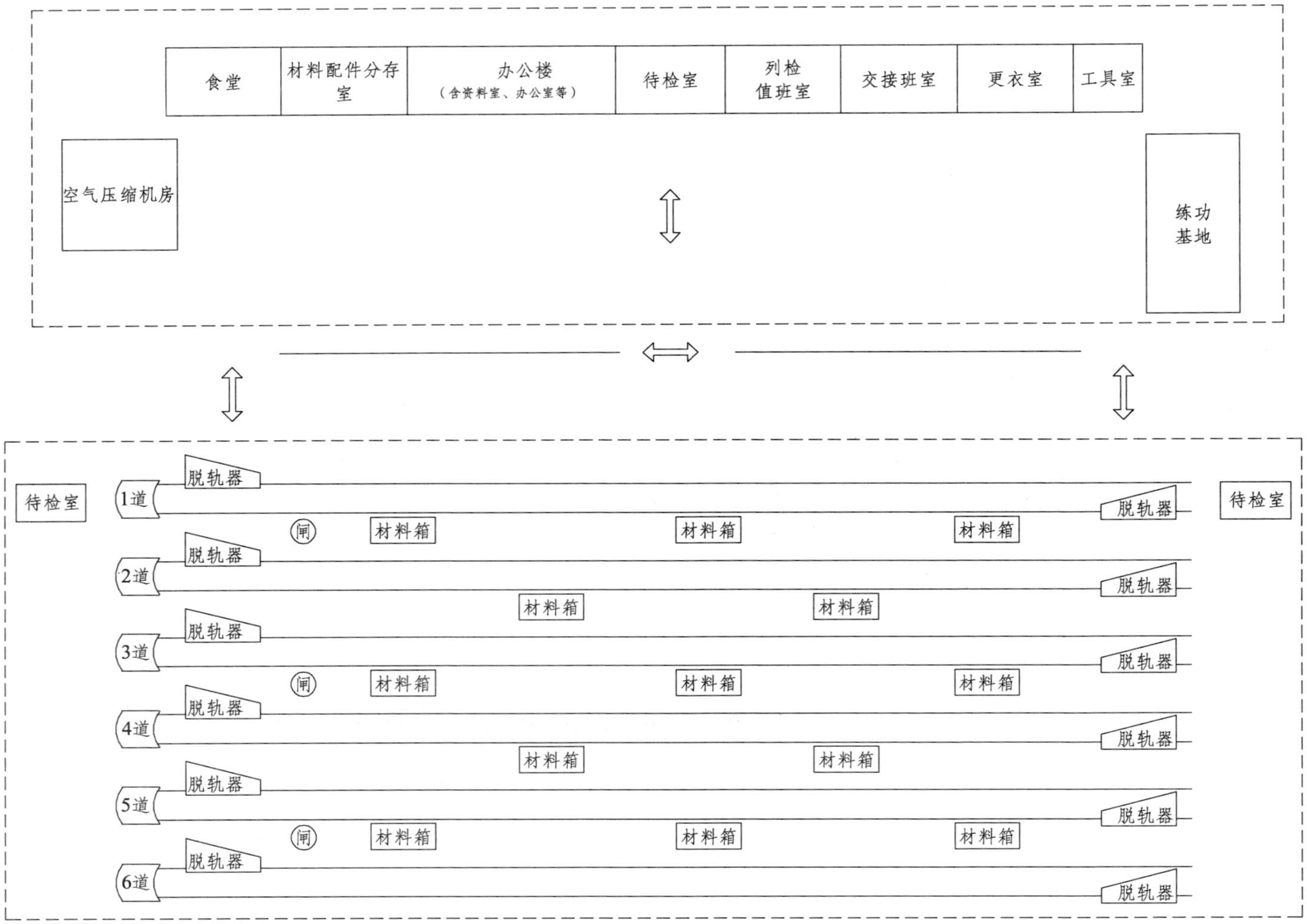

图 2-2　列检作业场布局示意图

列检作业场的作业线路须设灯桥（见图 2-3）或灯塔，照明范围覆盖全部作业区域，照度符合相关规定。在夜间及光线较暗的时间段进行列检作业时，灯桥或灯塔应处于照明状态。

图 2-3　列检作业场灯桥

列检作业场作业线路间及线群外侧（距线路中心 3.0 m）应以水泥预制板铺平至与轨枕上平面同高，宽度 1.0 m 左右，并具备良好的排水条件。线路应铺设混凝土平头轨枕，线群外侧设挡砟墙。同时，配备适应作业线路条件的工具、材料运输车，交叉设置工具材料分存箱，满足铁路货车故障修理需求。

（1）生产设施。

① 列检值班室。

列检值班室一般设置在列检作业场综合楼内或车站调度楼内便于瞭望列车到发的地方；待检室根据站场环境或车场内列检作业线路长度、数量设置。列检综合楼内应设待检室。当作业线路有效长 850 m 及以上时，还应在车场两端适当位置设待检室；当列检综合楼设在车场的一端时，应在车场中部和另一端设待检室；当列检作业线路 10 条及以上时，还应在站场或车场列检综合楼的另一侧适当位置设置待检室。待检室应配备 HMIS 运用子系统终端、打印机、与列检值班室直通电话、接发列车及安全信息揭示系统显示终端、座椅等。值班室、待检室应配备时钟，并与车站定期校准。

② 作业设备存放地。

充电室内须设存放台、工具台、控制台、充电设备，如图 2-4 所示；工具室配置工作台、钳工台、砂轮机、台式钻床等维修机具、设备配件及备品，如图 2-5 所示。

图 2-4　充电室

图 2-5　工具室

③ 教学及教具场所。

模具展示室须配备主型车辆零部件的剖件、模具、课件，如图 2-6 所示；故障展览室墙上应揭挂故障发现方法图示，摆放有代表性的铁路货车故障损品，如图 2-7 所示。

图 2-6　模具展示室

图 2-7　故障展览室

练功基地面积满足练功需要，应设置理论培训、实作演练、电化教学、配件实物、故障损品展示等不同区域。如图 2-8 所示。

图 2-8　练功基地

此外，列检作业场配备有交接班室、材料配件分存室、室外大型配件存放棚，与外界公路相通的道路，作业线路两端或一端应铺设平交运输道路，路面应硬化；运输道路与正线相交时，应设汽车和人员涵洞通道。对于列检作业需穿越正线或邻近正线作业的列检作业场，须安装列车接近语音报警提示装置和隔离设施。

（2）生产设备。

① 列检作业场的作业线路要安装具有安全防护功能的固定脱轨器（如图 2-9 所示），固定脱轨器应具备抗恶劣天气干扰和防雷功能，其安装位置应根据本固道的信号机、警冲

标及机车停车位置标的位置、机车长度等情况确定。根据站场实际情况，还须配置一定数量的移动脱轨器（如图 2-10 所示）。脱轨器是用于铁路防护区段的双向隔离设备，可靠地迫使线路两端闯入防护区段的机车车辆脱轨，保证作业人员人身安全。

图 2-9　固定脱轨器

图 2-10　移动脱轨器

② 列检作业场要安装微机控制列车制动机试验装置，试验执行器的数量和安装位置应根据列车制动机试验的需要确定安装。列车制动机试验装置是检验机车车辆成组运用时制动性能的设备，及时发现和处理车辆制动故障，保证车辆运行安全。如图 2-11 所示。

图 2-11　微机控制列车制动机试验装置

列检作业场应同时设置空气压缩机房，满足列车制动机试验最大用风量需要，并具备除尘、除湿、控温的功能，压缩空气管路须采用管径不小于 50 mm 的不锈钢等耐腐蚀材料，采取防冻措施，进入作业线路后须铺设在专用的地沟或地下管道中。

（3）列检作业场要安装列车车辆制动试验监测装置，并在列检值班室设监测终端和主机。如图 2-12 所示。

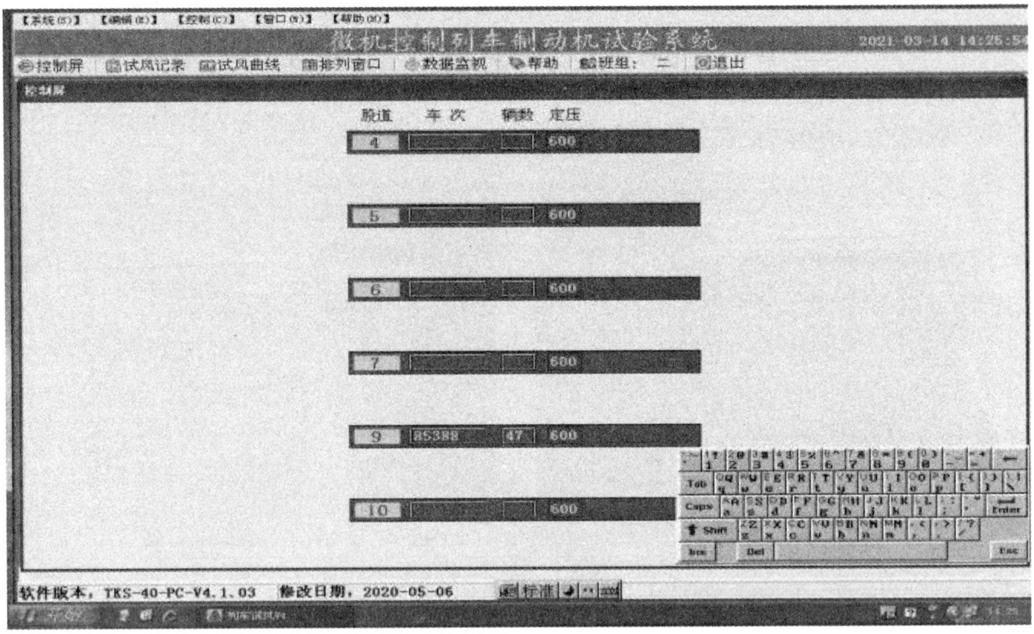

图 2-12　室内监测终端界面

（4）列检作业场配备货车车号自动识别系统列检复示终端、铁路货车管理信息系统（以下简称 HMIS）运用子系统、列检手持机系统、铁路货车运行安全监控系统等信息系统。

（5）列检作业场检车员应按作业要求配备检查锤、检车灯、无线对讲机、列检手持机、荧光分车牌、防护红灯或红旗、工具背带或腰带及相应工具等；列检作业场应配备列车队中处理铁路货车故障的专用工具、量具、机具，满足故障修理需要，并不断研发和更新列车队中新型的故障修理和抢修机具。

【复习题】

1. 简述货车运用作业场的分类。
2. 简述货车运用维修工作任务。

单元二　列检场技术作业

列检作业场按规定的检查范围和质量标准，对货物列车或铁路货车进行技术作业后，须保证铁路货车相应部位的质量标准符合规定，并在正常使用条件下安全运行到下一个负责检查该部位的列检作业场；承担相应的安全与质量责任。

【学习目标】

（1）掌握列检场的主要任务。

（2）掌握列检场列车技术作业范围。

（3）掌握列检扣车作业。

【学习内容】

1. 列车技术作业分类及方式

列车技术作业按作业性质分为到达作业、始发作业、中转作业、通过作业。其采用的作业方式、作业范围及质量标准有所差异。

1）到达作业

到达作业指对列检作业场所在车站到达列车进行的作业，采用人机分工检查或人工检查作业方式。列检作业场接入列车进路安装有 TFDS 的采用人机分工作业方式，执行“人机分工 TFDS 动态检查范围和质量标准”和“到达列车人机分工人工检查范围和质量标准”；列检作业场接入列车进路未安装 TFDS 或 TFDS 无法正常进行动态检查的采用人工检查作业方式，执行“人机分工 TFDS 动态检查范围和质量标准”和“到达列车人机分工人工检查范围和质量标准”。

2）始发作业

始发作业指对列检作业场所在车站始发列车进行的作业，列检作业采用人工检查作业方式。车辆技术检查实行人工检查作业，执行“始发列车检查范围和质量标准”。

3）中转作业

中转作业指对列检作业场所在车站且处在列检作业安全保证距离位置上的中转列车进行的作业，列检作业采用人机分工检查或人工检查作业方式。列检作业场接入列车进路安装有 TFDS 的实行人机分工作业，执行“人机分工 TFDS 动态检查范围和质量标准”和“中转列车人机分工人工检查范围和质量标准”；列检作业场接入列车进路未安装 TFDS 或 TFDS 无法正常进行动态检查的实行人工检查作业方式，执行“始发列车检查范围和质量标准”；对加挂的铁路货车，实行人工检查方式，执行“始发列车检查范围和质量标准”。

4）通过作业

中转作业指对上述情况以外的货物列车，利用 TFDS 进行的作业，实行动态检查方式，执行“通过作业 TFDS 动态检查范围和质量标准”，发现符合“通过作业 TFDS 动态检查范围和质量标准”的故障按拦停程序办理。

无列检作业场的车站编组始发列车，应在途经第一个列检作业场进行列检作业，执行中转作业有关规定。对铁路局集团公司无列检作业场的车站编组始发的列车，在本铁路局集团公司未途经列检作业场时，始发铁路局集团公司需通知接入铁路局集团公司安排途经第一个列检作业场进行列检作业，并在相关文件中明确作业地点。

2. 列检场检修范围

根据生产实际要求，在对铁路货车进行技术检查时可将车辆划分为以下几部分对其检查。

1）车　轮

车轮轮缘垂直磨耗、内侧缺损不超限，踏面擦伤、剥离、局部凹入、缺损、圆周磨耗不超限；轮缘厚度、轮辋厚度不超限，如图 2-13 所示。

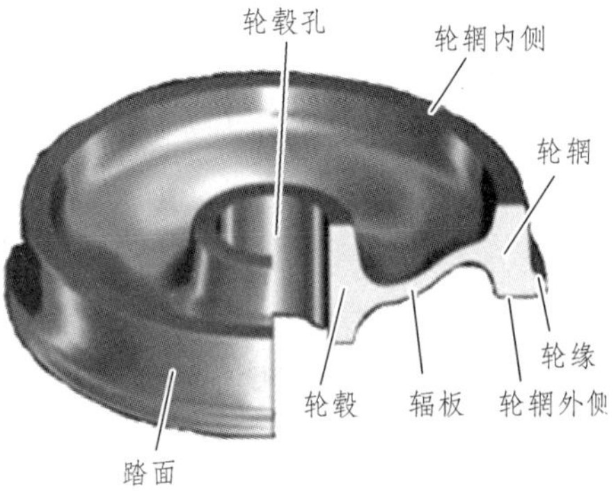

图 2-13　轮　对

2）轴箱及其附件

消除热轴故障；滚动轴承无甩油，外圈、前盖、承载鞍、轴箱无裂损，轴端螺栓无脱出；承载鞍无错位；轴箱盖螺栓无松动，如图 2-14 所示。

图 2-14　轴箱及其附件

3）转向架及其附件

侧架、摇枕及心盘无裂损；侧架立柱磨耗板及斜楔主摩擦板无破损、窜出、丢失；上、下心盘螺栓无折断、丢失；交叉杆盖板、杆体无弯曲、变形、裂损，安全链无脱落、折断，支撑座无破损，交叉杆端部螺栓无松动，防松垫止耳无折断；轴箱、摇枕弹簧无折断、窜出、丢失，如图 2-15 所示。

图 2-15　转向架及其附件

4）车　钩

钩体、钩舌及钩尾框无裂损；钩提杆及座齐全无破损，互钩差不超限；从板、从板座、缓冲器、冲击座无破损；钩尾框托板、钩尾扁销及安全吊架螺栓螺母无松动，开口销无丢失；钩尾销托板螺母无松动，车钩托梁及冲击座止挡块螺栓、螺母无丢失，如图 2-16 所示。

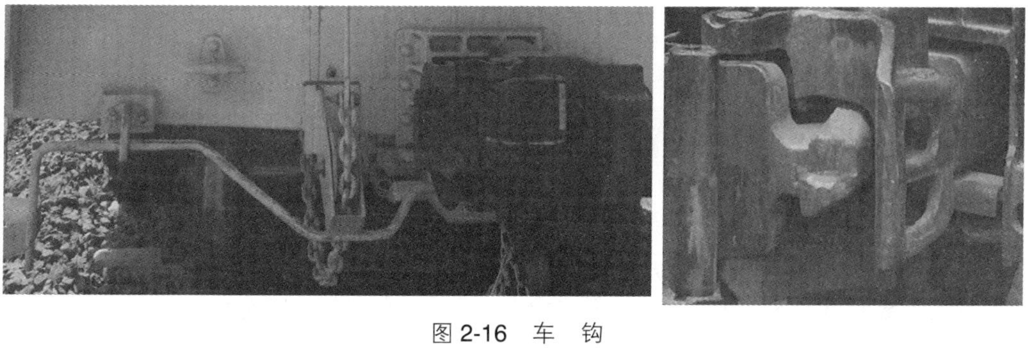

图 2-16　车　钩

5）制动装置

空气制动机作用良好；制动缸及风缸无裂损、脱落，吊架无裂损及紧固螺栓无松动、裂损；制动阀吊架螺母无松动、丢失；制动管、连接管无漏泄，卡子、螺栓无丢失；制动软管无破损、无丢失，制动软管吊链无丢失；折角塞门、截断塞门无破损，手把无丢失，如图 2-17 所示。

图 2-17　制动装置

制动梁梁架、支柱无裂损；制动梁梁吊无裂损，圆销开口销无折断、丢失；制动梁安全链无折断、脱落；闸瓦插销无折断、丢失，闸瓦磨耗不过限；各拉杆、杠杆、圆销、开口销无折断、丢失。

6）人力制动机

人力制动机配件齐全、无破损，如图 2-18 所示。

7）车　体

车体倾斜或外胀不超限；车号自动识别标签无失效、丢失；车门、车窗无破损、丢失；车门折页翻译时出错无折断，圆销、开口销无丢失；车门锁闭装置配件齐全、状态良好；绳栓无破损、丢失；脚蹬无破损，弯曲不超出车辆限界。如图 2-19 所示。

图 2-18　人力制动机

图 2-19　车　体

8）定检日期

空车定检不过期。

3. 列检扣车作业

1）扣定检车

非配属的货车定检到期或过期时，一律由发现的列检作业场进行扣留。扣留时，检车员在扣留车上插以规定的色票，并通知列检值班员办理扣车手续。

（1）按计划扣车：扣车应按车型、车种有计划地进行扣车，以保证全部车辆都能按时得到检修。

（2）按检修周期扣车：列检作业场必须按现车检修周期标记扣修定检车，厂修、段修车以月为准，辅修以日为准。厂修、段修、辅修同时到期时应做高级修程。

（3）按优先原则扣车：即在扣车时，如果遇到过期车和到期车，或者同期车中有破损程度大一些的车和破损程度轻一些的车，而按计划又不能同时扣修时，优先扣修过期车或破损程度严重的车辆。

（4）尽量空车扣车：扣定检车时，除重车有危及行车安全的故障不扣修不行外，一般在车辆处于空车状态或重车已抵达终到站才扣车。否则，对定检到期的重车车辆认真检查，在确保行车安全情况下，尽量放行至下一个列检作业场处置。

2）扣临修车

列检作业场发现车辆故障，应积极组织在列车队内进行维修；但对影响行车安全的在列车队内无法施修的较大故障或处理故障超过技检时间，影响解体作业或正点发车时，可以摘车临修。

3）扣车步骤

（1）掌握扣车计划：当班检车员首先应掌握在本班作业时间内，由值班员下达的扣车计划。严格按计划扣车(临修车除外)。

（2）检查车辆状态：检车员在对列车实施技检时，注意车辆的定检标记、技术状态和空重车状态，以便确定怎样扣车。

（3）确定扣车色票：根据车辆状态和扣车计划，确定对车辆的处置方法，选择色票。

（4）确认、填写色票：为防止发生人为差错，必须确认所用色票是否是正确，然后按规定正确、清晰、工整地填写。

（5）插票并记录：将色票插入车辆的色票框内，表示该车辆在运用中的身份。然后，将车种、车型、车号、扣车原因等信息记入“检车员工作手册”内。

（6）回所办手续：作业完毕归所后，立即将扣车情况向值班员汇报并登记，对插检修类色票者，如辅修、段修、厂修等，值班员必须填写“车辆检修通知书”。

【复习题】

1. 列检作业的任务是什么？
2. 简述列检场扣车程序。

单元三　货车单车技术检查

铁路货车单车技术检查是铁路货车检车员必须具备的基本功，要求检车员必须熟练掌握货车单车技术检查的步骤、方法和作业内容，熟知相关运用限度，以保证铁路运输安全。

【学习目标】

（1）掌握铁路货车运用限度。

（2）掌握铁路货车单车技术检查作业标准。

【学习内容】

1. 工装设备及检测器具

带反光带的黄蓝色长袖上衣、蓝色长裤、带反光带的黄色工作帽、臂章、劳保鞋、带反光条分体式雨衣、长筒雨鞋、300 mm × 300 mm 活动扳手、检查锤、检车灯、磁性防护红旗、频闪式防护红灯、对讲机、便携式红外线测温仪、车统-15A、车轮检查器、卷尺、作业记录仪等，如图 2-20 所示。

工作前必须按规定穿戴防护用品，着装整齐

工作前必须按规定穿戴防护用品，着装整齐

图 2-20　工作人员着装示意图

2. 铁路货车运用限度

（1）铁路货车车体运用限度如表 2-1 所示。

表 2–1　铁路货车车体运用限度　　单位：mm

序号	名称		限度	备注
1	侧梁下垂	空车	≤40	在两枕梁之间测量
		重车	≤80	
2	敞车车体外胀	空车	≤80	
		重车	≤150	
3	车体倾斜		≤75	
4	端墙板、侧墙板、地板、门板、浴盆板破损或腐蚀穿孔		≤50×50	
5	棚车、平车非金属地板破损		≤100×100	

（2）铁路货车转向架运用限度如表 2-2 所示。

表 2–2　铁路货车转向架运用限度　　单位：mm

序号	名称		限度	备注
1	间隙旁承同一转向架左右旁承间隙之和		2～20	铁路货车任何一侧旁承间隙须大于 0，载重 280 t 及以上铁路长大货物车须大于 2 mm
	双作用弹性上下旁承间隙		0	
2	双作用弹性旁承滚子或旁承尼龙支承板与上旁承间隙		>0	
3	各垂下品与轨面水平线垂直距离	钢轨内侧	≥60	钢轨上部垂下品不得小于 25 mm
		钢轨外侧	≥80	

（3）铁路货车轮对运用限度如表 2-3 所示。

表 2-3　铁路货车轮对运用限度

序号	名称		限度	备注
1	车轮轮辋厚度	无辐板孔	≥23	
		有辐板孔	≥24	
2	车轮轮缘厚度	棚车、集装箱平车、平车-集装箱共用车、小汽车运输专用车及 120 km/h 货物列车中的铁路货车	≥25	
		其他	≥23	3 轴及多轴转向架的中间轮对轮缘厚度列检可不掌握
3	车轮轮缘垂直磨耗（接触位置）高度		≤15	
4	车轮轮缘内侧缺损	长度	≤30	
		宽度	≤10	
5	车轮踏面圆周磨耗深度		≤8	
6	车轮踏面擦伤及局部凹下深度		≤1	
7	车轮踏面剥离长度	一处	≤50	1. 沿圆周方向测量。 2. 测量时规定如下： （1）两端宽度不足 10 mm 的，不计算在内。 （2）长条状剥离其最宽处不足 20 mm 的，不计算在内。 （3）两块剥离边缘相距小于 75 mm 时，每处长不得超过 35 mm；多处小于 35 mm 的剥离，其连续剥离总长度不得超过 350 mm。 （4）剥离前期未脱落部分，可不计算在内
		二处（每一处均）	≤40	
8	车轮踏面缺损	相对轮缘外侧至缺损部位边缘之距离	≥1508	从缺损部内侧边缘起测量
		缺损部位之长度	≤150	沿车轮踏面圆周方向测量
9	车轮辐板孔边缘周向裂纹		≤30	
10	滚动轴承温升		≤55 °C	

（4）铁路货车制动运用限度如表 2-4 所示。

表 2-4　铁路货车制动运用限度　　　　单位：mm

序号	名称				限度	备注	
1	制动缸活塞行程	装有闸调器的单式闸瓦	356×254 制动缸	空车位	115～135	未装闸调器	85～135
				重车位	125～160		110～160
			305×254 制动缸	空车位	145～165		
				重车位	145～195		
			254×254 制动缸	空车位	145～165		
				重车位	145～195		
			203×254 制动缸	空车位	115～145		
				重车位	125～160		
		装有闸调器的复式闸瓦	B_{21}、B_{22-1} 型车	空车位	120～130		
				重车位	150～160		
			B_{19}、B_{22-2}、B_{23} 型车		130～150		
		集成制动装置	BAB 系列		行程指示器在制动标志孔内		
			DAB 系列		行程指示器在行程标志环带内		
2	高、低摩合成闸瓦磨耗剩余厚度				≥20		
3	C_{100} 型敞车二、三位转向架闸瓦磨耗剩余厚度				≥25		
4	同一制动梁两端闸瓦厚度差				≤20	更换闸瓦后确认	
5	C_{100} 型敞车二、三位转向架同一制动梁两端闸瓦厚度差				≤10		

（5）铁路货车车钩运用限度如表 2-5 所示。

表 2-5　铁路货车车钩运用限度　　　　单位：mm

序号	名称			限度	备注
1	13 号钩舌与钩腕内侧距离	闭锁位置		≤135	—
		全开位置		≤250	
2	13A、13B 型钩舌与钩腕内侧距离	闭锁位置		≤132	—
		全开位置		≤247	—
3	16、17 型钩舌与钩腕内侧距离	闭锁位置		≤100	—
		全开位置		≥219	—
4	钩提杆链松余量			40～55	—
5	两连接车钩中心水平线高度之差			≤75	—
6	车钩中心高度	最高		≤890	—
		最低	空车	≥835	
			重车	≥815	

3. 列检作业责任划分

列检作业场按到达、中转和始发列车的作业性质，对一辆铁路货进行车技术检查作业时，以铁路货车纵向中心线为界，实行分面检查作业分工。为防止一辆作业过程发生漏检现象，对易混淆部位界限进行了划分：

① 车钩连接状态、首尾车钩三态作用、钩提杆及链、车钩防跳插销及吊链、下锁销组成，均由钩提杆所在侧检车员负责；车钩高度、两连接车钩高度差，两侧检车员负责；车钩上部、冲击座纵向中心线处破损，由非提钩杆所在侧检车员负责。

② 钩体底面（下锁销孔）、钩锁锁腿、车钩托梁、车钩支撑座、车钩支撑座含油尼龙磨耗板、钩尾销及安全吊架螺栓、制动软管吊链，均由跨轨检查的检车员负责。

③ 转向架旁承、心盘、摇枕、内侧枕簧（不含减振弹簧）、制动梁体及支柱夹扣螺栓、交叉杆、横跨梁及安全链（索）、空重车调整阀，均由跨轨检查的检车员负责。

④ 转向架内外侧以轮缘顶点划分。

⑤ 制动缸连通管漏泄由负责制动机试验的检车员负责。

⑥ 转向架内、外端固定及游动杠杆、上拉杆、固定杠杆支点及座、固定杠杆支点链蹄环及圆销、开口销（拉铆销套），均由所在侧检车员负责。

4. 中转列车人机分工人工检查一辆作业

中转列车人机分工作业时人工检查一辆的作业过程常采取“一跨、一俯、三探”分面检查方法，即一跨：制动软管所在侧端转向架外端跨轨检查；一俯：底架中部车下悬挂配件俯身顺车检查；三探：制动软管所在侧端转向架内端及另一转向架内、外端探身检查。检车过程如图 2-21 所示。

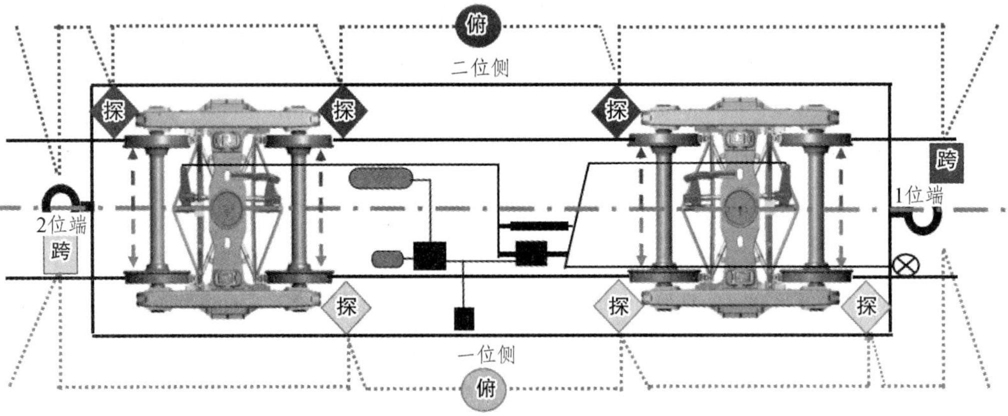

图 2-21　“一跨、一俯、三探”分面检查方法平面示意图

一辆作业人工检查具体内容及质量标准见表 2-1。

表 2-1　一辆作业人工检查作业方法

<table>
<tr><th>序号</th><th>步伐与姿势</th><th>检查内容</th><th>质量标准</th></tr>
<tr><td rowspan="2">1</td><td rowspan="2">左脚跨进钢轨，目视检查</td><td rowspan="2">本侧角柱、端梁，本侧冲击座、钩体，平车端板(渡板)折页及圆销开口销，端部布置空气制动装置，车端护栏等</td><td>① 角柱无裂损，端梁无折断；墙板破损或腐蚀穿孔不超限；车体外胀不超限。
② 钩体无破损，冲击座无破损，冲击座铆钉无折断、丢失；互钩差不超限。
③ 敞车上端梁无折断，绳栓无折断。
④ 平车端板、渡板折页及座无折断，圆销无丢失；绳栓无折断。
⑤ 罐车罐体无漏泄；罐体上部走板、防护栏等配件无脱落、窜出。
⑥ 矿石车、罐车、粮食车、双层集装箱平车（制动缸安装在底架上部车端处），根据底架上部制动装置构造实际检查各部：副风缸、加速缓解风缸、容积风缸、降压风缸缸体无裂损，吊架无折断、螺母无丢失；制动缸吊架无折断、螺母无丢失；制动阀中间体吊架螺母无丢失；制动主管卡子及螺母、法兰螺母无丢失；远心集尘器及组合式集尘器、缓解阀无破损，缓解阀拉杆吊架无裂损；截断塞门无破损</td></tr>
<tr><td></td></tr>
<tr><td rowspan="2">2</td><td rowspan="2">俯身，目视检查</td><td rowspan="2">（1）折角塞门、制动软管</td><td>折角塞门、直端塞门、制动软管无破损</td></tr>
<tr><td></td></tr>
</table>

<table>
<tr><th>序号</th><th>步伐与姿势</th><th>检查内容</th><th>质量标准</th></tr>
<tr><td rowspan="4">2</td><td rowspan="4">俯身，目视检查</td><td rowspan="2">（2）各梁、从板座铆钉、制动主管卡子</td><td>① 侧梁、端梁、枕梁、横梁及牵引梁无折断；从板座铆钉无折断、丢失。
② 制动主管卡子及螺母、法兰螺母无丢失</td></tr>
<tr><td></td></tr>
<tr><td rowspan="2">（3）脱轨自动制动装置、旁承、枕簧</td><td>① 脱轨自动制动装置调节杆无折断，拉环与车轴无接触，拉环圆销无丢失。
② 旁承体无破损、丢失，双作用弹性旁承上旁承与下旁承尼龙磨耗板无间隙、旁承滚子或旁承尼龙支承板与上旁承磨耗板不得接触，间隙旁承间隙不超限。
③ 装有弹簧托板转向架摇枕、上心盘铆钉无折断；副构架与连接杆连接用螺母及开口销无丢失。
④ 装有弹簧托板转向架内侧摇枕弹簧、减振弹簧无折断、窜出、丢失</td></tr>
<tr><td></td></tr>
</table>

<table>
<tr><th>序号</th><th>步伐与姿势</th><th>检查内容</th><th>质量标准</th></tr>
<tr><td rowspan="6">2</td><td rowspan="6">俯身，目视检查</td><td rowspan="2">（4）基础制动</td><td>① 制动梁吊无裂损，圆销及开口销无折断、丢失，转 K3 型转向架制动梁端头与闸瓦托组装开口销无折断、丢失；制动梁安装位置正确。
② 朝向本侧的基础制动装置的固定杠杆支点座、固定杠杆支点、固定杠杆支点链蹄环、上拉杆及圆销、开口销无折断、丢失，拉铆销套环无丢失</td></tr>
<tr><td></td></tr>
<tr><td rowspan="2">（5）集成制动装置</td><td>集成制动装置制动缸连接软管无破损，制动缸推杆及β型插销无丢失，制动缸活塞行程指示器、标志牌无丢失</td></tr>
<tr><td></td></tr>
<tr><td rowspan="2">（6）车轮</td><td>车轮轮缘内侧缺损不超限，辐板孔边缘径向无裂纹，周向裂纹不超限</td></tr>
<tr><td></td></tr>
</table>

<table>
<tr><th>序号</th><th>步伐与姿势</th><th>检查内容</th><th>质量标准</th></tr>
<tr><td rowspan="2">3</td><td rowspan="2">自由步跨出，站于定检标记相对处，目视检查</td><td rowspan="2">车体、侧梁、定检标记</td><td>① 侧梁无折断；敞车上侧梁无折断；侧梁下垂、车体倾斜或外胀不超限。
② 空车定检不过期（回送检修车除外）</td></tr>
<tr><td></td></tr>
<tr><td rowspan="2">4</td><td rowspan="2">自由步，俯身，目视检查</td><td rowspan="2">（1）车轮、轴承、承载鞍</td><td>① 车轮轮缘垂直磨耗不超限；踏面无碾堆，踏面擦伤、剥离、局部凹下、缺损、圆周磨耗不超限；轮缘厚度、轮辋厚度不超限；辐板孔边缘径向无裂纹，周向裂纹不超限；轮辋无破损。
② 滚动轴承外圈、承载鞍无破损，轴端螺栓无松动、脱出，转 K2 型转向架承载鞍顶面无金属碾出；侧架导框、副构架导框纵向与滚动轴承外圈无接触</td></tr>
<tr><td></td></tr>
</table>

续表

<table>
<tr><th>序号</th><th>步伐与姿势</th><th>检查内容</th><th>质量标准</th></tr>
<tr><td rowspan="2">4</td><td rowspan="2">自由步，俯身，目视检查</td><td rowspan="2">（2）车轮、瓦托</td><td>① 侧架立柱磨耗板折头螺栓、铆钉无折断、丢失。
② 车轮轮缘垂直磨耗不超限；踏面无碾堆，踏面擦伤、剥离、局部凹下、缺损、圆周磨耗不超限；轮缘厚度、轮辋厚度不超限；辐板孔边缘径向无裂纹，周向裂纹不超限；轮辋无破损。
③ 闸瓦上部无折断，闸瓦插销无折断、丢失，闸瓦磨耗不超限、无碾出金属镶嵌物。
④ 制动梁闸瓦托铆钉无丢失；制动梁吊无裂损，圆销及开口销无折断、丢失，转 K3 型转向架制动梁端头与闸瓦托组装开口销无折断、丢失；制动梁安装位置正确。
⑤ 交叉杆端部螺栓无松动、脱出</td></tr>
<tr><td></td></tr>
<tr><td rowspan="2">5</td><td rowspan="2">站立，目视检查</td><td rowspan="2">车体</td><td>① 侧柱无裂损；敞车上侧梁无折断；侧梁下垂、车体倾斜或外胀不超限。
② 车门、车窗无脱落、丢失；墙板、门板破损或腐蚀穿孔不超限；车门锁闭装置配件无破损、丢失；车门折页及座无折断，圆销无丢失。
③ 绳栓无折断；柱插无破损；集装箱锁头、门挡无破损、折断、丢失；罐体及阀无漏泄，罐车卡带无折断，紧固螺母及锁紧螺母无松动，圆销及开口销无丢失，罐体上部走板、防护栏无脱落、窜出</td></tr>
<tr><td></td></tr>
</table>

序号	步伐与姿势	检查内容	质量标准
6	自由步，俯身，目视检查	（1）立柱磨耗板、斜楔	① 侧架立柱磨耗板、斜楔及主摩擦板无破损、窜出、丢失。 ② 摇枕斜楔摩擦面磨耗板无窜出；摇枕斜面磨耗板折头螺栓无丢失

		（2）车轮、瓦托	同第四项第 2 小项

		（3）车轮、轴承、承载鞍	同第四项第 1 小项

<table>
<tr><th>序号</th><th>步伐与姿势</th><th>检查内容</th><th>质量标准</th></tr>
<tr><td rowspan="6">7</td><td rowspan="6">探身，目视检查</td><td rowspan="2">（1）各梁、制动主管</td><td>① 中梁、侧梁、枕梁、横梁无折断。
② 制动主管卡子及螺母、法兰螺母无丢失</td></tr>
<tr><td></td></tr>
<tr><td rowspan="2">（2）制动梁、空重车自动调整装置</td><td>① 制动梁吊无裂损，圆销及开口销无折断、丢失，转 K3 型转向架制动梁端头与闸瓦托组装开口销无折断、丢失；制动梁安装位置正确。
② 装有弹簧托板转向架摇枕、上心盘铆钉无折断；副构架与连接杆连接用螺母及开口销无丢失。
③ 空重车自动调整装置传感阀无破损</td></tr>
<tr><td></td></tr>
<tr><td rowspan="2">（3）脱轨自动制动装置基础制动各圆销</td><td>① 脱轨自动制动装置调节杆无折断，拉环与车轴无接触，拉环圆销无丢失。
② 朝向本侧的基础制动装置的固定杠杆支点座、固定杠杆支点、固定杠杆支点链蹄环、上拉杆及圆销、开口销无折断、丢失，拉铆销套环无丢失</td></tr>
<tr><td>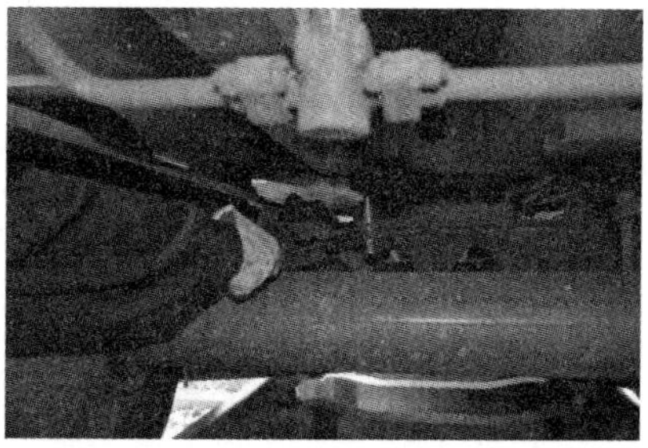</td></tr>
</table>

序号	步伐与姿势	检查内容	质量标准
7	探身，目视检查	（4）对侧轮缘内侧、旁承、枕簧	① 旁承体无破损、丢失，双作用弹性旁承上旁承与下旁承尼龙磨耗板无间隙、旁承滚子或旁承尼龙支承板与上旁承磨耗板不得接触，间隙旁承间隙不超限。 ② 装有弹簧托板转向架内侧摇枕弹簧、减振弹簧无折断、窜出、丢失。 ③ 车轮轮缘内侧缺损不超限 
8	自由步，目视检查	车体	① 侧柱无裂损；敞车上侧梁无折断；侧梁下垂、车体倾斜或外胀不超限。 ② 车门滑动轨道无折断，车门滑轮无脱出轨道，车门、车窗无脱落、丢失；墙板、门板破损或腐蚀穿孔不超限；车门锁闭装置配件无破损、丢失；车门折页及座无折断，圆销无丢失。 ③ 绳栓无折断；柱插无破损；集装箱锁头、门挡无破损、折断、丢失；罐体及阀无漏泄，人孔盖及安全阀无丢失，下卸式排油管、加热管及盖无脱落，罐体上部走板、防护栏无脱落、窜出 

续表

<table>
<tr><th>序号</th><th>步伐与姿势</th><th>检查内容</th><th>质量标准</th></tr>
<tr><td rowspan="6">9</td><td rowspan="6">自由步，俯身，目视检查</td><td rowspan="2">（1）中梁、侧梁、横梁</td><td>中梁、侧梁、横梁无折断；底开门转轴开口销无折断、丢失</td></tr>
<tr><td></td></tr>
<tr><td rowspan="2">（2）基础制动</td><td>制动缸后杠杆支点及圆销、开口销无折断、丢失，拉铆销套环无丢失</td></tr>
<tr><td></td></tr>
<tr><td rowspan="2">（3）人力制动机</td><td>人力制动机附加杠杆座及圆销、开口销无丢失</td></tr>
<tr><td></td></tr>
</table>

序号	步伐与姿势	检查内容	质量标准
9	自由步，俯身，目视检	（4）空气制动	副风缸、加速缓解风缸、容积风缸、降压风缸缸体无裂损，吊架无折断、螺母无丢失；制动缸吊架无折断、螺母无丢失；制动阀中间体吊架螺母无丢失；制动主管卡子及螺母、法兰螺母无丢失；空重车自动调整装置限压阀、调整阀无破损；远心集尘器及组合式集尘器、缓解阀无破损，缓解阀拉杆、空重车调整杆吊架无裂损，手动空重车位调整正确；截断塞门无破损

10	探身，目视检查	（1）各梁、主管卡子	同第七项第1小项

		（2）脱轨自动制动装置、基础制动各圆销	同第七项第3小项
			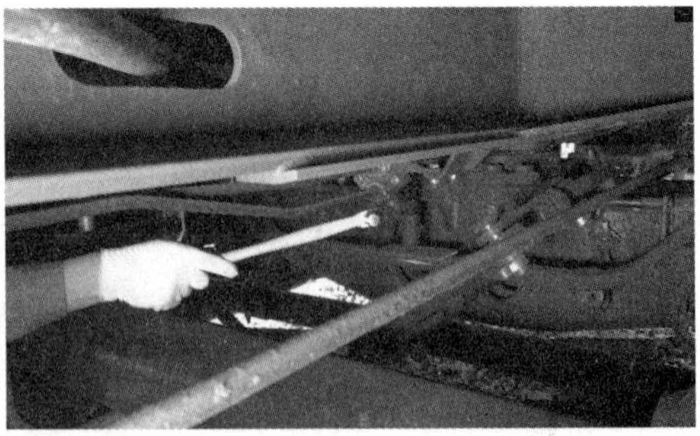

续表

<table>
<tr><th>序号</th><th>步伐与姿势</th><th>检查内容</th><th>质量标准</th></tr>
<tr><td rowspan="2">10</td><td rowspan="2">探身，目视检查</td><td rowspan="2">（3）对侧轮缘内侧、旁承、枕簧</td><td>同第七项第 4 小项</td></tr>
<tr><td></td></tr>
<tr><td rowspan="4">11</td><td rowspan="4">自由步，俯身，目视检查</td><td rowspan="2">（1）车轮、轴承、承载鞍</td><td>同第四项第 1 小项</td></tr>
<tr><td></td></tr>
<tr><td rowspan="2">（2）车轮、瓦托</td><td>同第四项第 2 小项</td></tr>
<tr><td></td></tr>
<tr><td rowspan="2">12</td><td rowspan="2">站立，目视检查</td><td rowspan="2">车体</td><td>同第五项</td></tr>
<tr><td></td></tr>
</table>

续表

<table>
<tr><th>序号</th><th>步伐与姿势</th><th>检查内容</th><th>质量标准</th></tr>
<tr><td rowspan="6">13</td><td rowspan="6">自由步，俯身，目视检查</td><td rowspan="2">（1）立柱磨耗板、斜楔</td><td>同第六项第1小项</td></tr>
<tr><td></td></tr>
<tr><td rowspan="2">（2）车轮、瓦托</td><td>同第四项第2小项</td></tr>
<tr><td></td></tr>
<tr><td rowspan="2">（3）车轮、轴承、承载鞍</td><td>同第四项第1小项</td></tr>
<tr><td></td></tr>
</table>

续表

<table>
<tr><th>序号</th><th>步伐与姿势</th><th>检查内容</th><th>质量标准</th></tr>
<tr><td rowspan="4">14</td><td rowspan="4">探身，目视检查</td><td rowspan="2">（1）各梁、从板座铆钉</td><td>① 侧梁、端梁、枕梁、横梁及牵引梁无折断。
② 从板座铆钉无折断、丢失</td></tr>
<tr><td></td></tr>
<tr><td rowspan="2">（2）脱轨自动制动装置、基础制动各圆销</td><td>同第七项第3小项</td></tr>
<tr><td></td></tr>
<tr><td rowspan="2">15</td><td rowspan="2">站立，目视检查</td><td rowspan="2">（1）脚蹬、车梯扶手及车端护栏</td><td>脚蹬、车梯扶手及车端护栏无破损、折断、丢失，脚蹬、车梯扶手弯曲不超出车辆限界</td></tr>
<tr><td></td></tr>
</table>

序号	步伐与姿势	检查内容	质量标准
15	站立，目视检查	（2）车体	角柱无裂损，端梁无折断；墙板破损或腐蚀穿孔不超限；车体外胀不超限；敞车上端梁无折断；平车端板、渡板折页及座无折断，圆销无丢失；绳栓无折断

		（3）人力制动机	折叠式人力制动机轴折页无折断，圆销及开口销无丢失，托架无折断

16	自由步，目视检查	（1）提钩杆座及链、互钩差	钩提杆座无裂损，螺母无丢失，钩提杆链松余量符合规定；互钩差不超限

<table>
<tr><th>序号</th><th>步伐与姿势</th><th>检查内容</th><th>质量标准</th></tr>
<tr><td rowspan="4">16</td><td rowspan="4">自由步，目视检查</td><td rowspan="2">（2）本侧冲击座、钩体</td><td>钩体无破损，冲击座无破损，冲击座铆钉无折断、丢失</td></tr>
<tr><td></td></tr>
<tr><td rowspan="2">（3）车列首尾端部车钩三态作用试验</td><td>车列首尾端部车钩钩舌 S 面无裂损、三态作用试验良好</td></tr>
<tr><td></td></tr>
<tr><td>17</td><td>同 1～16 项</td><td>同 1～16 项</td><td>同 1～16 项</td></tr>
</table>

【复习题】

1. 铁路货车运用时各部位的限度为多少？
2. 简述铁路货车单车技术检查作业内容。

单元四　始发列车制动机全部试验

列车制动机试验是在列车运行时，为调整列车运行速度和在指定地点停车，以及遇紧急情况下及时减速或停车，确保列车安全正点运行，防止列车冒进、冲突和人身伤亡事故的发生。列车中车辆空气自动制动机的性能好坏，是关系列车安全运行的重要因素。因此，列车中车辆空气自动制动机作用应确保良好、符合规定的技术标准。故列车在发车前，应对列车中车辆的空气制动机作用按规定进行列车制动机试验。

【学习目标】

（1）掌握列车制动机试验作业标准。

（2）掌握列车制动机试验手信号表示方式。

（3）掌握列车制动机手信号传递方法。

【学习内容】

1. 作业要点

列车制动机试验由现场检车员在列车运行方向左侧，按照分摊的辆数跑动检查，目视确认制动机制动、缓解状态。对因车辆结构影响现场检车员确认制动缸状态的车辆，整列编组时，现场作业组可调整为两个小组同时在列车两侧进行制动机试验；零星编入列车中的车辆，须向工长报告（由工长或工长指定专人在列车另一侧确认制动机性能）。在列车两侧进行制动机试验时，以列车运行方向左侧检车员作业为主，右侧检车员仅确认本侧制动缸状态和制动机性能，并在每个试验项目结束后向同段左侧检车员报告。

1）漏泄试验

关闭第一辆车前端折角塞门，列车管系保压 1 min，无线风压监测仪显示的列车主管压力下降不大于 20 kPa，试验完毕后开启折角塞门。

2）感度试验

置常用制动位，减压 50 kPa（编组 60 辆以上时减压 70 kPa），全列车须发生制动作用，并在 1 min 内不得发生自然缓解。然后置运转位充风缓解，全列车须在 1 min 内缓解完毕。

3）安定保压试验

置常用制动位，减压 140 kPa（列车主管压力为 600 kPa 时减压 170 kPa），不得发生紧急制动，并确认制动缸活塞行程须符合规定；同时保压，1 min 内无线风压监测仪显示的列车主管压力下降不大于 20 kPa。

2. 作业程序与标准

1）到达试风位置

现场检车员到达各自试风起始位置，按照列车制动机试验走行示意图进行列车制动机试验，如图 2-22 所示。

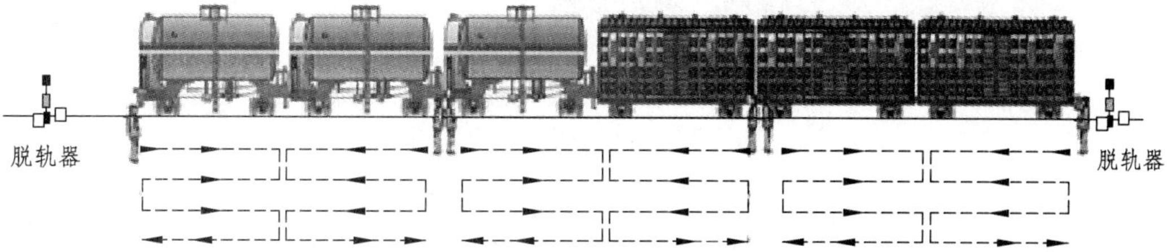

图 2-22　列车制动机试验走行示意图

图中所示，左侧为列车行进方向。第一个检车员是列首检车员，最后一个检车员是列尾检车员，因此，从左到右依次定为列首检车员、2 号检车员、3 号检车员、4 号检车员、5 号检车员、列尾检车员。

2）漏泄试验

（1）确认主管压力。

方式 1：尾部正号检车员目视确认无线风压监测仪显示的主管压力达到规定压力。

方式 2：尾部正号检车员使用对讲机与列检值班员联系，确认主管压力达到规定压力（标准用语："请确认 × 道 × 次风压"）。列检值班员在系统主界面，依据"压力"数值据实回复（标准用语："× 道 × 次风压 × × kPa"）；若达到主管定压，回复"× 道 × 次风压 × × kPa，符合要求"。

列车管压力：600 kPa。

（2）传递保压信号。

① 保压信号：昼间能见度能满足要求的须使用检查锤单臂平伸向列车方向平移，夜间或昼间能见度不能满足要求的须使用白色灯光的检车灯在胸前横向摆动，如图 2-23 所示。

② 恶劣天气、曲线线路可同时用对讲机辅助传递制动信号，标准用语：

传递人："× 道 × 段（或接收人姓名），保压。"

接收人："× 道 × 段（或传递人姓名），收到。"

③ 保压信号须依次逐段显示传递，不准越传、漏传、错传、代传，严禁臆测判断。

④ 禁止使用红旗（红灯）代替检查锤（检车灯）显示传递。

⑤ 保压信号传递程序和标准：

a. 尾部正号检车员站立于试风起始位置，面向列车首部，向中部正号、尾部负号检车员传递"保压信号"，确认对方不少于 2 次接收后停止显示。

图 2-23　保压手信号表示方式

b. 尾部负号检车员与中部正号检车员列队站立于试风起始位置，面向列车尾部，当尾部正号检车员传递“保压信号”时，不少于 2 次接收“保压信号”；转身 180°，面向列车首部，尾部负号检车员与中部正号检车员共同向中部负号、首部负号检车员传递“保压信号”，确认对方显示接收“保压信号”不少于 2 次后停止传递。

c. 中部负号检车员与首部负号检车员列队站立于试风起始位置，面向列车尾部，当中部正号、尾部负号检车员传递“保压信号”时，不少于 2 次接收“保压信号”；转身 180°，面向列车首部，中部负号检车员与首部负号检车员共同向首部正号检车员传递“保压信号”，确认对方显示接收“保压信号”不少于 2 次后停止传递。

d. 首部正号检车员站立于试风起始位置，面向列车尾部；当中部负号、首部负号检车员面向自己传递“保压信号”时，不少于 2 次接收“保压信号”。

（3）漏泄试验开始。

①首部正号检车员缓慢关闭第一辆车前端折角塞门，使折角塞门手把中心线与辅助管中心线呈 90°夹角（折角塞门开通线与辅助管中心线呈 90°夹角），并向列检值班员报告（标准用语：“×道×次折角塞门关闭”），如图 2-24 所示。

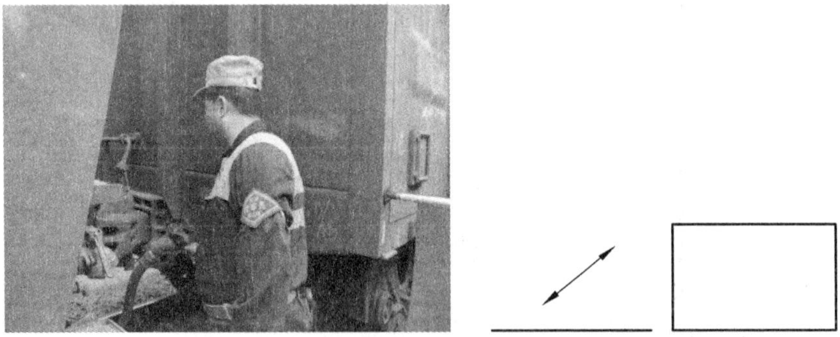

图 2-24　关闭折角塞门

② 列检值班员在系统主界面，使用鼠标左键点击“漏泄试验开始”按钮一次（“漏泄试验开始”按钮由凸起状态变为凹下状态）。

非正常情况：风压在上升阶段不能按漏泄试验按钮。若“漏泄试验开始”按钮按不下去（即按钮凸起状态无法变为凹下状态），则查看列车主管压力是否到达有效的定压范围内，未达到规定压力的使用车载台通知首部正号检车员，首部正号检车员打开第一辆车前端折角塞门，通知本务机车司机继续充风。

（4）传递确认信号。

① 确认信号：昼间能见度能满足要求的须使用检查锤，夜间或昼间能见度不能满足要求的须使用白色灯光的检车灯，朝向列车方向 45°斜行，如图 2-25 所示。

图 2-25 确认手信号表示方式

② 恶劣天气、曲线线路可同时用对讲机辅助传递制动信号，标准用语：

传递确认信号："×道×段（或接收人姓名），信号返过去了"。

接收确认信号："×道×段（或传递人姓名），收到"。

③ 确认信号须依次逐段显示传递，不准越传、漏传、错传、代传，严禁臆测判断。

④ 禁止使用红旗（红灯）代替检查锤（检车灯）显示传递。

⑤ 确认信号传递程序和标准：

a. 首部正号检车员站立于试风起始位置，面向列车尾部；向中部负号、首部负号检车员传递"确认信号"时，确认对方不少于 2 次接收后停止显示。

b. 中部负号检车员与首部负号检车员列队站立于试风起始位置，面向列车首部，当首部正号检车员传递"确认信号"时，不少于 2 次接收"确认信号"；转身 180°，面向列车尾部，中部负号检车员与首部负号检车员共同向尾部负号检车员与中部正号检车员传递"确认信号"，确认对方不少于 2 次接收后停止显示。

c. 尾部负号检车员与中部正号检车员列队站立于试风起始位置，面向列车首部，当中部负号检车员与首部负号检车员传递"确认信号"时，不少于 2 次接收"确认信号"；转身 180°，面向列车尾部，尾部负号检车员与中部正号检车员共同向尾部正号检车员传递"确认信号"，确认对方不少于 2 次接收后停止显示。

d. 尾部正号检车员站立于试风起始位置，面向列车首部，当尾部负号检车员与中部正号检车员传递"确认信号"时，不少于 2 次接收"确认信号"。

（5）确认漏泄量。

方式 1：尾部正号检车员实时观察无线风压监测仪显示的主管压力，确认 1 min 内无线风压监测仪显示的列车主管压力下降不大于 20 kPa，使用对讲机通知作业组作业人员。标准用语：“×道×次漏泄试验合格”。

方式 2：列检值班员实时观察“试风窗口”界面下方“漏泄试验”项目中显示的“保压”数值达到 60 s、“漏泄”数值不大于 20 kPa，使用车载台（或对讲机）通知现场作业人员（标准用语：“×道×次漏泄试验合格，漏泄量×kPa”），如图 2-26 所示。

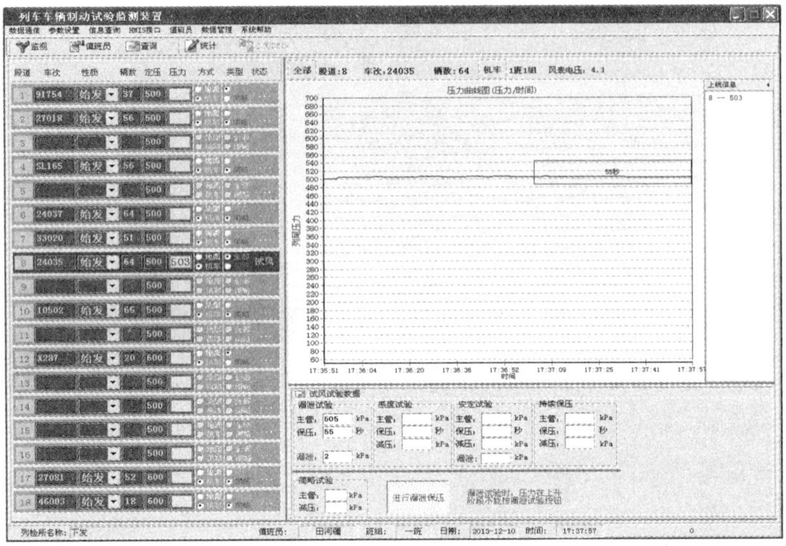

图 2-26　确认漏泄量

（6）漏泄试验结束。

首部正号检车员接到尾部正号检车员或列检值班员漏泄试验合格的通知后，缓慢开启第一辆车首部折角塞门，使折角塞门手把中心线与辅助管中心线方向一致（折角塞门开通线与辅助管中心线方向一致），如图 2-27 所示。

图 2-27　关闭折角塞门

3）感度试验

（1）确认主管压力。

方式 1：尾部正号检车员目视确认无线风压监测仪显示的主管压力达到规定压力

方式 2：尾部正号检车员使用对讲机与列检值班员联系，确认主管压力达到规定压力（标准用语："请确认 × 道 × 次风压"）。列检值班员在系统主界面，依据"压力"数值据实回复（标准用语："× 道 × 次风压 × × kPa，）；若达到主管定压，回复"× 道 × 次风压 × × kPa，符合要求"。

列车管压力：600 kPa。

（2）传递制动信号。

①制动信号：昼间能见度能满足要求的须使用检查锤高举头上，夜间或昼间能见度不能满足要求的须使用白色灯光的检车灯高举头顶上下摇动，如图 2-28 所示。

图 2-28　制动手信号表示方式

② 恶劣天气、曲线线路可同时用对讲机辅助传递制动信号，标准用语：

传递人："× 道 × 段（或接收人姓名），制动"；

接收人："× 道 × 段（或传递人姓名），收到"。

③ 制动信号须依次逐段显示传递，不准越传、漏传、错传、代传，严禁臆测判断。

④ 禁止使用红旗（红灯）代替检查锤（检车灯）显示传递。

⑤ 制动信号传递程序和标准：

a. 尾部正号检车员站立于试风起始位置，面向列车首部，向中部正号、尾部负号检车员传递"制动信号"，确认对方不少于 2 次接收后停止显示。

b. 尾部负号检车员与中部正号检车员列队站立于试风起始位置，面向列车尾部，当尾部正号检车员传递"制动信号"时，不少于 2 次接收"制动信号"；转身 180°，面向列车首部，尾部负号检车员与中部正号检车员共同向中部负号、首部负号检车员传递"制动信号"，确认对方不少于 2 次接收后停止显示。

c. 中部负号检车员与首部负号检车员列队站立于试风起始位置，面向列车尾部，当中部正号、尾部负号检车员传递“制动信号”时，不少于 2 次接收“制动信号”；转身 180°，面向列车首部，中部负号检车员与首部负号检车员共同向首部正号检车员传递“制动信号”，确认对方不少于 2 次接收后停止显示。

d. 首部正号检车员站立于试风起始位置，面向列车尾部；当中部负号、首部负号检车员面向自己传递“制动信号”时，不少于 2 次接收“制动信号”。转身 180°向司机显示“制动信号”，通知本务机车司机置常用制动位进行感度试验减压。允许用对讲机通知司机制动，标准用语：“×道×次感度试验，请减压 50(70) kPa”。

（3）确认感度试验减压量。

方式 1：尾部正号检车员实时观察无线风压监测仪显示的主管压力，确认感度试验减压量符合规定。

方式 2：尾部正号检车员使用对讲机与列检值班员联控确认感度试验减压量（标准用语：“请确认×道×次感度试验减压量”），列检值班员确认系统终端显示的感度试验减压量后向现场作业联系（标准用语：“×道×次感度试验减压量×kPa”）。

（4）确认制动性能。

列车达到规定减压量 1 min 后，现场检车员从试风起始位置开始，按照各自分摊的辆数跑动检查至试风碰头位置，逐辆弯腰探身、昼间用检查锤指（夜间用检车灯照）检查确认责任范围内的车辆发生制动作用，并确认 1 min 内未发生自然缓解，如图 2-29 所示。

图 2-29　制动性能确认

（5）监控试风曲线。

列检值班员实时观察系统终端显示的尾部风压曲线和提示信息，确认感度试验结果显示“合格”后，向现场进行作业联系（标准用语：“×道×次感度试验合格”），如图 2-30 所示。

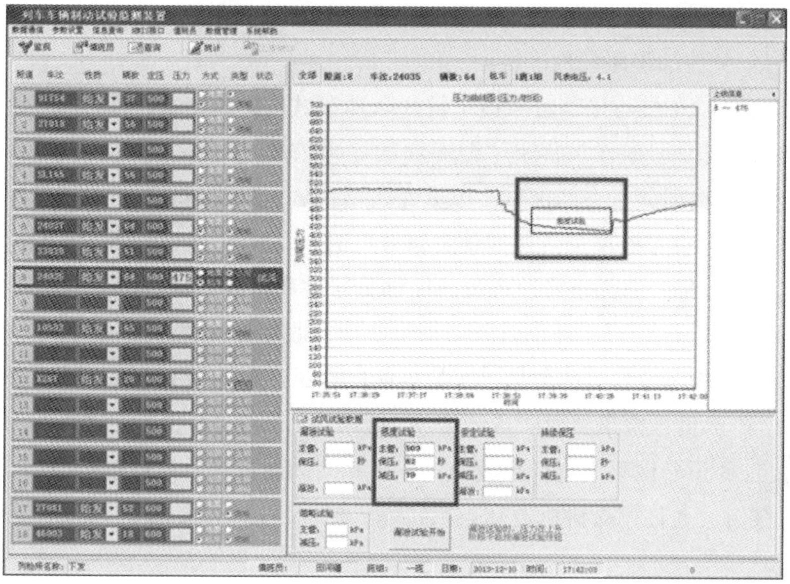

图 2-30　试风曲线

非正常情况：列检值班员发现试验项目未完成、试验不合格、试风数据中断等情况，通知现场检车员查清原因、处理后重新施行列车制动机试验。

（6）传递缓解信号。

① 缓解信号：昼间能见度能满足要求的须使用检查锤，夜间或昼间能见度不能满足要求的须使用白色灯光的检车灯，在下部左右摆动，如图 2-31 所示。

图 2-31　缓解手信号表示方式

② 恶劣天气、曲线线路可同时用对讲机辅助传递缓解信号，标准用语：

传递人："×道×段（或接收人姓名），缓解"；

接收人："×道×段（或传递人姓名），收到"。

③ 缓解信号须依次逐段显示传递，不准越传、漏传、错传、代传，严禁臆测判断。

④ 禁止使用红旗（红灯）代替检查锤（检车灯）显示传递。

⑤ 缓解信号传递程序和标准：

a. 尾部正号检车员与尾部负号检车员列队站在试风碰头位置，面向列车首部，向中部正号检车员、中部负号检车员传递"缓解信号"，确认对方不少于2次接收后停止显示。

b. 中部正号检车员与中部负号检车员列队站在试风碰头位置，面向列车尾部，当尾部正号检车员与尾部负号检车员传递"缓解信号"时，不少于2次接收"缓解信号"；转身180°，面向列车首部，中部正号检车员与中部负号检车员共同向首部正号检车员、首部负号检车员传递"缓解信号"，确认对方不少于2次接收后停止显示。

c. 首部正号检车员与首部负号检车员列队站在试风碰头位置，面向列车尾部，当中部正号检车员、中部负号检车员面向自己传递"缓解信号"时，不少于2次接收"缓解信号"。转身180°，首部正号检车员与首部负号检车员共同向司机显示"缓解信号"，通知本务机车司机充风缓解。允许用对讲机通知司机缓解。标准用语："×道×次缓解"。

（7）确认缓解性能。

列车充风后，现场检车员从试风碰头位置开始，按照分摊的辆数跑动检查返回试风起始位置，逐辆弯腰探身、昼间用检查锤指（夜间用检车灯照）检查，确认责任范围内的车辆须在1 min内缓解完毕，人力制动机拉杆链（闸缸链）处于松弛状态，如图2-32所示。

图2-32　缓解性能确认

4）安定保压实验

（1）确认主管压力。

方式 1：尾部正号检车员目视确认无线风压监测仪显示的主管压力达到规定压力。

方式 2：尾部正号检车员使用对讲机与列检值班员联系，确认主管压力达到规定压力（标准用语："请确认×道×次风压"）。列检值班员在系统主界面，依据"压力"数值据实回复（标准用语："×道×次风压××kPa，）；若达到主管定压，回复"×道×次风压××kPa，符合要求"。

列车管压力：600 kPa。

（2）传递制动信号。

① 制动信号：昼间能见度能满足要求的须使用检查锤高举头上，夜间或昼间能见度不能满足要求的须使用白色灯光的检车灯高举头顶上下摇动，如图 2-33 所示。

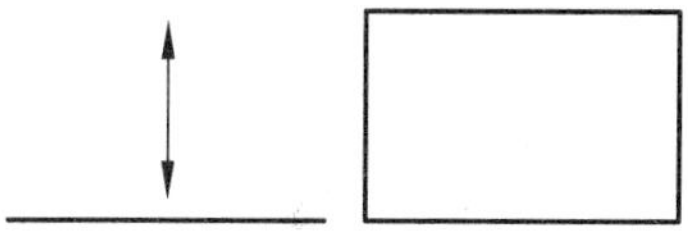

图 2-33　制动手信号表示方式

② 恶劣天气、曲线线路可同时用对讲机辅助传递制动信号，标准用语：

传递人："×道×段（或接收人姓名），制动"；

接收人："×道×段（或传递人姓名），收到"。

③ 制动信号须依次逐段显示传递，不准越传、漏传、错传、代传，严禁臆测判断。

④ 禁止使用红旗（红灯）代替检查锤（检车灯）显示传递。

⑤ 制动信号传递程序和标准：

a. 尾部正号检车员站立于试风起始位置，面向列车首部，向中部正号、尾部负号检车员传递"制动信号"，确认对方不少于 2 次接收后停止显示。

b. 尾部负号检车员与中部正号检车员列队站立于试风起始位置，面向列车尾部，当尾部正号检车员传递"制动信号"时，不少于 2 次接收"制动信号"；转身 180°，面向列车首部，尾部负号检车员与中部正号检车员共同向中部负号、首部负号检车员传递"制动信号”，确认对方不少于 2 次接收后停止显示。

c. 中部负号检车员与首部负号检车员列队站立于试风起始位置，面向列车尾部，当中部正号、尾部负号检车员传递“制动信号”时，不少于 2 次接收“制动信号”；转身 180°，面向列车首部，中部负号检车员与首部负号检车员共同向首部正号检车员传递“制动信号”，确认对方不少于 2 次接收后停止显示。

d. 首部正号检车员站立于试风起始位置，面向列车尾部；当中部负号、首部负号检车员面向自己传递“制动信号”时，不少于 2 次接收“制动信号”。转身 180°向司机显示“制动信号”，通知本务机车司机置常用制动位进行安定保压试验减压。允许用对讲机通知司机制动。标准用语：“×道×次安定保压试验，请减压 170 kPa 后保压。”

（3）确认安定保压试验减压量。

方式 1：尾部正号检车员实时观察无线风压监测仪显示的主管压力，确认安定保压试验减压量符合规定。

方式 2：尾部正号检车员使用对讲机与列检值班员联控确认安定保压试验减压量（标准用语：“请确认×道×次安定保压试验减压量”），列检值班员确认系统终端显示的安定保压试验减压量后向现场作业联系（标准用语：“×道×次安定保压试验减压量×kPa”）。

（4）确认制动性能。

列车达到规定减压量后，现场检车员从试风起始位置开始，按照各自分摊的辆数跑动检查至试风碰头位置，逐辆弯腰探身、昼间用检查锤指（夜间用检车灯照）检查确认责任范围内的车辆不得发生紧急制动作用，制动缸活塞行程符合下表规定，如图 2-34 所示。

图 2-34　确认制动性能

（5）监控试风曲线。

列检值班员实时观察系统“试风试验数据”界面“安定保压”试验项目下面显示的“保压”数值达到 60 s、“漏泄（kPa）”数值不大于 20 kPa（保压时间由系统自动计算），安定试验结果显示“合格”后，向现场进行作业联系（标准用语：“×道×次安定试验合格”）。

非正常情况：列检值班员发现漏泄量超标、试验项目未完成、试验不合格、试风数据中断等情况，须重新进行试验。

（6）传递缓解信号。

① 缓解信号：昼间能见度能满足要求的须使用检查锤，夜间或昼间能见度不能满足要求的须使用白色灯光的检车灯，在下部左右摆动。

② 恶劣天气、曲线线路可同时用对讲机辅助传递缓解信号，标准用语：

传递人：“×道×段（或接收人姓名），缓解”；

接收人：“×道×段（或传递人姓名），收到”。

③ 缓解信号须依次逐段显示传递，不准越传、漏传、错传、代传，严禁臆测判断。

④ 禁止使用红旗（红灯）代替检查锤（检车灯）显示传递。

⑤ 缓解信号传递程序和标准：

a. 尾部正号检车员与尾部负号检车员列队站在试风碰头位置，面向列车首部，向中部正号检车员、中部负号检车员传递“缓解信号”，确认对方不少于 2 次接收后停止显示。

b. 中部正号检车员与中部负号检车员列队站在试风碰头位置，面向列车尾部，当尾部正号检车员与尾部负号检车员传递“缓解信号”时，不少于 2 次接收“缓解信号”；转身 180°，面向列车首部，中部正号检车员与中部负号检车员共同向首部正号检车员、首部负号检车员传递“缓解信号”，确认对方不少于 2 次接收后停止显示。

c. 首部正号检车员与首部负号检车员列队站在试风碰头位置，面向列车尾部，当中部正号检车员、中部负号检车员面向自己传递“缓解信号”时，不少于 2 次接收“缓解信号”。转身 180°，首部正号检车员与首部负号检车员共同向司机显示“缓解信号”，通知本务机车司机充风缓解。允许用对讲机通知司机缓解。标准用语：“×道×次缓解”。

（7）确认缓解性能。

列车充风后，现场检车员从试风碰头位置开始，按照分摊的辆数跑动检查返回试风起始位置，逐辆弯腰探身、昼间用检查锤（夜间用检车灯照）检查，确认责任范围内的车辆处于缓解状态，人力制动机拉杆链处于松弛状态，如图 2-35 所示。

图 2-35　缓解性能确认

（8）涂打制动缸活塞行程检查标记。

现场检车员确认自动制动机缓解、基础制动装置缓解（人力制动机拉链处于松弛状态），按规定涂打“制动缸活塞行程检查标记”，如图 2-36 所示。

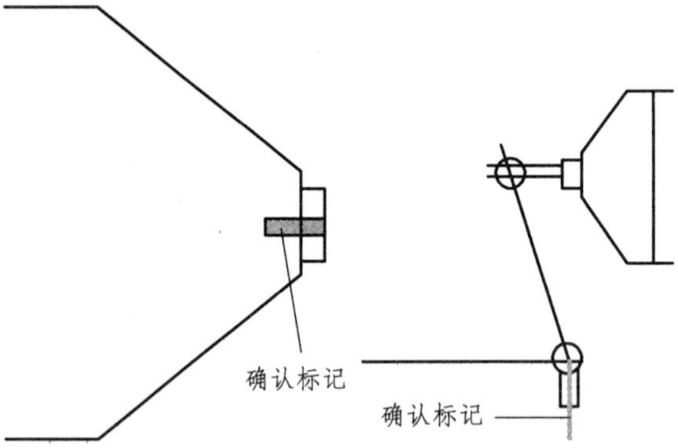

图 2-36　制动缸活塞行程检查标记涂打位置

制动缸活塞行程检查标记：逐辆在制动缸前盖、活塞筒上用粉笔画连线，长度不少于 100 mm；制动缸在车辆另一侧时，确认缓解后，逐辆在制动缸相对处的上拉杆头部用粉笔画连线。

5）试验结束

（1）确认主管压力。

方式 1：尾部正号检车员目视确认无线风压监测仪显示的主管压力达到规定压力。

方式 2：尾部正号检车员使用对讲机与列检值班员联系确认主管压力达到规定压力（标准用语：“请确认 × 道 × 次风压”）。列检值班员在系统主界面，依据“压力”数值据实回复（标准用语：“ × 道 × 次风压 × × kPa”）；若达到主管定压，回复“ × 道 × 次风压 × × kPa，符合要求”。

（2）保存试验结果。

现场检车员关闭无线风压监测仪后，“压力曲线图”自动保存。

（3）查看风压曲线。

列检值班员点击“查询”按钮，在弹出窗口单击相应车次，查看试风曲线，发现系统提示“已作业”或空白、试风项目不齐全、试风曲线不完整、试风曲线不规范等问题时，通知现场检车员查清原因、处理后重新施行列车制动机试验，如图 2-37 所示。

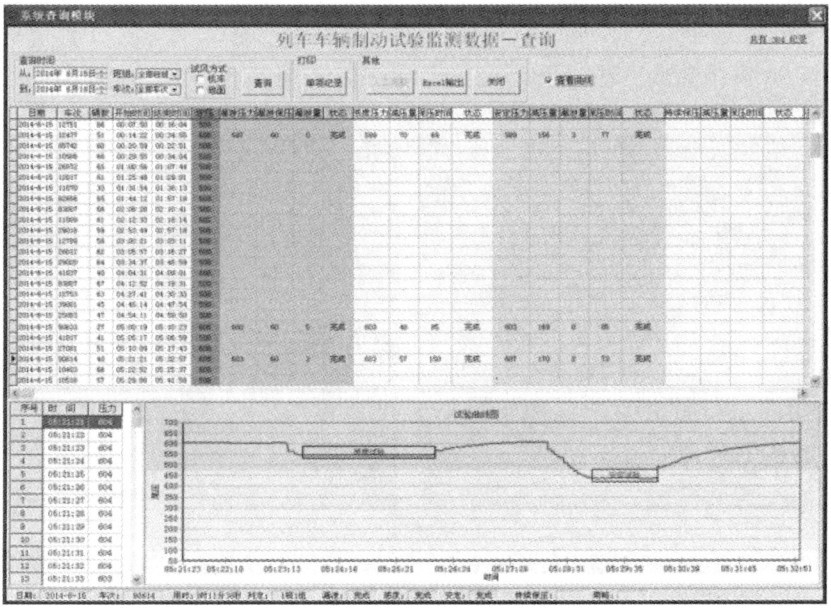

图 2-37　风压曲线

图 2-38　列车制动机试验标记涂打位置

（4）涂打列车制动机试验标记。

因停电或者临时故障影响列车车辆制动机试验监测装置正常使用时，列车制动机试验结束，确认最后一辆车缓解后，在尾部车辆制动缸前盖外侧涂打清晰的粉笔标记，标记格式：列检作业场简称、月、日，如图 2-38 所示。

（5）摘解无线风压检测仪。

a. 尾部正号检车员按下无线风压监测仪控制面板上的“关”键，关闭电源，如图 2-39 所示。

b. 尾部正号检车员关闭列车尾部车辆后端的折角塞门，使折角塞门手把中心线与辅助管中心线呈 90°夹角（折角塞门开通线与辅助管中心线呈 90°夹角），如图 2-40 所示。

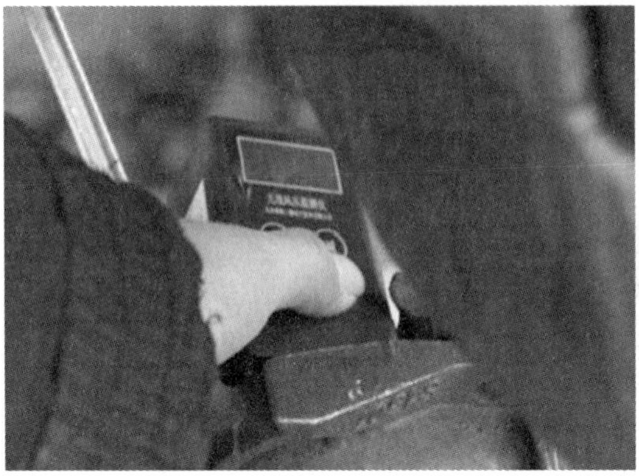

图 2-39　关闭无线风压监测仪电源

图 2-40　关闭折角塞门

c. 尾部正号检车员缓慢向风压监测仪方向搬动手柄（发射天线），排除尾部制动软管内的压力空气，如图 2-41 所示。

d. 无线风压监测仪挂钩离开软管连接器后，取下无线风压监测仪，如图 2-42 所示。

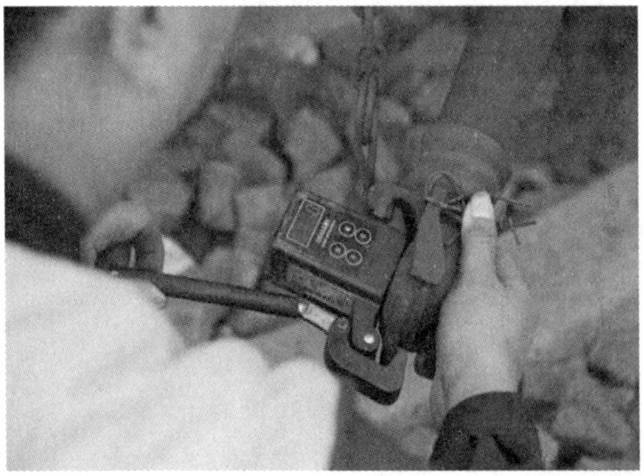

图 2-41　排除软管内压力空气

图 2-42　取下无线风压监测仪

（6）确认列车尾部标志。

以列尾装置作为列车尾部标志时，可不吊起尾车制动软管，尾部正号检车员须将车辆制动软管与列尾装置软管连接、打开最后一位车辆后端折角塞门，如图 2-43 所示。

图 2-43　列尾标志

（7）传递试验完了信号。

a. 试验完了信号：昼间能见度能满足要求的须使用检查锤，夜间或昼间能见度不能满足要求的须使用白色灯光的检车灯，由上部向车列方向做圆形转动，如图 2-44 所示。

b. 确认信号：昼间能见度能满足要求的须使用检查锤朝向列车方向 45°斜行，夜间或昼间能见度不能满足要求的须使用白色灯光的检车灯朝向列车方向 45°斜行，如图 2-45 所示。

图 2-44　试验完了信号

图 2-45　确认手信号

c. 恶劣天气、曲线线路可同时用对讲机辅助传递信号，标准用语：

传递试风完了信号：“×道×段（或接收人姓名），信号划过去了”。

接收试风完了信号：“×道×段（或传递人姓名），收到”。

传递确认信号：“×道×段（或接收人姓名），信号返过去了”。

接收确认信号："×道×段（或传递人姓名），收到"。

d. 信号须依次逐段显示传递，不准越传、漏传、错传、代传，严禁臆测判断。

e. 禁止使用红旗（红灯）代替检查锤（检车灯）显示传递。

f. 试验完了信号传递程序和标准。

- 尾部正号检车员站立于试风起始位置，面向列车首部，向中部正号、尾部负号检车员传递"试风完了信号"，确认对方不少于2次接收后停止显示。

- 尾部负号检车员与中部正号检车员列队站立于试风起始位置，面向列车尾部，当尾部正号检车员传递"试风完了信号"时，不少于2次接收"制动信号"；转身180°，面向列车首部，尾部负号检车员与中部正号检车员共同向中部负号、首部负号检车员传递"试风完了信号"，确认对方显示接收"试风完了信号"不少于2次后停止传递。

- 中部负号检车员与首部负号检车员列队站立于试风起始位置，面向列车尾部，当中部正号、尾部负号检车员传递"试风完了信号"时，不少于2次接收"试风完了信号"；转身180°，面向列车首部，中部负号检车员与首部负号检车员共同向首部正号检车员传递"试风完了信号"，确认对方不少于2次接收后停止显示。

- 首部正号检车员站立于试风起始位置，面向列车尾部；当中部负号、首部负号检车员面向自己传递"试风完了信号"时，不少于2次接收"试风完了信号"。向中部负号检车员、首部负号检车员传递"确认信号"，确认对方接收不少于2次后停止显示。

- 中部负号检车员与首部负号检车员列队站立于试风起始位置，面向列车首部，当首部正号检车员面向自己传递"确认信号"时，不少于2次接收"确认信号"；中部负号检车员与首部负号检车员转身180°，面向列车尾部；中部负号检车员与首部负号检车员共同向中部正号检车员、尾部负号检车员传递"确认信号"，确认对方不少于2次接收后停止显示。

- 中部正号检车员与尾部负号检车员列队站立于试风起始位置，面向列车首部，当首部负号检车员、中部负号检车员返回"确认信号"后，不少于2次接收"确认信号"；转身180°，面向列车尾部，中部正号检车员与尾部负号检车员共同向尾部正号检车员返回"确认信号"，确认对方不少于2次接收后停止显示。

- 尾部正号检车员面向列车首部，当中部正号检车员、尾部负号检车员面向自己传递"确认信号"时，不少于2次接收"确认信号"。

（8）撤除防护信号。

a. 首部正号检车员撤除机后一位车辆前端列车运行方向左侧车体上的停车信号，向列检值班员汇报，列检值班员复诵确认。防护红旗撤除后卷起，防护红灯撤除后关闭，并随身携带。标准用语：

首部正号检车员："×道×头，红旗（红灯）撤除。"

列检值班员："×道×头，红旗（红灯）撤除。"

b. 尾部正号检车员撤除尾部最后一辆车端列车运行方向左侧车体上的停车信号，向列检值班员汇报，列检值班员复诵确认。防护红旗撤除后卷起，防护红灯撤除后关闭，并随身携带。标准用语：

尾部正号检车员：“×道×头，红旗（红灯）、风表撤除。”

列检值班员：“×道×头，红旗（红灯）、风表撤除。”

6）作业完毕

试验完毕后，作业人员返回起始位置

【复习题】

1. 简述在进行列车制动机试验时，制动、缓解、保压、确认、试风完毕信号的手信号显示方法。

2. 感度试验操作程序是什么？

3. 漏泄试验操作程序是什么？

4. 安定保压试验操作程序是什么？

第三篇　客车运用维修

铁路客车是铁路旅客运输的重要运载工具，运用维修工作是铁路运输的重要组成部分，维修质量直接关系到旅客生命财产安全。提供良好设备，保证行车安全，为旅客运输服务，是铁路客车运用维修工作的基本任务。

客车实行固定配属管理，其运用维修工作包括客车车辆管理、运用维修管理及运用安全管理等工作，主要由客车技术整备所（库检）、旅客列车检修所和客车乘务负责，客车所属的铁路局、车辆段是客车运用安全、质量的责任主体。客车运用维修工作应贯彻养修并重、状态监测、预防为主的方针，持续强化运用基础，不断完善管理机制，实现“管理规范、作业标准、队伍专业、装备先进、质量达标、安全可靠”的客车运用工作目标。

单元一　客车技术整备所

客车技术整备所，是客车运用维修保养的重要基地，具有列车的辅修、入库检查、客车整修及临修等功能。客车经检修应达到《运用客车出库质量标准》，并保证列车在一个入库检修周期内不发生责任事故。

【学习目标】

（1）了解客车技术整备所的职责；

（2）掌握客车报废的条件；

（3）掌握客车技术整备所列车技术检查作业工序。

【学习内容】

1. 客车报废条件

客车凡自然耗损过限、腐蚀或事故破损严重，经鉴定符合下列条件之一者，可申请报废：

- 外墙、顶板须全部分解，并须更换铁立柱达 2／3。
- 需要更换中梁。
- 中、侧梁垂直弯曲超过 200 mm 或横向弯曲超过 100 mm。
- 两根侧梁折损或一根侧梁折损及两根端梁折损。
- 车底架扭曲，其倾斜度在车底架 1 m 以内超过 70 mm 或全部车底架超过 300 mm。

- 底体架破损程度较大和火灾事故后严重变形，经鉴定无修复价值。

2. 客整所检修作业程序

客整所检修作业程序及内容如图 3-1 所示。

（1）列车到达技术作业（乘务员、客列检）

（2）车底入库

（3）车辆乘务员交车（乘务员、库列检）

（4）车底改编

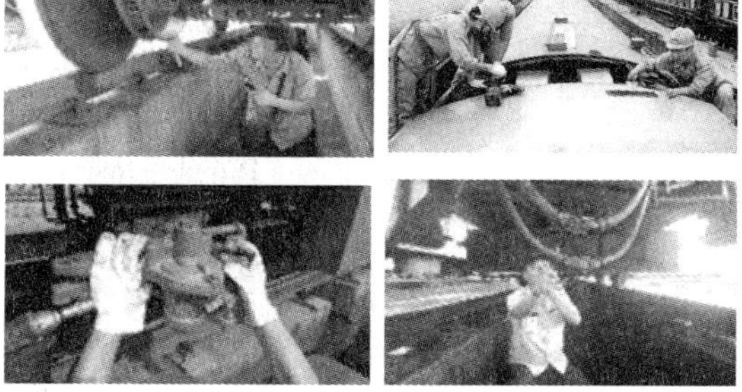

（5）车辆技术检查、车辆辅修、摘车临修等

（6）库列检交车（乘务员、库列检）

（7）车底出库

（8）列车始发技术作业

图 3-1　客整所检修作业程序及内容

3. 客整所列车技术检查作业

1）车底检修人员分工和作业路线

车底检修实行 4 人检车、4 人修理；检车 4 人编号为①～④号，两人一对，两对分别从车端两侧开始向中部作业，直至碰头为止。

修车 4 人编号为⑤～⑧号，两人一对，两对分别从车端两侧开始随相应检车员按标记向中部进行整修作业，直至碰头为止。①、⑤号两人分别为检、修车组组长。

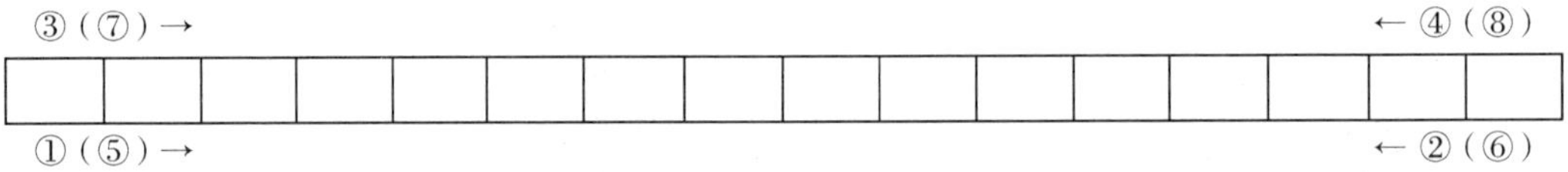

图 3-2　车底检修人员分工和作业路线示意图

2）列车技术检查作业安全注意事项

安全注意事项：① 在线路上检修、整备车辆的作业前后，应按照规定设置、撤除安全防护信号。② 按规定穿戴好工作服、安全帽等防护用品，禁止穿拖鞋、凉鞋、高跟鞋作业。③ 钻越车底应防止头碰配件，处理制动故障时应关门排风，严禁手指伸入圆销孔内。④ 作业时要作业到位，不简化作业。⑤站场作业要集中思想，严格执行“一站、二看、三确认、四通过”规定，作业过程中注意避让临线车列。⑥上下地沟注意安全，严禁跳跃。

3）列车技术检查作业工序

作业工序：下达任务→设置防护信号→检车技术检查→修复车辆故障→列车制动机全部试验→修竣后验收→撤除防护信号→回所填写台账。

（1）下达任务。

车底进库，工(组)长与回乘乘务员办理交接，回组召集本班(组)人员，包括修理人员，下达作业任务、传达注意事项及车底停放位置，检查每人随身携带工具、材料是否齐全，然后分对出发。

（2）插设防护信号。

由①、⑤号负责插设防护信号(安全牌、脱轨器)，在列车来车方向左侧钢轨上设置脱轨器，防护距离不少于 20 m，并在车端脱轨器同侧设置防护信号标志(白天红旗，夜间红灯)，挂好工种小牌。同时，接好列车制动试验器风源，对列车充风缓解(注意检查车底防溜措施是否到位)。向③、⑦号显示安全防护已安插好的信号后，开始作业。

（3）车辆技术状态检查。

从车底两端向中部检查，2 人 1 对，4 人平行作业，呼唤应答。发现故障，应在故障部位或明显处(但不得写在车皮上)用粉笔写明，并记于“车统-15”内。

（4）对故障的处理。

修理人员先处理“旅客列车技术状态交接簿(车统-181)”回乘乘务员交修的故障，然后跟随检车员按规定的质量标准依次逐辆处理检车员标画的故障。处理后，在原标记处划“√”。对需要施焊者，配合电焊工一起焊修。需要摘车修时，由工长确认后通知值班员。需要换轮对时，及时联系有关班组做好换轮准备工作，并向值班员提出送车计划。

（5）对车辆故障复查。

检车员对车底全部技检作业完毕后，要回头对修理人员处理的故障进行复查。合格者抹去标记；不合格者，通知修理人员再行处理。

（6）列车制动机试验。

列车全部检修完后 4 名检车员按规定的试验要求进行列车制动机持续一定时间的全部试验。对更换分配阀(三通阀)的车辆应先进行单车试验，确认良好后，再进行列车制动机持续一定时间的全部试验。经检修车辆，应达到客车出库质量标准。

（7）撤除安全防护信号。

作业完后，对号志，由尾部向前部逐个显示完工信号，白天用检点锤、夜间用白色灯光与车体成 45°斜摆动。①、⑤号接到全体完工信号后，撤除安全防护信号及工种小牌。

（8）回所、填写台账。

列队归所，通知值班室作业完毕。

由工(组)长汇总检修情况，填写“车统-181”，并向值班员汇报和递交“车统-181”。并填写其他台账（如“车统-81”等维修记录）。

（9）完工。

收集废旧材料、配件等，整理、保养工具，工长主持召开完工会。

4. 运用客车出库质量标准

客整所通过施行日常检修和专项检修，须保证上线客车达到《运用客车出库质量标准》，见表 3-1 所示。

表 3-1　运用客车出库质量标准

部位	质量标准
轮对	1. 轮轴各部不得有裂纹，轮毂无松动现象，各部尺寸符合规定限度。 2. 制动盘盘毂、盘座、半盘连接部无裂纹，散热筋（片）无贯穿裂纹，制动盘摩擦面无明显偏磨，制动盘磨耗及摩擦面热裂纹不超限，制动盘、螺栓、销套无松动，螺栓开口销无折损、丢失
转向架	3. 构架、摇枕、弹簧托梁及各安装座（含车体上与转向架配件相连的安装座）无裂纹、变形，摇枕吊及吊轴、横向控制杆、抗侧滚扭杆、牵引拉杆（横向拉杆）、牵引销、上下心盘、轴箱导柱、定位转臂及夹紧箍、各安全吊无裂纹，摇枕弹簧及轴箱弹簧无裂损。 4. 导柱弹性定位套无脱落、窜出；轴箱定位节点、牵引拉杆橡胶节点、横向挡等橡胶件无破损和脱胶；橡胶堆定位器不开胶，无裂纹，缺口方向符合规定；抗侧滚扭杆关节轴承及橡胶保护套无脱出、裂损。 5. 摇枕挡、旁承、横向挡间隙不超限；转向架各部安装螺栓无松动，防松铁丝捆绑良好；心盘垫板无破损窜出，摇枕挡磨耗板无脱落。 6. 空气弹簧高度测量块无缺失，橡胶囊与金属板的粘接面无脱离，橡胶囊及橡胶堆表面裂纹不超限、胶囊帘线不外露。 7. 高度调整阀及调整杆安装牢固、无裂损、无变形，调整杆护套完好；差压阀安装牢固、无裂损；防过充安全钢丝绳、圆销、开口销无折损；AM96 型转向架空气弹簧排风装置排风良好，钢索、操纵杠杆、弹簧、开口销等无折损。 8. 各油压减振器配件无缺失、安装牢固，无漏油、折损
基础制动装置	9. 盘形制动单元的杠杆和悬吊装置无裂纹，各杠杆转动灵活；各圆销、开口销无丢失、折损或磨耗到限，各圆销与套配合间隙不过限，销套不窜出。闸片厚度不超限，缓解时闸片离开制动盘或闸片无压力。 10. 踏面制动（含踏面清扫器）制动梁及吊、闸瓦托吊、各拉杆及杠杆无裂纹；杆件与托不抗劲，各托架安装牢固、无裂纹；缓解簧安装牢固、无裂损；闸瓦及托磨耗不过限；各圆销、开口销无丢失、折损，各圆销与套配合间隙不过限，销套不窜出、无裂损；闸瓦托防翻装置、闸瓦托吊销防脱挡齐全良好。 11. 制动缸活塞行程符合规定，自动间隙调整器、ST1-600 型闸调器作用良好，缓解时闸瓦不紧靠车轮，闸瓦不偏磨；各垂下品距轨面符合规定。 12. 手制动机作用良好，链条处于松弛状态；各磨耗部（含转向架、钩缓等各部）磨耗板齐全，润滑良好
空气制动装置及总风装置	13. 列车制动机试验符合规定。制动、缓解作用良好，制动管系泄漏不超限，单元制动缸、制动缓解显示器及防滑排风阀无漏泄；总风管系贯通良好，漏泄不超限。 14. 管系各管卡无松动、丢失；各阀、塞门、风缸配件无缺失；安装牢固、位置正确、作用良好；软管无鼓泡，安装无松动，连接状态良好，防尘堵悬挂牢固，防尘堵链垂下后不超过垂下品距轨面限度规定；折角塞门手把开口销无折损、丢失；制动缓解指示器清洁，显示正确，无裂损；风表不过期；紧急制动阀铅封齐全。 15. 单元制动缸及座无裂损，定位销轴定位良好，防尘套无破损，金属软管无松动、抗磨、破损。 16. 集成电空制动机箱、气路控制箱箱体及安装座无破损、松动，箱门关闭良好。 17. 客列尾例行检查试验良好，主机安装牢固，管路无漏泄，胶管无龟裂、老化，专用 DC48V 电源插座无松动、破损，工作正常

续表

部位	质量标准
车钩缓冲装置	18. 15 号车钩缓冲装置车钩、尾框、托板、摆块及吊、冲击座、从板及座无裂纹，缓冲器无裂损；托板螺栓、钩尾销横穿螺栓无松动，防松铁线安装良好；钩舌销无折断，螺母安装良好，开口销无折损；缓冲器无上翘，钩提杆落槽、不冲击下锁销连杆；下锁销及钩提杆按规定捆绑；车列首尾车钩三态作用良好，车钩高度符合规定；相连车钩钩差不过限。 19. 密接式车钩缓冲装置安装座、缓冲器壳体、钩体无裂纹和永久变形；各部螺栓无松动、丢失；两车钩连接间隙及缓冲器的内半筒相对外壳后端面的伸出量不超限；解钩手柄定位良好、无变形
车体及车顶设备	20. 车辆定检不过期；车端登车扶梯及防攀盒安装牢固，盒门锁闭良好；车体倾斜不超限；车底架各梁无裂纹，墙、顶板无破损。 21. 风挡弹簧、阻尼装置安装牢固、无折损；折棚式风挡拉杆组成松紧适度、连接牢固，篷布无裂损，车内折棚挂绳（簧）齐全，渡板无翘起；铁风挡折棚无弯曲、裂损和开焊；橡胶风挡胶囊裂损不超过 100 mm。 22. 脚蹬安装牢固，无腐蚀破损；手把杆无破损、丢失、松动；各裙板锁闭紧固。 23. 车底架各悬吊装置（含电器设备箱体悬吊）配件齐全、安装牢固、无裂纹、防松螺母无松动；车下各箱体（含电器设备箱体）外观无破损、箱门锁闭良好；油箱、水箱、污物箱无漏泄。 24. 各注水管、排水管及导管、排便桶安装牢固，无缺失；排水管朝向正确，避开轴箱、台车、轮对及基础制动装置；各类排水管、制动管、缓解阀拉杆等部件与车体间孔路封堵可靠，防寒材不外露。 25.车顶不漏雨；车顶设备安装牢固，车顶天线、车顶活盖、通风器、废排风帽、消音器帽等无缺失，固定螺栓无脱落、松动现象
车内设备	26. 按规定配备灭火器、消防锤；灭火器检修不过期，压力符合规定，铅封完好。墙板、地板、顶板完整无孔洞，通过台、厕所、洗面间、小走廊地板及墙板各压条齐全、间隙孔洞封堵良好。 27. 各折页门、拉门、翻板及簧、锁、门止及碰头配件齐全，作用良好；塞拉门作用良好，各锁开关正常，翻转脚蹬安装牢固、作用正常；自动内端门手动、电动控制位转换功能良好，作用灵活，防挤压功能良好。 28. 活动车窗配件齐全，升降、锁闭作用良好；门窗玻璃安装牢固、无破损；外嵌拉铆结构车窗窗框无破损、松动。 29. 座席、卧铺及吊带、扶手、扶梯、茶桌、行李架、衣帽钩安装无松动；座席及卧铺面布无破损；车内身高标志牌、座号牌、铺号牌、残疾人专用座席标牌齐全、清晰，位置符合规定；车内地板及地板布无影响行走的塌陷、鼓泡现象。 30. 给水管系及阀不漏水、作用良好；洗面盆、洗手盆、便器安装牢固、裂损不影响使用；水位表（液位仪）显示准确，检修不过期。 31. 采暖装置配件齐全，作用良好。温度表、水位表指示准确；管系各阀、塞门、接箍、弯头无漏水、冻结。燃煤温水锅炉、茶炉及餐车炉灶作用良好，烟筒及防火隔热装置完整。 32. 集便装置作用良好，便器冲水均匀、无外喷

续表

部位	质量标准
	33. 测试列车干线绝缘符合规定；车端电气连接器各插头、插座外观无变形、破损，标记清晰、正确；连接线护套无损伤，密封垫无破损；各连接器连接牢固；首尾安装尾部标志灯的车辆 DC 48 V 侧灯插座导通良好。 34. 各分线盒、配线槽、配线管安装牢固；各传感器（包括制动供风系统压力传感器、车体及转向架加速度传感器、防滑器速度传感器、轴温传感器、蓄电池温度检测传感器）、排风阀安装牢固，配线无破损，各引线套管连接良好、无抗磨；轴端接地装置、车体接地线安装牢固，螺栓无松动、丢失。 35. 轴端发电机各部配件齐全，作用良好；大小皮带轮安装无松动、裂纹，螺栓无折损，悬吊装置配件齐全，无裂纹，吊销与销孔间隙符合规定、润滑状态良好；皮带安装松紧适度，不磨底槽；整流元件表面无烧痕，导线无脱焊。 36. 蓄电池无松动、漏液，电解液面符合规定；接续线牢固，无硫化，导电良好；电解液比重及电压符合规定，熔断器容量符合规定，定检标记清晰；排水、排气通畅；单块电池电压符合规定，DC 110 V 蓄电池组放电电压不低于 92 V
车上电气装置	37. 电气综合控制柜、电源柜、空调控制柜、照明配电柜（盘）、厨房电器控制柜等电器控制柜门锁状态良好、关闭严密；触摸屏及指示灯正常，各开关、按钮操作灵活、接触良好；各传感器、热继电器、PLC、触摸屏、在线绝缘检测装置的设定值符合规定、作用可靠；各电气开关、接触器、继电器等电气元件安装牢固、作用良好；接线端子无松动、脱焊、烧损，测温胶贴齐全、无变色；各配线无外露、绝缘良好；各熔断器容量符合规定。 38. 充电机、逆变器输出电压、频率正常；充电机、逆变器与电气综合控制柜通信正常，触摸屏上显示正常信息代码；电气综合控制柜的车下电源箱指示灯显示为绿色。 39. 通电后控制柜电源转换及空调控制电气动作及指示正常，各项功能符合要求；各功能单元工作电流正常；DC 600 V 单车漏电电流不超过 100 mA，AC 380 V 单车漏电电流不超过 150 mA；首尾车 DC 600 V 干线在线绝缘监测装置 CF 卡完好，触摸屏无故障或错误显示，任一路干线对地电压不得低于 130 V。 40. 空调装置各部配件齐全、作用良好、安装牢固；蒸发器网、回风网清洁；机组空气预热器安装牢固，无烧损；根据外温通电试验检查相应功能，系统功能作用须良好，各电机运转正常无异声。 41. 电加热器安装牢固、作用良好，防护罩与墙板间无异物，与加热板（管）不密贴；温水箱、伴热装置工作正常；电开水器出水阀无松动、漏水，加热及保护功能正常。 42. 照明灯具配件齐全，型式统一，照明正常。旅客信息显示系统车厢显示屏显示正确；48V 应急电源整流、充电、应急输出功能正常。顺位号调节器作用良好。厕显开关配件齐全，安装牢固，作用良好。隔离变压器、电铃、排气扇、电动水泵、插座、播音呼唤公共系统等装置作用良好。 43.电气化厨房电蒸饭箱排水阀和排气阀开闭正常（自动排气阀开启压力不大于 0.05 MPa），管件连接处无渗漏；通电后，设备工作正常。电炸锅、排油烟机通电后，控制面板按键控制作用良好，设备工作正常。电磁灶控制旋钮档位控制灵活，工作正常，进、出风口通畅，通风管道清洁，空气通过冷却盘无阻碍，风扇、冷却盘安装牢固。保鲜加热柜箱门开关灵活，通电工作正常。电冰箱配件齐全、无泄漏，箱体及门无破损、密封良好，换热器及滤网清洁；配套逆变装置电源输出可靠，通电后冰箱工作正常。

续表

部位	质量标准
车上电气装置	44. 影视系统电视画面清晰、频道正常、安装可靠；影视控制器功能正常，表面清洁。播音系统电源开关处于工作位，音量开关工作正常。 45. 电子防滑器主机与电气综合控制柜的 PLC、行车安全监测装置的车厢级主机通信正确、可靠；电气综合控制柜触摸屏上防滑器的信息显示应为正常信息代码；与塞拉门联锁信号（<5 km/h）作用良好。 46. 轴温报警器、记录仪轴位显示准确，轴温及外温显示功能正常，声光报警可靠；同侧静态轴温温差<5 °C；报警器车厢顺位号、记录仪时钟、记录时间间隔设置正确；记录仪通信功能正常；报警器与电气综合控制柜中的 PLC 通信正常，在电气综合控制柜触摸屏上无“故障”信息显示。 47. 烟火报警器主机声光报警功能良好，电源开关处于工作位，与电气综合控制柜中的 PLC 通信正常，在电气综合控制柜触摸屏上无“故障”信息显示。 48. 行车安全监测装置：车厢级电气设备监控网络网关、代理节点各指示灯显示正常；电气综合控制柜触摸屏显示本车电气设备信息正常，车厢顺位号与实际编组相符；列车级电气设备监控网络主控站触摸屏显示正常，无离线车辆及故障信息。列车级主机显示的列车编组数，车厢顺位号应与实际编组相符，防滑器、制动、转向架的“报警/故障”报告内容不得出现黄色标志

【复习思考题】

1. 客车报废的条件是什么？
2. 客整所的主要职责是什么？
3. 在客整所进行列车技术检查作业时，怎么插设防护信号？

单元二　客车单车技术检查

【学习目标】

（1）掌握单车技术检查作业方法。
（2）掌握铁路客车运用限度。

【学习内容】

客车单车技术检查是铁路客车检车员必须具备的基本功，要求检车员必须熟练掌握客车单车技术检查的步骤、方法和作业顺序以及有关车辆运用限度，以保证铁路运输安全。

1. 作业方式

根据现场场地条件，单车技术检查作业分为不带地沟作业和带地沟作业两种作业方式，其作业路线示意图如图 3-3 和图 3-4 所示。总体上来讲，其作业工序为：插红旗→按操作过程进行客车技术检查作业→发现故障口述→作业完了撤红旗。

1）不带地沟作业

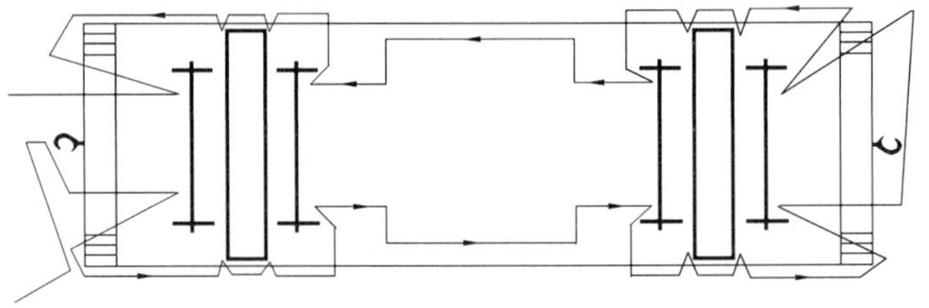

图 3-3 不带地沟单车技术检查作业线路示意图

2）带地沟作业

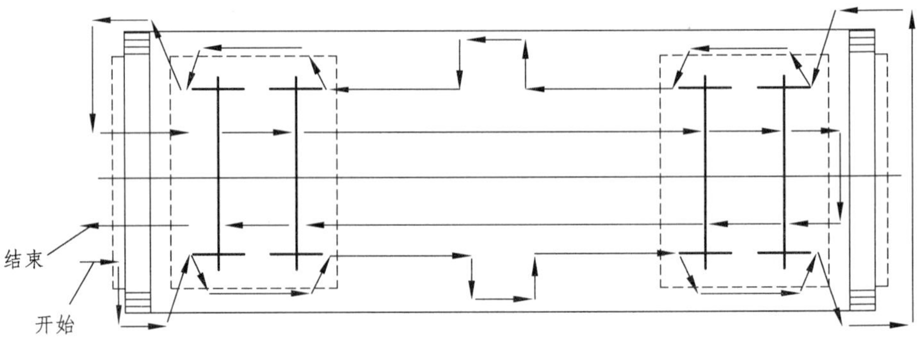

图 3-4 带地沟单车技术检查作业线路示意图

2. 作业步骤及质量标准

在作业时，须保证红旗须插牢且展开，作业中衣帽穿戴整齐，戴好手套，作业过程中身体不能滑倒，身体任何部位不能划伤出血。作业质量标准及作业步骤见表 3-2。

表 3–2 普通客车技术检查内容及质量标准

序号	检查顺序	质量标准
1	风挡	风挡、弹簧不折，螺母、圆销、开口销不失 

续表

<table>
<tr><th>序号</th><th>检查顺序</th><th>质 量 标 准</th></tr>
<tr><td rowspan="2">2</td><td rowspan="2">转头定检倾斜望</td><td>厂、段修不过期；车体倾斜不大于 50 mm</td></tr>
<tr><td></td></tr>
<tr><td rowspan="2">3</td><td rowspan="2">车钩提杆试三态</td><td>摇动钩提杆不碰下连杆，钩提杆座不松动，杆与座凹槽间隙不大于 3 mm。钩舌销与钩舌销孔间隙不大于 7 mm</td></tr>
<tr><td></td></tr>
<tr><td rowspan="2">4</td><td rowspan="2">折角塞门、制动软管、车钩托梁螺栓、螺母，螺栓、支撑座</td><td>软管不变质、起泡，水压试验不过期，配件无裂损，连接无漏泄，卡子螺栓有松余量，折角塞门作用灵活、正位无松动</td></tr>
<tr><td></td></tr>
</table>

续表

序号	检查顺序	质　量　标　准
5	钩颈摆块风杆簧	螺栓不松动，磨耗板不破不失，风挡杆不弯曲，簧不折断，摆块及吊、钩颈无裂纹，卡子无松动 
6	进车主管及各梁	管系无漏泄，管卡齐全无松动，风挡杆插销开口销不折不失，钩托不松不裂，各梁无裂纹，地板无腐蚀 
7	钩身从板钩尾框	钩身、缓冲器、从板及座无裂纹，钩体下部、尾框各部磨耗不大于 6 mm，托板无松动、无裂纹 

序号	检查顺序	质 量 标 准
8	心盘三横制动梁	心盘销不失，螺栓不松，心盘、摇枕、枕簧托梁、构架、制动梁无裂纹，制动梁不弯曲 
9	杠杆拉杆开口销	各圆销磨耗不大于 3 mm，各垂下品距轨面不少于 50 mm，各杠杆、拉杆不抗衡，不磨轴身、轮毂
10	轴身轮背缓解簧	轮轴无裂纹，轴身磨耗深度不大于 1 mm，轮缘内侧缺损长不大于 30 mm，宽不大于 10 mm；轮对内距（1353±3）mm，三处差不超过 3 mm，缓解簧不裂、不松
11	跨轨蹲姿看闸件	瓦托吊平直部分和瓦托各部磨耗不大于 4 mm，制动梁端轴磨耗不大于 3 mm，组装间隙不大于 4 mm，各扁开口销磨耗剩余厚度不小于 1.5 mm，瓦托距轨面不小于 25 mm，闸瓦厚度不小于 10 mm，同一制动梁闸瓦厚度互差不大于 20 mm，闸瓦不紧靠车轮
12	踏面轮辋轴箱簧	轮缘垂直磨耗高度不大于 15 mm，轮缘厚度不小于 23 mm，踏面圆周磨耗深度不大于 8 mm，轮缘顶部无碾堆；踏面擦伤局部凹入深度不大于 1.5 mm。踏面剥离长度：一处不大于 30 mm，二处每处不大于 20 mm,连续剥离长度不大于 350 mm。踏面缺损：相对轮缘外侧至缺损部之距离不少于 1 508 mm，长度不大于 150 mm。轮辋厚度不少于 25 mm。轴箱后部不甩油，各螺栓不松动，圆簧不折不裂，定位套、支持环、缓冲器不串，不失不破，支柱插销开口销不失
13	车端出来看脚蹬	脚蹬不腐蚀、不变形，车门扶手不松动，排便筒各配件作用良好 

<table>
<tr><th>序号</th><th>检查顺序</th><th>质 量 标 准</th></tr>
<tr><td rowspan="2">14</td><td rowspan="2">移步蹲下看轮辋</td><td>轴箱无裂纹，螺栓无松动，轮辋无裂纹</td></tr>
<tr><td></td></tr>
<tr><td rowspan="2">15</td><td rowspan="2">起身轴箱轮面望</td><td>圆簧、定位套良好，轮辋、踏面、轮缘良好</td></tr>
<tr><td></td></tr>
<tr><td>16</td><td>圆簧轮面及闸件</td><td>同 12、13 两项</td></tr>
<tr><td rowspan="2">17</td><td rowspan="2">转身挡吊安全托</td><td>螺栓不松动，安全托、摇枕吊、吊座无裂纹，枕簧、摇枕挡良好不裂不破</td></tr>
<tr><td></td></tr>
</table>

续表

序号	检查顺序	质　量　标　准
18	吊轴托板摇动簧	吊轴无裂纹，吊轴螺栓无松动，枕簧无裂纹折断，组装螺栓良好，簧上下要入槽，承台托板良好、无裂纹 
19	减振器到摇枕挡	减振器配件齐全，不漏油，不松动，牵引拉杆螺母不松，止铁、胶垫良好 
20	构架轴检不漏检	构架无裂纹
21	旁承心盘看两边	心盘、旁承螺栓不松动，心盘无裂纹 

序号	检查顺序	质 量 标 准
22	蹲看另侧摇枕挡	同 19、18、17 三项
23	同左顺序到轮面	同 12、13、14、15 四项
24	探身主管及各梁	主管无腐蚀、无漏泄，管卡齐全，各梁、地板无裂纹、腐蚀 
25	再进台车里到外	同 8、9、10 三项
26	拉杆托架看仔细	托架无裂纹，螺栓不松动，杠杆不抗衡 
27	管系横梁向前看	同 24 项
28	支管塞门集尘器	管系无漏泄，螺栓无松动，塞门、集尘器正位，把手不折不失 

续表

序号	检查顺序	质 量 标 准
29	调整器阀及风缸	调整器不卡死，安装螺栓无松动，阀螺栓无松动，阀不漏泄，紧急阀防尘胶垫不失，压力风缸无漏泄，吊带不松动，排风塞门良好

30	辅修标记制动缸	制动缸不漏泄，螺栓不松动

31	行程托架各种销	手闸拉杆、托架无裂纹，开口销良好
32	拉杆向前地板梁	中拉杆、手闸拉杆配件齐全，花篮螺母不松，地板梁良好

续表

序号	检查顺序	质 量 标 准
33	看到台车同前样	同 8、9、10、12～25 项
34	手闸配件不能忘	螺栓不松动，圆开口销良好，闸链应在松弛状态 
35	连缓车端看半边	同 7、6 项
36	钻出车端风杆簧	同 5 项
37	钩头舌销吊链堵	钩舌销开口销齐全，软管吊链及堵齐全无裂纹
38	看清标记和风挡	同 1 项，标记清楚
39	扶手脚蹬半边完	同 11 项

【复习思考题】

1. 结合实际，模拟客车单车技术检查下部作业过程。

单元三　旅客列车检修所

旅客列车检修所（简称“客列检”）是确保旅客列车安全运行的重要部门，承担始发、通过、终到旅客列车技术作业，及对站折、通过旅客列车进行重点技术检查，排除危及行车安全故障等工作。

【学习目标】

（1）掌握旅客列车检修所的职责。

（2）掌握旅客列车检修所检修范围。

（3）掌握旅客列车技术检查作业程序。

【学习内容】

1. 旅客列车检修所职责

旅客列车检修所主要职责为：

（1）客列检是确保旅客列车安全运行的重要部门，承担对终到、始发、通过旅客列车走行部进行重点技术检查，及时排除危及行车安全故障等工作。

（2）客列检对发现或预报的车辆故障，必须积极修复或妥善处理，保证行车安全。故障车辆应否摘车由客列检确认并负责处置。

（3）客列检人员工作时必须佩戴臂章。

（4）对始发旅客列车，负责机车与机后第一辆客车的软管、车端电气连接线的连接，并进行制动机简略试验。

（5）对终到旅客列车，负责列车机车与机后第一辆客车的车钩摘解及软管、车端电气连接线的摘解。对不入库检修的站折返列车，按库列检技术检查作业范围检修，并进行制动机全部试验。

2. 旅客列车检修所作业范围

1）通过旅客列车的技术检查作业范围

（1）列车车辆技术状态交接。

（2）轴温：轴温达到 90 °C 或超过外温加 60 °C 时摘车处理；超过外温加 45 °C 时，通知车辆乘务员重点监控并预报前方客列检重点检查，站折返列车须开盖检查，发现轴承零件破损、油脂变质、混砂、混水、混有金属粉末等异状，不能保证行车安全时应做摘车修理。

（3）车轮缺损，踏面剥离、擦伤。

（4）摇枕悬吊装置、基础制动装置。

（5）轴箱弹簧、摇枕弹簧、空气弹簧装置。

（6）配件丢失、脱落或损坏。

（7）车钩、制动软管、总风管的连接状态。

（8）按规定施行列车制动机试验。

2）通过旅客列车的不摘车修范围

（1）标记速度 120 km/h 及以下客车、装有 209HS 转向架的客车轴箱弹簧折损时更换，支承圈折损在确认无其他相关故障时，可一次运行到终点站更换。其他客车轴箱弹簧折损可一次运行到终点站更换。

（2）处理基础制动故障。

（3）处理空气制动故障。

（4）更换钩舌，调整钩差。

（5）更换处理牵引拉杆故障（25T 型客车除外）。

（6）处理配件丢失、脱落或损坏故障。

客列检对发现或预报的车辆故障必须积极修复或妥善处理，保证行车安全。故障车辆是否摘车由客列检确认并负责，车辆乘务员应服从客列检的决定。

3）旅客列车检修所责任划分

（1）属于客列检不摘车修范围的故障，未做处理或摘车处理为客列检责任。

（2）经客列检处理的故障，属于不摘车修范围的，应保证安全运行到终点站。

（3）属于客列检检查范围的检查部件保证及其安全运行到下一个客列检。

4）旅客列车技术检查作业程序

旅客列车技术检查作业安全注意事项：

① 作业人员列队出待检室须集中思想，严禁钻车底，通过线路执行“一停、二看、三确认、四通过”规定，确认安全后方可迅速通过平交道，严禁抢越轨道，不得从待发的列车前通过，列车进站时要站在安全白线外侧。

② 作业人员在接到列车预报后，提前 5 min 到达接车位置。

③ 作业前作业人员要严格做好防护号志插设工作，白天用红旗、夜班用红灯，防护号志要作用良好、颜色鲜明。

④ 非站台侧作业时，要注意邻线有无列车通过，如遇作业列车邻线有列车或单机通过时，要在安全处躲避，不得侵线。值班员和列车首尾作业人员要用对讲机及时通知现场作业人员注意安全，并做好呼唤应答，相互提醒。遇特快、动车组通过时，必须提前 10 min 停止邻线作业，在安全地方躲避，带列车通过后方可作业。

⑤ 严禁在高站台随意跳上跳下，防止滑落摔伤。

1）通过旅客列车技术检查作业程序

作业工序：准备→接车→技检作业→制动机简略试验→送车→归所。

（1）准备。

客列检人员当班作业时，应佩戴规定的臂章，接到值班员的作业命令后，立即按分配检查列车的辆数、确定的作业位置和规定的时间，在列车进站前到达岗位，分立于列车到达线两侧安全地点，等待列车进站。班前点名与传达作业任务、列队出发如图 3-5、3-6 所示。

图 3–5　班前点名与传达作业任务

图 3–6　列队出发

（2）接车。

列车进站时，客列检检车人员在作业位置面向列车进入方向立岗接车。待机车越过本位置时，以 45°角面向列车进入方向，进行“三觉”检查（目视有无配件脱落；耳听有无异声及车辆不正常跳动声；鼻闻有无异味）。发现问题必须准确记录位置。待列车停稳后及时到达故障部位进行确认并积极妥善处理。接车、插设防护信号如图 3-7、3-8 所示。

图 3-7　接车

图 3-8　插设防护信号

（3）安插防护号志。

客列检检车人员在列车抵达停妥后，列车首部检车员向列车尾部检车员显示技术检查开始信号(中间检车员负责信号传递)，尾部检车员收到信号，安插防护号志。

（4）技术作业。

充分利用技检时间，对列车进行技术检查，对发现的故障及时修复、处理。对车队内无法修复的故障车辆是否摘车，应认真确认、果断决定。车辆技术检查如图 3-9 所示。

（5）制动机简略试验。

对始发列车及换挂本务机车后的列车，由列车尾部检车员安装好校对风表，打开列车尾部车辆的折角塞门，开始进行列车制动机试验。当机车与尾部风表达到定压时(与尾部车辆风表误差不超过规定)，列车尾部检车员向首部检车员显示列车制动信号；当列车尾部车辆制动良好后，再向首部检车员显示列车缓解信号；待列车尾部车辆缓解作用良好，列车主管风压达到定压后，关闭折角塞门，卸下校对风表，装好风管防尘堵并挂好风管，向首部检车员发出列车制动机试验完毕信号，撤除防护号志，各就各位准备送车。

图 3-9　车辆技术检查

（6）撤除防护号志。

作业完毕对号志，确认车下无人作业后，列车首尾检车员撤除安全防护号志。

（7）送车、归所。

列车发车铃声响时，应分立列车两侧安全地点；列车启动时，面对列车成 45°角下蹲送车；列车通过作业人员位置后，作业人员起立，面向列车方向继续目视列车，待列车尾部越过警冲标(或出站信号机)后，从头部向尾部对号志后归所。送车示意图如图 3-10 所示。

图 3-10　送车

2）始发旅客列车技术检查作业程序

作业工序：准备→连挂机车→列车制动机简略试验→作业结束。

（1）准备。

检车员接到作业命令后，立即按分配检查列车的辆数、确定的作业位置提前 20 min 进入岗位。

（2）连挂、检查。

前部检车员检查机后车辆车钩“三态”作用及风管连接状况是否良好。机车连挂后，确认连接状况并连接制动软管及电气控制连线，打开折角塞门向列车充风，各检车员复查各车辆管路无漏泄。

（3）制动机简略试验。

当列车制动主管达到定压后，按规定进行列车制动机试验，完好后装好风管防尘堵并挂好风管。

（4）作业结束。

全部作业完毕后，列车首尾作业人员联系撤除安全防护号志，列首作业人员在非站台侧机车车辆连接处、列尾作业人员站在列车尾部、中部作业人员站在中部位于安全地点按规定送车。

3）旅客列车终到（入库）技术检查作业程序

作业程序：准备→接车→机车摘结→作业结束。

（1）准备。

检车员按规定准备，提前 5 min 到达接车位置，等待接车。

（2）接车。

进入岗位后，打开对讲机监听本次列车进站情况，列车进站时按规定进行接车。发现问题准确记录，列车停稳后再次进行确认并处理。

（3）机车摘解。

作业人员在列车前端侧面设置安全防护信号，打开机后一辆车前端的“三捆绑”，先关闭车辆折角塞门，再关闭机车折角塞门，排出机车和车辆软管内空气后，摘解制动软管、车钩及电气控制连线。

（4）作业结束。

作业完毕后，作业人员向待机车离开后向值班员汇报，返回待检室，接受下个任务。

【复习思考题】

1. 客列检的职责是什么？
2. 客列检要检查通过旅客列车的哪些部位？

单元四　旅客列车乘务

车辆乘务组是确保旅客列车运行安全的最后防线，是对外展示车辆部门形象的窗口，负责列车运行状态的动态监控、设备故障的应急处置和职责范围内的技术作业。各单位应按照强化值乘的原则，积极推行库乘分离，逐步取消车辆乘务人员的包修范围。

旅客列车车辆乘务工作原则上实行包乘制。车辆包乘组由车辆乘务长和车辆乘务员、发电车乘务员组成，统称为车辆乘务人员，配备标准按相关规定执行。

车辆乘务人员工作中要统一着装且保持整洁，言行举止要文明礼貌，当班车辆乘务人员应在左上臂规范佩戴臂章（式样如图 3-11 所示），自觉遵守劳动纪律、作业纪律以及路风规定。跨局旅客列车在外局要接受当地铁路局的领导，服从命令、听从指挥。

图 3–11　旅客列车乘务式样

【学习目标】

（1）了解车辆乘务主要职责。

（2）掌握车辆包乘作业要求。

（3）学会处理旅客列车运行途中突发故障。

【学习内容】

1. 车辆包乘作业要求

1）出乘前

车辆包乘组在出乘前应到值班室报到，接受酒精测试，听取命令指示，在列车出库前按技术作业过程对列车干线绝缘、DC 110 V 母线电压、车下各箱门锁闭情况、发电车油量、水位、机油油位及柴油发电机组运行状态进行检查，对车下油箱管系各阀状态进行确认，对火灾报警器报警功能进行试验，核对并签认车统-181 记录故障的处理情况。

2）值乘中

在列车始发前，按照本规程“车辆摘挂”有关规定作业；负责尾部标志灯的设置，建立客列尾连接。按规定参加列车制动机试验。

运行中，车辆乘务员每 3 h 左右对全列车厢进行一次巡视，巡视重点是列车运行状态、电气系统工作状态及“两炉一灶”。空调列车始发后的第一次巡视、接班后的第一次巡视及终到前最后一次巡视，车辆乘务员须打开控制柜，对电源柜主接线排处、主接触器进出线接线处、主空气开关进出线接线处温升状态等进行检查。

巡视间隔期间，车辆乘务员应在固定地点值乘，值乘位置原则上为首尾车乘务室（不得长时间固定占用），编挂工程师车的须在工程师室值乘。

在无客列检作业站车辆乘务员须下车瞭望，观察车辆有无冒烟、倾斜等异状，对途中巡视时发现的重点故障进行确认、处理；有客列检作业站还需与客列检办理列车车辆技术状态交接。

机车换挂、列车换向时按照本规程“车辆摘挂”有关规定作业，解除、建立客列尾连接。列车换向时负责列车尾部标志灯的摘挂。

列车发生紧急制动停车后，车辆乘务员须联系机车乘务员（运转车长），了解停车原因，必要时下车对车轮踏面、车钩连接等技术状态进行检查，符合安全运行条件后，通知机车乘务员（运转车长）开车，开车后加强运行状态监控。

客列尾装置发生故障时，确认为机车 LBJ 故障的应就近更换机车，确认为 KLW 主机故障需要更换的，应在站停时进行。KLW 故障运行期间，车辆乘务员根据机车乘务员通知按有关规定核对风压。

发电车乘务员应在监控室值乘，非巡视需要离开监控室时，不得超过 10 min。每间隔 30 ~ 60 min，进入发电车机房、冷却间进行一次巡视检查，每间隔 1 h 填写一次“发电车运用记录”。

发电车乘务员途中换班，原则上应在站停时办理交接，接班乘务员负责对站台侧发电车的电力连接器的连接状态及温升、对柴油机排烟有无异常情况进行重点检查，非高站台车站还须对下油箱剩余油量进行确认。

值乘中遇有紧急情况需要汇报时，车辆乘务长凭臂章发铁路电报。非经主管部门准许，任何人不得撤换、中止车辆乘务员的工作。

3）终到后

列车终到后，车辆乘务员应解除客列尾连接，按照本规程“车辆摘挂”有关规定作业，摘除列车尾部标志灯。发电车供电旅客列车终到停车 10 min 后，还须进行卸载、断电、停机。

无客列检作业的站折列车，车辆包乘组利用本务机车进行列车制动机全部试验。同时，按照因列车牵引、超员超载、异物击打等可能造成故障的部位必须重点检查的原则，按客列检对通过列车技术检查范围进行作业，对途中出现异常的车辆进行重点检查，处理 TVDS、THDS 预报的故障（含热轴故障）。

对入库折返的旅客列车车辆包乘组随车入库到库列检值班室进行签到，接受酒精测试，办理车统-181 故障交接；车底出库前，车辆包乘组到值班室报到，接受酒精测试，听取传达有关事项。按本属出库作业范围对列车进行技术检查，并核对车统 181 故障处理情况，随车出库。

本属终到后，车辆乘务组随车入库并向值班员汇报列车运行状态，接受酒精测试，交接“旅客列车技术状态交接簿”（车统-181），重点故障须将途中发现及处置情况向库列检工长当面交接。

2. 旅客列车运行途中车辆故障应急处理

1）运行途中发生火灾时的处理

（1）立即采取措施，拉下紧急制动阀，使列车停车，并拨打当地火警电话。

（2）协助列车长有组织地疏散失火车辆内的旅客。

（3）迅速采取有效措施，切断电源、使用灭火器等灭火工具，及时将火扑灭。

（4）根据需要分解列车，先将失火车辆与后部车辆分离，再将失火车辆与前部车辆分离，分离时不要将失火车辆停留在桥梁、隧道及主要建筑物附近。

（5）及时向上级汇报，报告火情、初步原因和已采取的措施。

2）运行途中发现轴温升高时的处理

（1）轴温升高的原因。

轴承零件破损，组装不良，润滑失效以及车轮踏面等外部故障都会引起轴温升高。

（2）检查、判断、处理方法。

① 发现个别轴位温度升高时，乘务员一定要及时下车验证，对轴箱进行“一摸二看三对比”，用手摸轴箱顶部，将摸得温度和其他轴箱比较，必要时用点温计测量轴箱顶部温度，确认该轴箱温度是否超过外温 40 °C。

② 开盖检查、处理方法：

- 如开盖检查发现轴端压板螺栓松动，应及时紧固防松。
- 如开盖检查发现缺少油脂，应及时加添轴承脂。
- 如开盖检查发现轴承油脂变质，用手检查油脂内混有金属粉末，说明该轴承零件已严重磨损，应特别注意跟踪检查。
- 如开盖检查发现该轴箱混砂、混水，应检查前盖密封圈是否失效，有密封圈备品时，及时更换，关盖前适量补充新油脂。
- 途中开盖检查发现滚动轴承零件破损、卡死，直接影响行车安全时，应采取果断措施，和当地段、分局或路局联系作解车处理，并按当地局、段调度命令办理。

轴承故障和处理情况，必须按规定做成详细记录，到达终点交列检或库检处理。

3）运行途中因机车与车辆车钩分离而停车时的处理

（1）车辆乘务员应会同机车乘务员、运转车长认真确认机车与车辆的分离情况：是机车端车钩在全开位置，还是车辆端车钩在全开位置，或者两钩都在闭锁位置时的互钩差情况。如机车端车钩在全开位置或测量后机车钩高不合要求或机车车钩故障，应由机车乘务员处理并取得证明，记录车次、时间、地点、机车型号、号码，以及司机、运转车长姓名。

（2）如属车辆端情况，乘务员要认真检查车钩的技术状态，检查车钩的闭锁位钩舌与钩腕内侧面的距离是否大于 135 mm，捆扎的第二防跳装置是否失效，下锁销防跳装置是否良好，锁铁、推铁是否磨耗，钩提杆捆扎情况，是否跳出槽外，钩提杆座与提钩杆间隙是否过限，提杆与下锁销连杆距离是否不足（规定为不大于 15 mm），等，特别注意易导致开锁的配件及周围各类装置、部件有否遭到过外力打击的痕迹和人为的损坏、丢失。

（3）如车辆钩舌拉断，乘务员应检查钩舌断面是否有旧痕，新、旧痕的百分比。同时应注意分离前后的有关情况，特别是要分清是紧急停车后超动时分离，还是运行中分离后造成停车。根据情况做出分析判断，并进行相应的检查、处理，认真详细记录情况和数据、描绘简图，妥善保管损品。

4）当全列旅客列车风表压力达不到规定时的处理

（1）如全列车风表压力在 500 kPa 左右，又不上升，一般为货车机车牵挂客车时，压力没有调整，要求司机调整风压，再观察风表压力。

（2）如机车已用缓解位充风，风表压力仍达不到规定时，应检查车辆主、支管系有无漏泄、制动软管连接处及各风缸排风塞门是否在大量排风，发现漏泄及时处理。

（3）如分配阀有非正常排风时，应更换分配阀。

5）当列车运行途中发生紧急制动停车时的处理

（1）车辆乘务员应了解发生紧急制动停车的原因，及时下车对车辆进行详细技术状态检查。检查重点是：车钩、缓冲、牵引部位，轮对和转向架各部位配件。检查轮对有无擦伤，配件有无裂损、脱落等，如发现车辆有不良部位和损坏时，及时修复或做临时处理。

（2）确认车辆配件无损坏后，如停车时间隔超过 20 min 时应会同司机、运转车长进行制动机简略试验。

（3）如系动用紧急制动阀而停车，则除对车辆进行必要的检查和做有关记录之外，还应对此项做成记录，并告到达客列检所补封。

（4）开车后，乘务员应加强上部巡视，了解车辆运行状态。

6）最高运行速度超过 120 km/h 的旅客列车，在双管供风时，列车管破损不能修复时的处理

（1）在途中，因意外障碍物将列车管打坏无法修复时，应将破损车辆的总风管连接软管连接在相邻车辆的列车管上，该车作为过桥作用。

（2）在这种情况下，必须将破损车辆及以后各车辆改成单管供风。但必须捆扎好各塞门把手，以防异物打击，造成事故。

7）双管供风时，因故障需改成单管供风时，各塞门的位置

（1）关闭总风管通往空气弹簧（总风缸）管路上的塞门。

（2）开启副风缸通往空气弹簧（总风缸）管路上的塞门，保证空气弹簧用风。

（3）因分配阀故障需关闭截断塞门停止空气制动机作用时：

①关闭副风缸通往空气弹簧（总风缸）管路上的塞门。

②开启列车管通往空气弹簧（总风缸）管路上的塞门，保证空气弹簧正常用风。

8）在运行途中，空气弹簧漏泄时的处理

（1）首先确认是胶囊漏泄还是管路漏泄，若是胶囊漏泄则关闭高度调整阀前面的小塞门，停止空气弹簧供风。

（2）在停止破损空气弹簧的供风时必须停止全车空气弹簧的用风。这是因为：如果只关闭破损的空气弹簧，其他空气弹簧仍在供风会引起车体倾斜和车钩高度差，所以说要关闭全车的空气弹簧。

（3）按规定通知司机和运转车长，列车需限速 120 km/h 运行。

（4）如属管路漏泄时，必须立即紧固管路上漏泄处。

【复习题】

1. 简述车辆包乘组主要职责。
2. 简述列车运行途中发生紧急制动停车时的处理方法。

第四篇　车辆部门生产安全

铁路运输安全是运输生产系统运行秩序正常、旅客生命财产平安无险、货物和运输设备完好无损的综合表现，也是在运输生产全过程中为达到上述目的而进行的全部生产活动协调运作的结果。铁路运输生产的根本任务就是把旅客和货物安全及时地运送到目的地，而铁路运输生产的作用、性质和特点，决定了铁路运输必须把安全生产摆在各项工作的首要位置。

车辆部门应遵守国家有关法律法规，以保障铁路运输安全、车辆设备质量安全、劳动安全等生产安全为目标，坚持“安全第一、预防为主、综合治理”的方针，全面推行安全风险管理，提高安全生产管理水平。

【学习目标】

（1）掌握车辆部门生产安全要求。

（2）掌握现场作业“十不准”。

【学习内容】

1. 一般作业安全

（1）上班前，严禁饮酒，要充分休息好，保证工作时精力充沛，思想集中。工作前必须按规定穿戴好防护用品，禁止穿拖鞋、凉鞋、高跟鞋作业。下班前，要关闭风、气、水、电等开关，工具、材料要收拾整齐，打扫周围环境。

（2）两人以上从事同一作业时，必须指定专人指挥，统一行动，互相配合，呼唤应答。

（3）顺线路行走时，不走轨道中心和枕木头，如图 4-1 所示。横越线路或道口时，注意瞭望机车、车辆，执行一站、二看、三确认、四通过制度。严禁抢道、抓车、跳车、钻车，如图 4-2 所示。

图 4-1　严禁在道心行走

图 4-2　严禁钻车

（4）横越停留车辆的线路时，应先确认无调车作业及车辆无移动的可能，再由车钩上方通过，手抓牢，脚踩稳，严禁脚踩钩锁、钩颈和折角塞门手把。从停留车辆的端部横过线路时，要留有安全距离：徒手通过时不少于 3 m；搬运材料、工具时不少于 5 m。要迅速通过，不得在轨道上停留。

（5）搬运材料、配件应在两线间行走，不得紧靠线路。

（6）在站场上作业和行走时，要随时注意邻线来往的机车车辆。严禁在枕木头、轨道心、车底下、车端部和站台边坐、立、闲谈、休息、避雨或乘凉。

（7）严禁私接电源线。机械设备的电部分发生故障时，要立即关闭电源开关，通知电工进行修理，严禁非电工人员检修电器。

（8）氧气瓶与乙炔发生器的距离应在 5 m 以上。氧气瓶和乙炔发生器距明火应在 10 m 以上。氧气瓶不得沾染油脂、暴晒和碰撞。

（9）全体职工除严格遵守安全用电外，必须懂得触电急救知识：

① 使触电者迅速脱离电源。发现者迅速把就近电源开关切断或用绝缘钳、木柄斧切断电源线，或用绝缘物将触电者与带电体分开。

② 在切断电源的同时，要考虑触电者脱离电源后防止摔伤的措施。

③ 触电者脱离电源后，应就地迅速进行人工呼吸，如需送医院抢救，在送往医院途中也不能停止人工呼吸，一直做到复活或交给医生抢救为止。

2. 列检作业场作业安全

（1）列检人员要熟悉本站内线路、设备、建筑物以及调车作业情况。进出作业场要严格按照指定路线行走。

（2）上班前，特别是上夜班前要充分休息好，保证工作时精力充沛，思想集中，班前和班中严禁饮酒。

（3）列检作业要统一着装，佩戴臂章。雨雪天时，穿戴要注意保持视、听觉的良好，并注意防滑。

（4）接发列车作业要严格执行整队出发，作业完后列队归所制度。

（5）列检作业场应按检修列车股道数，配备带有脱轨器的防护信号，保持状态良好，并指定专人负责维修保管。

（6）在站内线路上检查、修理、整备车辆时，必须有专人按规定插设脱轨器和防护信号，禁止在无防护信号情况下进行车辆检修工作。风雪雨雾等不良天气要严格执行安全联控制度。

（7）列车作业完了时，在列车两端对号志，确认车下无人时，由专人撤除脱轨器及防护信号。

（8）在站场内行走，应顺线路走行在两线路中间的安全处，不准走轨道中心和枕木头，并注意来往车辆；禁止互相打闹或两人以上并列行走；禁止扒乘站内调车机车或车辆代步，更不许飞上飞下扒乘。

（9）横过线路时，严格执行“一站、二看、三确认、四通过”的制度，确认左右及邻线无车，安全时迅速通过；严禁与来往机车、车辆、车列抢行；严禁在无防护信号的车列下通过。

（10）横越列车（车列）时，应先确认无调车作业和车辆移动的可能，再由车钩上方通过，严禁钻越车底。通过时严禁脚踩上锁销、钩颈和折角塞门手把。

（11）从停留车辆端部跨越线路时，要留有安全距离，徒手通过时不少于 3 m ；搬运材料、工具时不少于 5 m。

（12）在站内抬运笨重工具、材料或在车底下传递工具、配件时，要呼唤应答、步调一致，并注意列车动态。

（13）接发列车时，应站在两线间安全地点，要目迎目送，注意酸、碱罐车运行、货物装载、篷车绳索等状态，防止意外伤人。

（14）在检修车辆上部时，应确认装载货物状态及车门关闭状态，确保安全后，再进行工作。

（15）处理一切制动装置故障（换阀、换闸瓦、洗制动缸、换制动梁等），必须首先关闭截断塞门（关门），排净副风缸余风（排风），作业结束后注意恢复；调整制动缸活塞行程时，严禁用手摸探孔装销；清洗制动缸卸缸盖螺栓前要套上安全套，插上安全销；卸缸盖螺母时，头部要闪开。此外，大件修理时，还必须遵照相应的安全操作规程作业。

（16）在站场内休息或待检时，不得坐在钢轨上、站台边缘上或在车底下休息、避雨、乘凉。

（17）在旅客列车通过时，严禁对其相邻线路的列车进行检修作业。

（18）在对列检设备的轨边设施进行检修作业时，必须设专人防护，不得单人作业。

3. 检修作业安全

（1）在站内线路上检查、修理、整备车辆时，应在列车两端来车方向的左侧钢轨上，设置带有脱轨器的固定或移动信号进行防护，前后两端防护距离应不少于 20 m。旅客列车在到发线上进行技术检查时，用停车信号防护，可不设脱轨器。列检作业线路应平整，不得铺设凹型水泥轨枕，不得铺用大块石渣。

（2）列检所应按最大作业量备足防护装置（红旗、红灯、脱轨器）并指定专人保管交接，经常保持良好状态。

（3）列检人员要熟悉本站内线路、设备、建筑物，以及列车运行、调车作业、车辆取送等情况。到达、始发列车检修，要按作业过程进行。严格执行整队出发，列队归所制度，严禁单独行动。

（4）列检作业在开始和结束前，要严格执行插、撤防护信号联锁传递办法，严禁在无防护信号的情况下进行检修作业，严禁在列车运行中处理故障。

（5）接车时要提前到达接车地点，蹲在两线中间安全地点接车。狭窄路线，邻线上、下行同时到发列车时，要在两线外侧接发列车。

（6）接发列车要目迎目送，并注意车辆运行、货物装载、蓬布绳索状态，防止意外伤人。

（7）在线路上作业时，禁止戴妨碍视觉、听觉的色镜、帽子。有冰冻时可在脚上绑扎草绳或草鞋，以防滑倒摔伤。

（8）更换大型配件时，工组长要亲自组织指挥和负责安全工作。

（9）处理制动故障时，要先关闭截断塞门，排尽副风缸余风后方可进行。作业结束后恢复开通位置。调整活塞行程时，严禁用手指探摸圆销孔。清洗制动缸前要先装设安全套，插上安全销。卸除制动缸盖螺母时，头部要闪开。更换折角塞门时，要关闭本车与另一端及邻车的折角塞门。更换闸瓦时，严禁将手伸入闸瓦与车轮踏面间。

（10）非列检人员在列车队中实行轴检、扣车或其他检查作业时，应事先与有关人员联系，采取有效安全防护措施后方可进行。

（11）对线路旁的红外线探测装置及固定脱轨器进行检修、清扫时，要设专人防护来往车辆；遇有列车通过时，必须停止作业。

【复习题】

1. 举例说明现场作业安全“十不准”。

参考文献

[1] 中国铁路总公司. 铁路货车运用维修规程[M]. 北京：中国铁道出版社，2018.

[2] 中国铁路总公司. 铁路车辆安全管理规则：铁总运〔2015〕304 号[M]. 北京：中国铁道出版社，2015.

[3] 王秋鹏，等. 车辆运用与管理[M]. 成都：西南交通大学出版社，2018.

[4] 吴海超. 车辆运用与管理[M]. 北京：中国铁道出版社，2014.

[5] 中国铁路总公司. 铁路货车站修规程[M]. 北京：中国铁道出版社，2012.